Billy The Kid: An Autobiography

BILLY THE KID
An Autobiography

By Daniel A. Edwards

CREATIVE TEXTS PUBLISHERS
Barto, Pennsylvania

Creative Texts Publishers products are available at special discounts for bulk purchase for sale promotions, premiums, fund-raising, and educational needs. For details, write Creative Texts Publishers, PO Box 50, Barto, PA 19504, or visit www.creativetexts.com

BILLY THE KID: AN AUTOBIOGRAPHY
by Daniel A. Edwards

Portions of this manuscript have been published previously in the book *Alias Billy the Kid* by C.L. Sonnichsen and William V. Morrison published by University of New Mexico Press, Copyright 1955.

Published by Creative Texts Publishers, LLC
PO Box 50
Barto, PA 19504
www.creativetexts.com

ISBN: 9780692437254

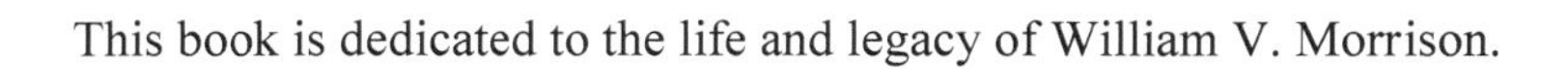

This book is dedicated to the life and legacy of William V. Morrison.

You were right, Bill.

TABLE OF CONTENTS

"I want a pardon so I can die a free man. I wasn't no outlaw.
I never robbed banks or stagecoaches"
William H. Roberts

AUTHOR'S PREFACE

In 1882 a notorious outlaw finally walked out of a Texas jail a free man. He had just completed serving a prison sentence for the murder of a Texas Ranger and decided prison was not for him. His debt to society paid, he walked out of the prison and disappeared, never to be heard from again…or so we were told.

The outlaw was Jesse Evans, founder of the notorious "Jesse Evans Gang" that terrorized the Wild West during the 1870s and early 1880s. This gang, also more famously known as "the boys", committed innumerable acts of armed robbery, violence and cattle rustling. Its members included such prominent western names such as Frank Baker, Jim McDaniels and "Curly Bill" Brocius, among others. Each of these men have carved their names into western history and have become notable in their own right, but none of them are so well known as the gang's most famous occasional member and Jesse's childhood friend; the legendary desperado Billy the Kid.

Billy "the Kid" is one of the Wild West's most controversial figures. In a matter of months during the years 1880 and 1881, he was transformed from a relatively minor player in a small-town cattle war to the most wanted outlaw in the West. The circumstances of this transformation were simple. When the sides were drawn in the cattle dispute that became the Lincoln County War, poor Billy ended up on what would become the losing side. As his friends and colleagues were killed and scattered around him, Billy eventually found himself the last man standing against what was then known as the "Santa Fe Ring", a corrupt group of politicians, businessmen, and lawmen that operated on both sides of the law.

The Santa Fe Ring used all of the power under their control to brand Billy an outlaw. Not that Billy, or perhaps anyone involved in the Lincoln County War, was an angel, but he certainly was not responsible for all of the many depredations that he was accused of and that were attributed to him by the press. Regardless, although by this time he was alone and outnumbered, Billy continued to fight on to avenge his friends and for what he thought was right. He even appealed many times to Governor Lew Wallace for his assistance and offered to testify regarding the corruption that was rife in the territory. The governor had originally taken

Billy's side and promised him a pardon, but in the end the governor reneged on his promise and left Billy to die.

But Billy did not die, and much to the consternation of the establishment of the time, Billy's courageous, almost single-handed, struggle against a rigged system inspired a folk hero type following among the citizens of his time. As his legend and exploits grew, he became the archetype of a young rebel unafraid to face the world on his own. Nevertheless, although Billy was captured and sentenced to hang, he escaped…multiple times…before traditional history tells us that Billy eventually lost the battle. He was said to have been tracked down and "brought to justice" by virtue of a gunshot by Sheriff Pat Garrett's pistol in Ft. Sumner, NM in 1881.

In 1948, however, almost seventy years after Billy's childhood friend Jesse disappeared, Jesse's brother passed away and his estate needed to be settled. It was then that Jesse Evans quietly re-appeared and revealed that he had been living in Florida under the alias Joe Hines. Joe Hines was able to prove to the satisfaction of a court of law that he was the one and only Jesse Evans of legend. You see, his brother had left a parcel of land to Jesse and he intended to get what was rightfully his, and he did.

Jesse told the lawyer handling the case that he was one of three surviving participants of the Lincoln County War, a cattle war so out of control that the President of the United States got personally involved in putting an end to it. Jesse claimed that one of the other survivors was his childhood friend William H. Bonney, alias "Kid" Antrim, alias Billy "the Kid". This was a startling claim from someone who had himself been considered long dead and it was against the odds that two surviving old men, both of whom were now of meager means, would have the methods or energy to correct the almost 70 years of established storyline that had developed around the disappearance of Jesse Evans or the exploits of Billy the Kid.

Nevertheless, the lawyer, William V. Morrison, contacted the Kid who was now himself living under an alias and approaching ninety-one years old. At first the old man was reluctant to share his story, especially since he was technically still wanted and condemned to hang for the murder of Sheriff William Brady, a crime he claimed he didn't commit. However, after some consideration he decided it was more important to make an attempt to secure the pardon that he was promised more than seventy years earlier than it was to remain a fugitive outlaw hiding in the shadows. In the end, after a lifetime of hiding and running from the law, Billy wanted to die a free man.

Morrison learned that the Kid's true name was not William H. Bonney, nor was it William H. Antrim, although he had used all of those names. In fact, he had used many aliases over the years but his Christian name was William H. Roberts and he had the family bible to prove it. The Kid's story was remarkably normal. He discussed the events of the Lincoln County War and some of his infamous shootouts, but he also spoke equally as proudly of his skill as a cowhand and bronc buster. He spoke with deep emotion regarding his friends who had been killed and filled in many details of the era that had escaped the historians of the time and were only found out to be true many years later.

He also provided physical evidence of his identity, both on his own body and in the form of artifacts. With Morrison's help, he was even able to procure five signed affidavits from surviving witnesses who personally knew Billy the Kid that supported his claim. He spoke to these people in person and was recognized by all of them (and more). When they spoke together they were able to speak conversationally about the old days, each reminding the other of specific events when they were together as old friends do. After these meetings, they were each individually and collectively certain that this man was Billy the Kid.

Morrison prepared his evidence and brought the ninety-year-old Billy the Kid before the Governor of New Mexico to obtain his pardon. In the end, however, the Governor made a media circus and a mockery of the proceedings and used it as a publicity stunt rather than treating it as a serious legal matter. It was thus that the testimony of two genuine living legends was discarded for the convenience of popular history as they chose to accept it. Discarded perhaps, discredited for a time, but not before their story was told in full.

William H Roberts, aka Billy the Kid personally collaborated on his autobiography with William V. Morrison and you are now invited to sit down with him and listen as he tells his story once and for all. Mr. Roberts' was a treasure trove of first hand testimony regarding life in the Wild West. Like all credible living witnesses of the period he would have no doubt been widely pursued and quoted if it were not for the fact that he claimed to be Billy the Kid.

Many men have from time to time come forward to claim that they were famous historical figures. No one, however, has ever been able to do so with the mountain of evidence that Mr. Roberts was able to provide that he was, in fact, the authentic Billy the Kid of legend.

In addition to the living witnesses who signed sworn affidavits, Mr. Roberts physically matched the description of Billy the Kid on all counts, including height, weight, eye color, boot size and stature. He also shared scars from gun and knife wounds that exactly matched those known to have been inflicted to the Kid during his famous battles. All of these evidences were available at the time to support his claim. However, despite these things no one of his era except Mr. Morrison was willing to investigate them during his lifetime.

What follows is the original tale put forth in collaboration with Mr. Roberts himself before his unfortunate death in 1950. His story is remarkable both in detail and simplicity. After all, Billy the Kid was a period of only a few years out of a life of ninety. Life, it seems, moves on, and much of life does not consist of adventure or amazing exploits but rather hard work and too often scrambling to get by. The story of Brushy Bill Roberts, therefore, is a story that in its entirety makes perfect sense. It explains with great credibility how a very human Billy the Kid began and ended life as a real person and not as a comic book character or dime novel hero.

My hope as you read this narrative is that you consider all of the evidence for yourself and that you keep in mind what Mr. Roberts said during this first meeting with Mr. Morrison.

He said simply "I done wrong like everyone else did in those days. I have lived a good life since I left New Mexico. I have been a useful citizen. I want to die a free man. I do not want to die like Garrett and the rest of them, by the gun. I have been hiding so long and they have been telling so many lies about me that I want to get everything straightened out before I die. I can do it with some help. The good Lord left me here for a purpose and I know why he did. Now will you help me out of this mess?"

Here's to you Brushy, and here's to getting this mess all straightened out once and for all.

Daniel A. Edwards

INTRODUCTION

The year was 1950 and it was about seven o'clock in the morning when Bill Morrison and his elderly friend, William H. "Brushy Bill" Roberts, walked into the restaurant to get breakfast. The two men had shared a table many times together over the past year, but this time would be different. This particular time would be their last together before Mr. Morrison, acting as Mr. Roberts' advocate, would present him to the Governor of New Mexico as an outlaw and a fugitive from justice—a man seeking a pardon for a death sentence handed down in a court room almost seventy years earlier.

Aside from television and the various Hollywood movies that were still coming out and playing across the country, by 1950 most Americans had all but forgotten about the real Wild West. World War I and World War II had both come and gone and the world had moved into the Atomic Age. Life was now electric powered, complete with radio, television, and airplanes, and the industrial revolution had been in full swing for decades. The two men couldn't know it at the time but within another twenty years men would walk on the moon. It was an exciting time for the country and everyone was looking to the future, not the past. This is certainly understandable because by 1950 most people in America really had no connection to what was now being called the "Wild West". Aside from a very few old timers that were still around, pretty much everyone that had lived through that era was long dead and gone.

That made the task before an almost ninety-year-old Brushy Bill Roberts even more difficult and confusing. Securing an interview with the Governor of a State is tricky enough, and convincing the Governor to grant a pardon for murders committed almost 70 years prior would be trickier still, even in normal times. But these were not normal times and the reason that the Governor had agreed to meet the old man was only because he had claimed to be none other than the notorious desperado Billy the Kid.

Billy, "the Kid", was a young man in a grown man's world. Only about 5'8" tall with prominent buck teeth and large, goofy-looking ears, Billy was all alone on the western frontier in the 1870s at a very young age. He worked off and on at various cattle ranches throughout the southwest and for a time made a living as a monte dealer. The fact that he was able to navigate the treacherous times of the Wild West on his own is impressive enough, but do so while looking like a school boy and to be accepted by the rough and violent men of the frontier speaks powerfully to the unique abilities of Billy the Kid.

The fact is that Billy the Kid was an exceptional individual. He inherently possessed qualities that suited him for life in the Wild West. Among these were lightning quickness, a good-natured charm, and an uncanny accuracy with both a rifle and a pistol. Billy also was cunning, and he possessed almost superhuman instincts during combat situations. His achievements in battle are legendary because he defied all of the odds and accomplished things that were almost unbelievable, both then and now, and yet they did happen and are well documented.

By the time Billy was seventeen he was already known by many as a "bad man", which meant simply someone that was not to be trifled with, not necessarily that the person referred to was an outlaw. Understandably, there were quite a few men in the west, each of whom were legitimately tough in their own right, that couldn't manage to see past the outward appearance of young Billy. Unfortunately for them, Billy's outward appearance and his naturally friendly disposition disguised very well the sociopathic demon that lived within him, and by the time that demon came out for them to see, they were dead. It has been said that by the time he was twenty-one years old, he had killed twenty-one men, one for every year of his life. Whether or not this is exactly true, there is no doubt that when he believed the situation dictated it, he had no hesitation or compunction about taking human life.

But there was another side to "the Kid". His friends would say that he had a great sense of humor and that he loved to have good clean fun. He was known joke and dance, play cards, and chat for hours about any number of sociable topics with his friends. He spoke fluent Spanish, and he was very popular with the Mexican senoritas and their families that lived throughout New Mexico, usually conducting himself as a perfect gentleman. He was not a big drinker, and he was no fool either. In everything he did he was calculating and cautious. In the early days of the frontier, there were lots of men who were "bad men" or killers, but despite his diminutive size and youthful years, Billy could outdo them all.

But what effect would advancing age have on a personality like Billy the Kid's? This must have been a question on Mr. Morrison's mind as he looked at the old man across the table from him and tried to reconcile what he saw with what he knew of the Kid's reputation. Brushy seemed calm enough, and unfortunately, he no longer had his prominent buck teeth that would have made him easier to identify. Aside from that, however, he was the spitting image of "the Kid", and still matched his physical description down to his boot size.

Of course, the main problem with old man's claim was obvious; Billy the Kid was dead. Everyone knew that. The tale of how the brave Sheriff Pat Garrett had shot him down in a darkened bedroom on a moonlit night way back in 1881 had become legend. It was a feel-good story of how good had finally won over evil and how the law had finally brought the lawless "Billy the Kid" to justice. Yet over time Morrison became convinced that Brushy really was the Kid, and after many months he believed that his evidence would prove it. Perhaps this is why Governor Thomas Mabry agreed to a private interview with the pair.

As they entered the restaurant that morning for breakfast, Morrison saw the headlines on the front page of the Albuquerque Tribune as he passed the cashier's desk. He had the paper in his hand as they sat down, and the more he read, the less he felt interested in food. "**GOVERNOR MABRY TO INTERVIEW BILLY THE KID CLAIMANT**," the story said.

"The chat is the result of a recent request from an El Paso legal firm that the Governor pardon their client, who claims he is the notorious desperado."

It was the next paragraph which took away Morrison's appetite.

"Several historians have been invited by Mabry to attend the interview. One is W. A. Keleher of Albuquerque who takes a definite stand for the story Garrett killed Billy. Others are Paul A. Walter of Santa Fe and Will Robinson of Albuquerque.

"Also invited is Wilbur Coe of Glencoe. He is the son of Frank Coe, who with his brother George took part in the Lincoln County War, in which the Kid figured prominently. Frank and George Coe are dead.

"Mabry said the El Paso law firm said it did not want its client "molested" by reporters, but the Governor said reporters would not be barred from the meeting and could question the aged man after the official interview.

"Meanwhile, Radio Station KGGM in Albuquerque suggested the Governor, rather than pardoning the Kid, if the old man proves to be the famous desperado, should insist that he face trial. Billy had a murder charge hanging over him."

"What's the matter, ain't you hungry?" Roberts asked, already chomping away at his breakfast.

"No," said Morrison. "I don't believe I'll eat till after this interview is over."

Over the long-distance telephone in Ted Andress' law office back in El Paso, Morrison had told the governor that he would introduce his man if the conference could be private. Roberts was afraid- afraid of being hanged or, at least, of being trapped somehow. He would go if he could see the governor alone. Not otherwise. There was no telling what might happen now.

At this moment, the ancient warrior seemed unworried. He had dressed for the part he had to play- the big hat with "Brushy Bill" on the front of the leather sweat band- the red silk handkerchief around his neck (he loved red things)- the fringed buckskin jacket with the horseshoe-shaped trim around the pockets- blue jeans- shiny cowboy boots. He looked many years younger than the ninety-one years he claimed, and seemed steady enough.

Well, they would have to go on now and take things as they came. The stopped at La Fonda hotel, in Santa Fe, to call the governor and let him know they had arrived. Morrison was politely indignant about the way the interview was being handled, and Mabry was apologetic.

"I had to give them a statement," he said, "but I told them I was to see your man at ten. You come to my house early and I'll give you a private conference, as I promised. I'll let you in the back door about 9:40."

They dodged the reporters and photographers, who were already bunched at the front of the governor's mansion, and were admitted at the kitchen door. Mabry met them as they stepped into the central hallway and greeted them cordially, but they could not fail to notice that a good many people were assembled in the front room at the end of the hall, including two uniformed state policemen, with pistols on their hips.

Roberts surveyed the assembled multitude and began to go a little shaky. "Step in here," said Mabry, and took him in to the governor's study, where there was a place to lie down. For twenty minutes, they conferred alone behind a closed door.

The chain of events which brought Brushy Bill Roberts to that conversation in the governor's mansion in Santa Fe, on November 29th, 1950, was weird enough. It began in Florida in 1948 with a man named William V. Morrison, who was working as an investigator for a legal firm. Morrison was a graduate lawyer with a good nose for evidence, an earnest collector of odd bits of fact from bygone days, and a member in good standing of the Missouri Historical Society. He was delighted when it fell to his lot to handle a case for an old man who went under the name of Joe Hines. Joe had never thought of reassuming the name he was born with until a brother died in North Dakota, leaving some property behind. In order to get his share, Joe had to establish his real identity and Morrison was assigned to work up the documents.

It turned out that he was a survivor of the Lincoln County War, in the seventies, and had fought against Billy the Kid. Morrison himself was a direct descendant of Ferdinand Maxwell, brother of the famous Lucien Bonaparte Maxwell, and had some information about New Mexican history. He mentioned the fact that Billy the Kid had worked for the Maxwells and added that Billy had been killed in Pete Maxwell's house on July 14, 1881.

"Garrett did not kill the Kid on July 14, 1881, or any other time," said Hines with great emphasis. "Billy was still living somewhere in Texas last year. The reason I know is that a friend of mine, now living in California, stops over to visit with me here every summer. He and Billy and me are the only warriors left of the old Lincoln County bunch."

Morrison tried to find out who this old man was, but Joe Hines would never tell his name. However, another old-timer came along who knew all the parties concerned. This was an ancient Missourian named Dalton, who already had startled the country by declaring that he was Jesse James. Dalton knew the whereabouts of the man Joe Hines said was Billy the Kid, and Morrison got his directions without waiting for the annual visit of the mysterious Californian. A correspondence began between him and a man using the name O.L. (Brushy Bill) Roberts, of Hamilton, Texas, and finally, in June of 1949, he went out for an interview.

He located Roberts in an unpretentious part of his little county-seat town and made notes on his first impression.

"When I stepped to the door of his home, he greeted me wearing a sleeveless sweat shirt, blue jeans, and cowboy boots. I was amazed to see a man ninety years old in excellent physical condition, stranding as straight as an arrow. He was about five feet eight inches tall and weighed about 165 pounds. He was smiling, blue-gray eyes dancing into my eyes, with right hand outstretched for a very firm handshake. I noticed that he had a small, neat hand with well-shaped fingers, unusually large wrist, heavy forearm, and well-developed biceps. His shoulders were heavy, square, and shapely. His thinning gray hair had dark streaks running through it. He had a high forehead, prominent nose, and large ears, the left ear protruding noticeable farther from the head than the right ear. He seemed to be a happy, sympathetic, warm-hearted man, but unusually alert."

They went inside, and Morrison met Mrs. Roberts. In her presence, he remarked that it was difficult for him to believe that he was talking to Billy the Kid.

The old man turned red and replied, "Oh no, you've got me all wrong. Billy the Kid is my half-brother. He is still living down in Old Mexico."

So, they talked about the half-brother, and Morrison let it be known that he might make a trip to Mexico for an interview. Roberts drove back with him to his hotel and arranged for another talk the next morning. "I have much more to tell you if we can talk alone," he said.

Early next morning he sent Mrs. Roberts off to visit a neighbor. When he and Morrison were by themselves, he pointed his left forefinger at the lawyer and said, "Well, you've got your man. You don't need to look any farther. I'm Billy the Kid. But don't tell anyone. My wife does not know who I am. She thinks my half-brother is Billy the Kid, but he died in Kentucky many years ago.

"I want a pardon before saying anything about this matter. I don't want to kill anyone any more, but I'm not going to hang."

He became excited as he talked, and tears began to course down his lined cheeks.

"I done wrong like everyone else did in those days. I have lived a good life since I left New Mexico. I have been a useful citizen. I want to die a free man. I do not want to die like Garrett and the rest of them, by the gun. I have been hiding so long and they have been telling so many lies about me that I want to get everything straightened out before I die. I can do it with some help. The good Lord left me here for a purpose and I know why he did. Now will you help me out of this mess?"

"I'll help you," Morrison answered, "if you can prove to me that you are Billy the Kid. I don't believe you are old enough."

"I have taken good care of myself all my life. I do not drink or use tobacco. I was never drunk in my life. Of course, I did drink a little when I was young, but I figured that a drunken man could not take care of himself. Some of my boys were heavy drinkers. I never had any trouble with them, though. They minded me when we were in tight places."

"Well," Morrison said, "there's one way to tell, Peel off that sweat shirt and those pants and let me look you over."

Without a word of protest, the old man did as he was told and stood there in his boots and nothing else. Morrison noted his fine firm muscles. "All right, what do you want," he said.

"Tell me about that mark on your right hip."

"That scare was from the time I run into the street at Lincoln to take the guns off the body of Sheriff Bill Brady. Billy Matthews ran behind an adobe wall and fired. His shot went through the flesh of this hip and then hit Wayte. I was not hurt, but Wayte was laid up a few days.

CLIPPED THROUGH THE LEG
Fred Wayte, who sided Billy the Kid when Sheriff Brady was killed.

"Here's one I never took out. You can feel it right here. The slug entered just inside my left knee, doing downward and lodging in my calf muscle. I got it in a fight in a mountain pass northwest of Tularosa, where we sold them stolen cattle to that man."

Morrison figured out that he meant Pat Coughlan, of the Three Rivers ranch.

"The toughest battle in my life was at the Maxwell house that night. Garrett and his posse could see me out there in the moonlit yard, but I could not see them in the shadow of the house. One of their bullets struck here in my lower jaw, taking out a tooth as it passed through my mouth."

He displayed a depression in his jaw- he had no teeth and had never worn a denture.

"When I turned to jump over the yard fence, a bullet hit here in the back of my left shoulder, making this scar. Put your finger in there. After I got over the fence I stopped to fire back at them, and another of their bullets hit me across the top of my head, about an inch and a half back of the forehead, and made this scar. That was the shot that knocked me out."

Morrison added up twenty-six scars from bullets and knives. One crossed the back of his right hand just behind the knuckles, and there was another across the first joint of the trigger finger on the same hand.

"I emptied this one in a fight once," he explained, patting his left hip, "and had to draw the right one. I wasn't as fast with my right hand as I was with the left. I could fire the pistol with both hands. I fired the Winchester and both pistols from the hip. My left hand was never hit because the man never lived who could beat me to the draw with that left. I wore my pistols in the scabbard with the butts toward the back. I fanned the hammer at times. I have been ambidextrous all my life, but I am left handed naturally."

"What about the story that you could pull your hands through a pair of handcuffs?" Morrison asked.

Bill laid his thumbs inside his palms and held out his hands. The big wrists merged into the small hands without a bulge. "Did you ever see anybody else could do that?" he demanded.

Morrison said he hadn't.

He made note, among other things, that Bill wore a size seven boot; that he was thirty-eight inches in the waist, with small hips; that his chest measured forty inches; and that he wore a size seven hat.

They talked for six continuous hours, going over all the events of those far-off times and finally arriving at the trial in Mesilla, New Mexico, where Billy the Kid was convicted, on circumstantial evidence, of the murder of Sheriff Brady on the main street of Lincoln, and sentenced to hang. Brushy Bill complained bitterly, and with more tears, that the trial was unfair, that subpoenas were never served on his witnesses, that Governor Wallace had let him down by failing to come forward with a pardon, as he had promised.

"But they didn't hang me, they didn't!" He concluded. "I wasn't born to hang."

PHOTOGRAPHIC COMPARISON

Above is a comparison of the face of a 27-year-old William Henry Roberts with both halves of the face of a 21-year-old Billy the Kid from the famous tintype. Note the left and right eyebrows are both an uncanny exact match, despite the fact that the right and left eyebrows each have a slightly different unique shape. The eyelids are also an exact match in size and shape although in the tintype the Kid is slightly squinting or perhaps the camera caught the Kid in the middle of blinking. The unique nature of the eyes are identical in both photos as are the nose, mustache pattern, hairline, jawline and length of the face, clearly indicating that these two photos are of the same man.

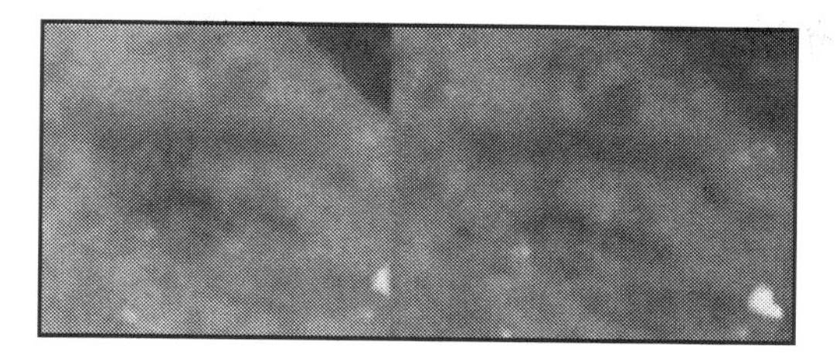

Close up of the right eye of both men. Again, the Kid is slightly squinting in the tintype but the eyes and eyebrows are an exact match.

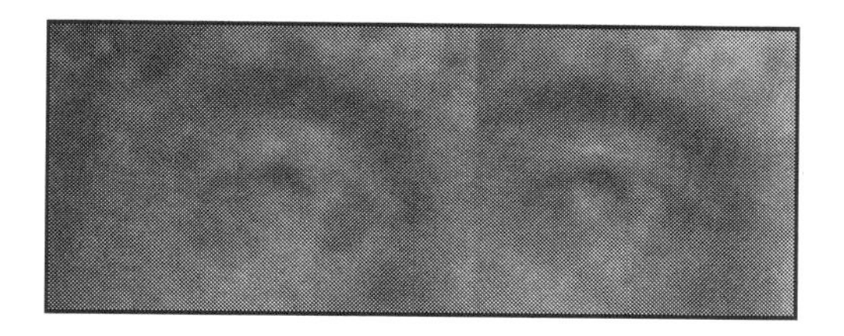

Close up of the left eye of both men.

Billy the Kid tintype on the left with a later photo of Billy the Kid (Brushy Bill) imposed on the right.

Billy the Kid tintype on the right with a later photo of Billy the Kid (Brushy Bill) imposed on the left.

The two images merge perfectly into one face, the face of Billy the Kid

Before leaving for Beaumont to report at his headquarters, Morrison made an agreement with Roberts that he would arrange an interview with the head of his firm, Mr. R.F. Roberts; that Morrison himself would work up the records for the case; that nothing would be disclosed until a pardon was obtained-no pardon, no disclosure of the old man's identity. Mrs. Roberts was not to know what was going on.

On August 16, Morrison came to Hico, Texas, where Roberts and his wife had moved, and the two of them set off on a jaunt through Texas and New Mexico, intending to go over the ground where Billy the Kid had ranged and to get copies of papers necessary for carrying out their purpose. Roberts reminisced as they traveled, dredging up many a hitherto-unrecorded fact from his memories. He made mistakes and contradicted himself sometimes. He was "still running," as Morrison puts it, and dodged questions which were too pointed. He was never easy in his mind about what he was getting ready to do, but he went ahead anyway, talked to people who might have helpful information, and even submitted to having his picture taken alongside his own grave.

"They think they've got me there, buried like an outlaw with my feet to the west," he growled on this occasion, "but that won't get it. They didn't get me yet, they didn't."

He looked at the graves of O'Folliard and Bowdre and went on: "They shot down O'Folliard like a dog in the night. They shot Bowdre down like a dog at sunup a few days later. Neither one of them had a chance. Bowdre was wearing a large hat like mine when he stepped out the door that morning. Without saying a word, they shot him down, thinking he was Billy the Kid. It was not my time to go, I guess. I never was afraid to die like a man fighting, but I did not want to be shot down like a dog without a chance to fight back. They knew that I was not afraid to die, and they knew that some of them would do down with me. I always hoped I would not die by the gun, nor be hanged with a rope. I wasn't born to be hanged, I wasn't. I want a pardon so I can die a free man. I wasn't no outlaw. I never robbed banks or stagecoaches."

Morrison took the old man home and moved to El Paso to be near the records he would have to use. By the summer of 1950, he thought he had enough evidence. Since he was not a member of the bar, he went to the firm of Andress, Lipscomb, and Peticolas, of El Paso, and convinced them that he had something to go on. With their help, he got together a brief to present to the governor of New Mexico.

The contentions they sought to establish were as follows:

That Billy the Kid had voluntarily surrendered to Sheriff Kimbrel in 1879 and had received a promise that, in return for his testimony in the case of the murder of lawyer Houston Chapman, at Lincoln, he would be pardoned in the event that his own trial resulted in a conviction.

That Billy had carried out his part of the agreement to the letter.

That General Wallace had only partially fulfilled his part, failing to come to the rescue when Billy was convicted and sentenced at Old Mesilla for the murder of Sheriff William Brady.

That Billy the Kid was not killed by Pat Garrett and had now reappeared. And that it had now become the duty of the present governor to carry out the terms of the original agreement, entered into by Lew Wallace, to pardon this man and restore him to good standing in the state.

And that was how Brushy Bill Roberts came to be lying on a bed in the governor's study in Santa Fe that November morning in 1950. As things turned out, he might just as well have stayed at home.

When the private interview was over, Governor Mabry brought him out and took him into the dining room. They both sat at the big round table, Bill nearest the door. The two state policemen took up stations on either side of the entrance. The rest of the visitors stood around the walls about twenty men in all, every one skeptical of the old man's claim, though they treated him courteously.

Pat Garrett's sons Oscar and Jarvis were there, indignant about the whole proceeding. Near them stood Cliff McKinney, son of the Kip McKinney who came to Fort Sumner with Garrett and Poe the night Billy supposedly was shot. There, too, was Arcadio Brady, grandson of Sheriff Brady, for whose murder Billy was condemned to hang. Others included Will Robinson, the Albuquerque historian, and General Patrick Hurley. One at a time they turned their batteries on Ollie L. Roberts, of Hico, Texas, alias Brushy Bill Roberts, alias Rattlesnake Bill, alias the Texas Kid, alias the Hugo Kid, alias William Antrim, alias William Bonney, alias Billy the Kid.

Roberts made a poor showing and we now know that he had a stroke on the spot. Perhaps it was the stress of the armed State Troopers or perhaps it was the stress of the media circus that the Governor orchestrated, but the end result was the same. The strain on Brushy Bill was too much for his ninety-year-old body to handle and it resulted in his death a month later.

To his credit, despite his stroke or perhaps prior to it, Roberts maintained as much of his dignity as he could. As a 90-year-old man, Roberts was understandably balding and apparently sensitive about it. He also had a long scar from front to back across the top of his head. A scar he claimed he received the night Pat Garrett shot the wrong man in his place. At one point in the meeting he had taken his hat off when a reporter attempted to take a photo of his bald head. Roberts banged his fist on the table and said threateningly to the man "Don't you dare take any pictures of me with my hat off! I won't have pictures taken with my hat off!"

The photo was not taken.

ROBERTS AT THE GOVERNOR'S MANSION

This whole situation is very telling about the personality and nature of Brushy Bill Roberts. Here is a 90-year-old man in front of a hostile crowd of several dozen people, under the threat of a death sentence with armed state troopers and the governor present, and yet he had no hesitation to lose his temper, bang his fist on the governor's table with eyes blazing, and intimidate at least one of the reporters to not go too far in disrespecting him.

Something in that exchange must have resonated with the reporter because the photo was not taken. Perhaps the photographer was just being respectful of the old man's wishes, or perhaps there was something more intimidating about the immediacy of the old man's flashing anger or the intensity of his blazing eyes. One can't help but wonder if this incident was a shadow that still remained in Brushy of a much younger Billy the Kid. A shadow, perhaps, that provides some insight into what it was like to find oneself unexpectedly on the wrong side of the Kid's anger. Unfortunately for Brushy, this was the old man's only moment of strength.

Earlier in his career, noted writer E.B. Mann attended the meeting and wrote the following in the July 1981 issue of *Field and Stream* magazine: *"On November 29, 1950, I was one of the fifty or more avid witnesses in the Governor's mansion when Brushy Bill and his attorney appeared to plead their case. The little man was sick, and scared. Small wonder that he was scared, confronted as he was by Pat Garrett's towering sons, Oscar and Jarvis, by clusters of state and local police, by yammering newsmen and flashing cameras. He denied knowledge of, or gave wrong answers to, the questions fired at him; and he finally collapsed and had to be carried from the room. The news media made a joke of it, and Governor Mabry denied action on the petition for pardon "because I do not believe this man is Billy the Kid." No one could have believed it, on the basis of the little man's performance."*

To anyone with a conscience, this scene could only be described as extremely unfortunate and sad. To mock an elderly man who couldn't remember Pat Garrett's name or the places they asked him about because he was literally in the middle of a stroke is unconscionable. At this point, Brushy must have known that he couldn't win this battle and unfortunately neither his body or his psyche could handle the hostile crowd that faced him. When Will Robinson asked him if he killed Bell and Olinger when he escaped from the Lincoln jail, Brushy said he didn't do any shooting- just got on his horse and rode off. He watched the policemen at the door and was upset when the governor pointed out one of the guests as the Sheriff from Carlsbad.

The only point he scored was making Will Robinson admit that he was pretty hazy himself about things that happened sixty years ago. When Oscar Garrett was asked to take his turn, he answered: "I do not wish to dignify this claim with any questions."

Probably everyone at the conference was convinced that Roberts was an impostor. That may explain why no one commented on the size of his hands and wrists or asked him to show any of his scars- why there was no question about any of his physical peculiarities except the present whereabouts of his famous buck teeth.

The carefully prepared brief which had been sent to the governor was not brought out for examination and apparently had never been given thoughtful consideration by anyone in the room. Of course, what Morrison didn't know at the time and what many people today do not realize, was that Governor Thomas Mabry was a relative of the famous storyteller Walter Noble Burns, who had made his legend on telling his version of the life of Billy the Kid.

It is highly likely, therefore, that Mabry's mind was made up before Morrison and Roberts had even arrived. Far from being an impartial judge, Mabry had a vested interest in protecting his family member's legacy. What's more, it is interesting to know that, following the meeting,

Mabry held on to the evidence file, telling Morrison that it would need to become part of the official record and that he could obtain a copy through official channels.

What actually happened, however, was that Mabry buried the file and it was never entered into the official record, which is why one cannot write to the State and obtain a copy today. When he attempted to obtain copies, Mabry's office gave him the run around and attempted to redirect him from office to office. Finally, Morrison appealed directly to Mabry himself, who did not respond. It is uncertain if Morrison was ever able to get the original or if he had copies made before he submitted the file, but this is all captured in period correspondence with the Governor's office.

But, at the time, it all appeared to the world the way the Governor had intended it to appear. With great indignation, he proclaimed to the assembled crowd "I am taking no action, now or ever, on this application for a pardon for Billy the Kid because I do not believe this man is Billy the Kid."

The newspaper men went off to tell the world about it. "The bubble burst today for the buckskin-clad vain little man who claims he is 91 years old and is the one and only, the true Billy the Kid." That was the sort of comment made by all the reporters present. Morrison took his client back to El Paso, expecting to renew his application when the next governor took office.

Brushy Bill was bitterly disappointed. It seemed ironic that yet another governor, like the old members of the Santa Fe Ring, had once again used his power to attempt to humiliate and discredit Billy the Kid in the minds of the public. He did not think he had been given a square deal. He felt worse because he had left for Santa Fe without telling his wife who he claimed to be, and he was afraid she would leave him now that the cat was out of the bag. There was only one bright spot in the whole gloomy business- the fact that he would not have to go back to jail and was not going to be hanged. Otherwise it had been a bad show for him.

He returned to his little house in Hico, Texas, and went to bed for a while. In a few days, he was up and around again, but the strain had been too much for him. About one o'clock on December 27 he went out to mail a package for his wife. Just as he was passing the office of the *Hico News-Review*, his heart stopped ticking and he died in the street with one arm across the bumper of a car parked at the curb.

That might have closed the chapter. For most people, it did. But Brushy Bill was not giving up, even on the wrong side of the grave. He had made some attempts at writing his autobiography and had spent some time with Morrison correcting this narrative just before his death. Morrison had got some more of his recollections on a tape recorder and had taken notes on their innumerable conversations, especially the ones they had while traveling through New Mexico together. In his files were certified copies of legal papers, affidavits from old men and women, letters, and records of interviews with people who knew something about Brushy Bill. He was convinced that Roberts was really what he claimed to be and made up his mind that his man should have a hearing even if it had to be posthumous.

He showed his material to C.L. Sonnichsen, of the staff of Texas Western College, at El Paso, a transplanted Northerner who had made a hobby of Southwestern history and folklore. Sonnichsen had met Roberts for a few minutes once, before the fiasco in Santa Fe, and was not too much impressed by Brushy Bill's buckskin, boots, and badges until he reflected that a little exhibitionism was probably a normal part of the character of any frontier outlaw, including Billy the Kid.

He, naturally, was bothered by the fact that this sort of thing had happened so many times before. Old desperadoes never die; they do not even fade away. They arise from their ashes, full of strength and stories. Every year some graybeard comes forward claiming to be this or that notorious character of the past and many of the great killers have provoked impersonation even before they were dead. John Wilkes Booth supposedly died in Texas long after he should have been moldering in his grave. Jesse James supposedly passed on at one hundred seven, not long after the demise of his friend Brushy Bill Roberts, and other men have appeared who called themselves by the name of the fabulous Jesse. Even such an innocuous but notorious figure as Oscar Wilde was said to have survived his funeral. Billy the Kid, himself, has been reported ever since 1881 as living in Mexico, in California, in Arizona, in New Mexico, in Texas, and in South America. Old men seem to fall naturally into these delusions. It is said that in recent years the caretaker at Roy Bean's old saloon in Langtry, Texas, grew a beard and began passing himself off as the original Law West of the Pecos.

This story could hardly be anything but a hoax, like all the rest of them- not worth paying any attention to. And yet, Sonnichsen thought, in this age of scientific attitudes, could one afford to be positive? Inductive reasoning establishes only a strong probability. Nine hundred and ninety-nine hoaxes do not prove that the thousandth case will be a hoax too. There are always exceptions to confound the skeptic and make him skeptical of his skepticism.

And there were things in Brushy Bill's story that made one wonder. How did he know that negro soldiers from Fort Stanton took positions on the hillside and joined in the firing that day when the Murphy men burned McSween's house? Not many people know about that. How could he be sure of the layout of the second story of the Lincoln courthouse and jail when the experts argue about it? Billy was not the type to read up on these matters and remember every little detail, nor would he have had the opportunity while living destitute in his poor little shack in rural Texas.

And what about the killing of Jim Carlyle, the day the posse cornered Billy the Kid at the Greathouse ranch? The stories say that Billy shot him when he dived through a window. Brushy Bill maintained that Carlyle was shot by the posse men, who thought it was the Kid crashing headfirst into the open. The Kid wrote a letter to Governor Wallace afterward- a letter that historians know about but ordinary readers do not- telling it exactly that way.

If Brushy Bill was not Billy the Kid, he must have been at the Kid's elbow when some of these things happened. His account would, at least, shed valuable light on what actually took place.

And suppose the old man turned out to be an impostor- he would be interesting for that very reason, if for no other. Of the thousand and one fakes who have tried to edge into the limelight, here was the only one who could be investigated; the only one, as Morrison puts it, "who had the guts to go before the governor of his state and ask for a pardon." Here was a Western Lazarus, risen from the dead with a six-shooter in each hand, who was willing to tell of his experiences behind the veil. Such a phenomenon had never been heard of before.

And there was one final thought. How strange it would be if the most famous American of all time should really survive into the Atomic Age; how ironic if, after almost seventy years of lying and running and hiding, he decided, with tears and tremors, to come out of the shadows- and nobody would believe him.

There would be a real story. If it were not true, it ought to be, and somebody should look into it.

Oscar Garrett, son of the immortal Pat, argued that to believe Brushy Bill is to question the veracity not merely of his father, but of "a whole generation"; for if Billy was not killed, practically everybody in southern New Mexico must have heard something about it and must have been accessory to a lie by keeping silent.

It may be so. But before we talk about that let's let Brushy Bill tell his own story.

CHAPTER ONE

BRUSHY BILL'S STORY

"MY GRANDFATHER, Ben Roberts, settled in Nacogdoches, Texas, in 1835. In 1836, he helped Sam Houston free Texas from Mexico. My father was born eight miles from Lexington, Kentucky, March 8, 1832. He fought in the Civil War in the Southern Army, under Ross, until 1863. Then he joined Quantrill. After the war, he went west as a cowboy.

My mother's maiden name as Mary Adeline Dunn. Her native state was Kentucky. Sometime in the late fifties my father moved to Buffalo Gap, Taylor County, Texas. I was born at the Buffalo Gap on December 31, 1859, the last hour of the last day of the year."

Thus begins Brushy Bill Roberts' account of his own life, as set down in a series of paper-covered notebooks and corrected not long before his death.

Historians have accepted without much question the statement that Billy the Kid was born in New York City on November 23, 1859, the William H. and Kathleen Bonney, and that the birth announcement appeared in the New York Times on November 25. Morrison asked the Times for a photo static copy of the announcement and was told that no information about births appeared in that issue.

Morrison was not alone. For over 100 years no one has been able to locate a matching historical record that verifies the Kid's birthplace as New York City. The original source of the information was Sherriff Pat Garrett's book *The Authentic Life of Billy the Kid,* published several years after Garrett claimed to have killed Billy. Garrett's book, mostly written by Ash Upson, has been looked upon negatively by many due to its many historical errors and obvious bias towards self-promotion. Regardless, Garrett's source, he claims, was Billy the Kid. As we shall see, Brushy

Bill Roberts claims that he did tell Garrett that he was born in New York, but that it was not true; as a young man out on the prairie it merely sounded good to tell people he was born back east in New York City.

It is worthy of mention that in more recent times it has become *en vogue* among some to attribute an entirely different New York City family to Billy the Kid in order to circumvent the fact that there is no actual evidence of him there. The creative genealogical gymnastics that allows this is simply to choose a different, but similar name from the census and claim the reason that it is different is a spelling mistake on behalf of the census taker. Given the masses of Irish immigrants in New York in the mid-1800s, finding a family that is "close enough" is not really that difficult, but this certainly cannot be considered serious scholarship.

When Morrison quizzed Brushy Bill, the old man told him that nobody would ever find a record of his being born in New York- that he never saw New York until he was a man. Morrison's notes then record the following conversation:

"Do you know why they think Billy the Kid was born in New York?"

"Yes, because I first told them that in that country up there when I went up there in New Mexico. That's the reason they think it, yes."

"You told them that you were born in New York?"

"Yes, and that I came with Mrs. Antrim."

"You told the Coe boys that you were born in New York?"

"Yes, and I told them Mrs. Antrim was my mother, and that I wanted to go back home to see my mother."

"Well, what did they say?"

"I guess they believed it, but they should have known that Mrs. Antrim died in '74 before I went to that country. My mother died when I was about three years old, but I did not tell them."

"Do you know if other people in the country told stories [lies] about their family and whereabouts?"

"Why yes. I wasn't the only one who ran away from home and landed in that country. I wasn't the only bad man, either. Lots of fugitives went there to live under different names. Just like the James boys and Belle Starr. They came to Lincoln at times, but they did not tell who they were and why they were there. You know as well as I do that they have no proof on record that Billy the Kid was born in New York. Neither do they have any proof that Billy the Kid is dead. They will never find any record that he was born in New York. In those days people did not care where you come from. Not many of them bothered to ask. Sometimes when they talked too much they didn't live very long. No, they didn't live very long. Garrett didn't bother to tell them everything he done before he came to that country either. He was just like the rest of us. He wasn't no angel either."

His real name, the old man said, was William Henry Roberts. At the age of three he changed it for what seemed adequate reason.

J.H. Roberts, his father, was not a suitable person to control the destiny of any child, least of all his own. "Wild Henry" was a rough and violent follow, and his Civil War experiences, particularly his service with the bloodthirsty guerilla leader Quantrill, were not of the sort to civilize and refine him. This fact was plainly, and probably painfully, apparent to his relatives. Consequently, when Mrs. Roberts died, in 1862, while her husband was gone to the wars, her kinfolks came to the baby's rescue. Mrs. Roberts' half-sister, Mrs. Kathrine Ann (Kathleen) Bonney, came down from the Indian Territory and took him away with her, being careful to avoid leaving her address lest the father should follow and claim his child.

They went first to Trinidad, Colorado, then to Santa Fe, and finally to Silver City, New Mexico. Young Billy Roberts lived with Mrs. Bonney (later Mrs. Antrim) and her mother until he was twelve years old, and passed as her son.

Apparently, Mrs. Bonney covered her tracks well, for when the Civil War was over and Wild Henry Roberts came back to Buffalo Gap, he was unable to learn where his son had been taken. Soon he was married again-this time to Elizabeth Ferguson, of Tennessee. She became the mother of James Roberts, who was some six years younger than his half-brother Billy. In later years Billy consistently called his father's second wife "Mother," carefully omitting all reference to the things that happened to him before he was twelve years old.

Morrison was unable to find any verification for the story that Billy left Silver City at the age of twelve after committing his first murder. He left, according to Roberts' story, in 1872, at that age, but it was to go back to Texas to see his people. He first stopped at Buffalo Gap, only to find that his father and step mother had moved. He located them at Carlton, Texas, and lived with them for about two years, which was as long as he could stand it. During this period, he was known as "Kid Roberts," since he was small for his age.

The only good thing that could be said for old man Roberts was that he made his son proficient in roping, riding, and shooting and this would serve young Billy well as he faced survival in the brutal west.

But there is more, this early experience with his father no doubt helped shape the dual nature of his personality. Up until this time Billy had spent many years around gentle, caring women. Moving forward, he would increasingly spend time with more and more ruthless, tough men.

It is no wonder, therefore, that Billy's character reflected the best of both worlds, so to speak, for a western man. He was both a fun loving, gentle, and loyal friend but he could also be an extremely tough, ruthless, and cold as ice killer when needed.

"From the time I was big enough to ride, I've been in the saddle," he wrote in his old age. "Beginning by riding behind my father on the old Chidam [Chisholm] trail on cattle drives, seeing thousands of head in a single drive. I was a pretty good rider for a kid, riding most of the yearlings that they would run up. From that I began riding the two-year-old colts that the older boys would run up from the range. That was great sport to my boy friends. An old man stepped up to my dad one day and said, "That boy of yours is going to get some of these boys killed." He was a Baptist preacher from Arkansas. My father told him if he didn't want his boys around where other boys were learning to ride, that he could keep them at home. "My boy is learning to be a bronc buster, and I believe he will learn if he don't get his neck broken."

"My father raised a goodly bunch of horses. I would step out in the herd and get one and break it by him helping me. By the time I was fourteen I would bar no common horse. I picked a four-year-old black out of the bunch and broke him. He could pace or single-foot as fast as a common horse could run. Coming in one Sunday evening, he said, "You will have to let the doctor have that horse." I told him that I had already broken fourteen horses and would have to go back to the heard to get another. "If that is the way you feel about it, I can break horses for the other man as well as for you, and get paid for it." He drew a whip from his cow horse and like to have beaten me to death. It taken me about a month to get well. My mother doctored me up, but I didn't go back to the herd to get another horse.

"I left home as soon as I was well enough to travel, which was in May of 1874. From there I went to the Indian Territory by the way of the old Chisholm Trail with a herd of cattle."

KATHRINE ANN McCARTY
Brushy Bill said this woman was Billy the Kid's aunt

"As my father had warned me that he would have the Rangers to bring me back home, I took precautions to climb from my horse and get into the chuck wagon and cover up lest he find me as we passed through the towns, which was very few and far between.

"I quit this herd at Briartown. As I was prodding along the trail, a big dark-featured man on a bay horse came dashing up."

"Where you going, Son?"

"I could see no use in lying to him so I told him very bluntly, 'I'm running away from home.' And I told him why." He said, "Climb up, Son; you may have a place to stay with me." So, I figured that would be jail.

"We rode up to a place where I was sure he lived. He told me to go into the corral and throw a saddle on one of the horses there and bring it out. He called his cow dog and rode down across the prairie and drove up four good milk cows. Then he told me, 'Put the horses away and I'll tell you what will be done with you in the morning.'"

"So, you may be sure I didn't rest good that night, as I figured I was jail bound next day."

"But early next morning, very much to my surprise, I found I had fell into the hands of Belle Reed, later known as Belle Starr, the great outlaw. She told me very plainly was I was to do. I was to go up on a mountain which overlooked the surrounding country, with a pair of field glasses, and be a sentry or guard for her. My instructions were if I seen one man or rider approaching, blow one blast upon a bugle. Or if two men were approaching, blow two blasts, and so forth. And she, Belle, would do the rest."

"My job was a general chore boy around the place. They would go away lots of times leaving no one there but Aunt Ann, the negro cook, and me. I would take a pack horse and go to town for provisions and ammunition for them. She would go with me to the Canadian River and see me across and meet me there coming back. During the time I was there I met all the outlaws in the territory. It seemed to be a holdout for outlaws there. I got acquainted with the James boys and the Younger boys, Joe Shaw's bunch, Rube Burrow and Jim Burrow and their bunch. I have seen them bring in sacks of money and throw it on the bed and Belle would count it out and say, "This is your part and this is my part." Two men would be sitting there holding six shooters."

"At one time, an outlaw ordered me to saddle his horse, talking pretty rough to me, and Belle overheard him. She told him that I was her kid and she would protect me. She told him to saddle his own horse and the quickest way to get away was too slow, for she was marking him off her list. She said, 'Blackie, you keep away from that boy or I'll blow your brains out.'

BELLE STARR

"In my practice Belle discovered I was a good shot with a rifle or six-gun and offered me a job as her right-hand man. The offer I at once refused, as I told her I did not like the outlaw trail. She saw that she could not make an outlaw of me and told me when I got ready to go I could go. At the end of three months she gave me nice clothes and fifty dollars in money, saying "Texas Kid, any time you want to come back, you have a home with me." She carried me within about a mile of town and set me down."

"After leaving her, I went to my aunt's home in Silver City for a few months. When my aunt died, I went back to the Indian Territory and fell in with a bunch of cattle rustlers and I was just a lackey boy for them. I had to black their boots, clean up their saddles, and anything they said to do. They beat me, they banged me, they swore they would hang me if I didn't do it. One of the rustlers took a shine to me and gave me a small gun to protect myself from the other rustlers."

"They were fixing to beat up on me one day when I took a shot at a big rowdy, grazing his temple. My friend who had given me the gun stepped up and said, "Here, here, you have beat that boy enough. Try me for a change." At which he fell in and whipped four of them."

"The boss also liked me. He told me, 'Son if you can ride that buckskin hoss in there in the corral, I'll give him to you. Also, the pick of them saddles in the shed. But mind you, Son, that hoss is a killer.' I rode him after a nasty fight. He sunned his sides and his belly too. I tell you that hoss could buck."

"I left the ranch next morning for Dodge City, and at the end of five days, I reached that place. The wagon yard is the place I stopped to leave my horse and hunt something to eat. There was four men sitting by a camp fire eating supper, and they invited me to eat with them. I was thankful for the meal. One of the men said, 'Son, you have a nice hoss and saddle there.' I told them, 'Yes, and a high bucker, too."

"Next morning when I brought him out for a rub down, he began to buck at the end of my lariat. At which one of the men said, 'Son you cannot ride that hoss. There's not one in twenty that can.' I told them, "I rode him here. I'll ride him away."

"Well, Son, if you ride that hoss you need not look further for a job. You already have one with me." At which he gave me ten dollars saying, "Son, make yourself to home. We'll leave here in about four days. We're starting on a long trip to the Black Hills of South Dakota."

"Someone who was acquainted with my father notified him that I was seen in Dodge City, Kansas. He at once wired to the officials to catch and hold me two months at which time he would come after me. But the city marshal only had a brief description of me. So, he jailed the wrong lad. It was a lucky break for me as it gave me two months start on my dad. But never again could he get a trace of me, for I was on my way north- four of us and two pack horses."

The rest of Roberts' account of these early days is hard to follow. He fell into the company of a man he calls Mountain Bill, who decided to make a career of betting on Billy's skill as a rider. According to one of Billy's notebooks, they covered practically the entire West, Billy riding the worst horses the ranchers and show people could dig up for him, while Mountain Bill placed bets which netted him plenty. They were in Arizona and Montana and Oregon and Wyoming and Nebraska. No horse was too much for the Texas Kid, and he attributed his success to the fact that Mountain Bill had placed him with a band of Cheyenne and Arapaho Indians for training. "I trained with the Indians four months and came out an expert rider. They taught me to ride with a one-hold surcingle or a two-hold surcingle. Also, they taught me to ride with a mane hold." He was not at his best riding in a corral, but preferred to stage his contests "on the bald prairie. I learned to ride a lick saddle with one girt, without a choke rope. Neither did I use hobbled stirrups. I used loose-rowel O.K. spurs. I was supposed to ride anything that wore hair and contest it according to Cheyenne rules after the Indians turned me loose."

Apparently, the boy started his career as a bronco buster at a place called the Daugherty ranch, in the Oklahoma Indian Territory. He concluded this chapter of his life by taking a trip to Arizona with Mountain Bill. "Bill and I went to Arizona to visit with Bill's sister and brother-in-law. This was about the first of April, 1877. We worked a few months on the Gila ranch. I think that was the name. I left Mountain Bill here and went down to Mesilla, New Mexico, where I ran into Jesse Evans and the boys I had known before. I met Jesse in Silver City about 1870 or 1871 and went with him down into Old Mexico when I left Silver City. I knew Mel Segura right after I knew Evans. Jesse and me stayed at the ranch of Segura's uncle in Chihuahua State, Mexico.

"When I broke Segura from jail at San Elizario, we rode to his uncle's ranch in Chihuahua, where we hid for a few days. I don't remember how long. We stayed there lots of times. Segura went down into Mexico and I rode back to Mesilla, that summer of '77. Met Jimmy McDaniel, Billy Morton, Frank Baker, and Tom O'Keefe there."

CHAPTER TWO

THE FEUD BEGINS

AS FATE would have it, the life of Billy the Kid was about to dramatically change forever as he was plunged into the bloodiest cattle war in western history. The Lincoln County War was a conflict between a group of men known as the Murphy-Dolan faction, which included some of the prominent citizens of Lincoln County, New Mexico, and a newly arrived Englishman named John Tunstall and his allies and followers, one of whom was Billy the Kid. By the time the conflict had ended more than a dozen men were dead and the President of the United States himself had removed the governor of the state to restore order.

Many books have been written on this subject, and many men have shared their first-hand accounts. Never before Morrison's interview with William Henry Roberts, however, had anyone had the first-hand account of the most famous participant in that war, Billy the Kid.

Brushy began, "In the summer of '77 Tom O'Keefe and I left Mesilla for the Loving's Bend near Phoenix, New Mexico. We had a run-in with some Indians in the Guadalupe mountains and I got lost. Lost my horse in the mountains during the fight. I struggled through the mountains and wound up at the Jones place at Seven Rivers. My feet were all cut up. I had walked several days through mountain brush.

"Jim and John Jones were working for Chisum, so I went to work with them- I think up at Bosque Grande. Frank McNab was foreman. Later Chisum moved to South Spring, I think. Tom Storey, Miles Fisher, Walker, Goss, Black, and Ketchum worked there too, I think. Sally Chisum was already there when I went to work for Chisum. Sally was not Old John's daughter. She was his niece. Her daddy was all right then, though."

"I made a cattle drive to Dodge City that fall with Chisum's outfit. We went up the Loving Trail, I think. Or the Goodnight Trail; I don't remember now. Maybe both of them run cattle on that trail. That was before my time. It was a good wide trail that connected with the other trails further up."

"This was the time we had the tintype picture made at the end of the cattle trail in Dodge City."

AT THE END OF THE CATTLE TRAIL

Copy of the tintype Brushy referenced that was made in Dodge City in the fall of 1877. Left to right: Jim Jones, Bob Speaks (trail boss), John Jones, and Billy the Kid- the latter identified by Bill and Sam Jones, brothers of Jim and John Jones

"I bought my first horse in that country from Chisum when I went to work with the Jones boys. He had that little roan that was wild and could run, so I bought him and paid for him out of my pay from Chisum."

"I left Chisum and worked for Maxwell a short time at Bosque Redondo. Then I went over to Frank Coe's place on the Ruidoso. While there I run into Jesse Evans and Baker again. They took me to Murphy's cow camp in the Seven Rivers country. Evans and his gang stole cattle from Chisum, and some horses too. They still had some of the horses when I went to work with them at Murphy's Seven Rivers camp that winter. They had stolen this roan, too, but he got back to the ranch."

"Later on, we got into an argument about my share of the bunch of cattle we cut out, and one of the horses I was supposed to get, and they welshed on the deal. Baker accused me of stealing the little roan that I rode up there on when I went to work with them. I told him I bought the horse from Chisum with my own money, and I aimed to keep him too, I did. I had both six-shooters on him when I said it, but Jesse knocked the right one down. I swung the other over with my left hand and held it right in his ribs while I told him. He told the boys to keep still or suffer the consequences, and begged me to leave peacefully.

"You know Jesse and I were nearly like brothers. We had roamed New Mexico, Arizona, Texas, and Old Mexico together. Jesse and I argued, and I nearly killed him one day in Lincoln, but I always felt close to him. I tried to spring him from jail in Stockton one time after they killed Chapman."

"I almost killed Baker and Morton that time. Guess I should have done it, but I didn't."

"Well, after Jesse told them to keep still, I jumped on my little roan pony and rode back toward Tunstall's ranch on the Feliz. I was on my way to Coe's place. I stopped at Tunstall's to get something to eat. We always rode up to ranch houses when we got hungry. I knew some of the boys there. Dick Brewer was foreman. Bowdre had left Chisum and went to Tunstall's. John Middleton, Doc Skurlock, Bob Widenmann, and lots of others were there too. Dick Brewer, the foreman, was a friend of Coe, and I told him I was headed back there, as I had had trouble with Murphy's men. After eating that day, Tunstall said that I might as well stay there with the boys, so he hired me to ride for him. That's the way I met Tunstall."

"John Middleton was lots older than the rest of us. He was as mean as hell, a heavy drinker. Tom O'Folliard was about the age of Jesse Evans and me. Tom was a big fellow. Jesse and me were small. Tom was good, but liked to drink some. Charlie Bowdre was older than us. He was a good man- could shoot quick. Rudabaugh was the toughest man I ever knew. He was older and rougher and had been through lots of trouble. I saw him in Sonora after that shooting at Maxwell's when they thought they had killed me. He was calm; not easily excited. Tom Pickett and Wilson were not bad men. I don't remember of seeing them in that war up there. Skurlock wasn't a bad man. He was in the war, though. Hank Brown was from a good family, but he was mean. So was Fred Wayte. They left me on a cattle drive just before Skurlock or just after him. I don't remember now."

"Selman fought on our side in that cattle business in '78. I knew him in '77. He was always in trouble and my men helped him, too. He was a good shot and had lots of nerve, too, he did. I don't think he worked for Chisum on that ranch. But I don't know. He was up there with the rest of us."

"Tunstall had a store in Lincoln in opposition to Murphy and Dolan. McSween became a partner with Tunstall. Then Old John Chisum joined them. Murphy men had been rounding up Old John's cattle and selling them to the army at Fort Stanton. Then Chisum would pay us boys a dollar a head to get his cattle back. That is how the cattle war got started, if you want to know it. Tunstall got mixed up in it through McSween and Murphy's troubles. McSween had worked for Murphy as his lawyer. Later McSween joined forces with Chisum and the trouble got worse."

"The Murphy bunch had come to Lincoln before McSween and Tunstall got there. Murphy and Dolan had been filling government contracts for beef and provisions. McSween was hired by Murphy to prosecute the Chisum cowboys for cattle rustling. McSween found out that Chisum was only taking his own cattle from the Murphy boys, so he quit Murphy and started up with Tunstall, who had come in from England to settle in this country. He raised blooded horses and ranched cattle on the Feliz."

"From this time on there were two factions fighting to get the business. Each accused the other of cattle stealing. I guess both of them were right about it."

"The Murphy bunch had the backing of the Santa Fe Ring, which included Tom Catron, U.S. District Attorney, and his brother-in-law. Of course, they were not out in the open with it, but during the cattle war Old Tom took over the Murphy-Dolan property. All the politicians belonged to the Santa Fe Ring, even judges and attorneys."

"Brady, the Sheriff, wasn't any better than anyone else up there. He was a Catron man and he did just as they told him. He had threatened to kill Tunstall several times. That attorney that prosecuted me in Lincoln County that time and the judge too were Catron men. How could a person get justice among them? The law wasn't no good."

"Later on, the governor was put out of office by the President of the United States."

"Tunstall and McSween were ranching together on the Feliz ranch of Tunstall's. McSween was taking care of the estate of Old Man Fritz. He collected on an insurance policy, and Murphy claimed that Fritz, his former partner at Stanton, owed the money to him. They had a lot of trouble about McSween's law fee. Finally, Murphy got a judgment or attachment against McSween and started to pick up partnership property of Tunstall's. We turned the cattle over to the law. Tunstall had a herd of fine horses of his own. He decided that we would drive the horses over to Lincoln and surrender them until the case was cleared up."

"On the eighteenth of February Tunstall picked Dick Brewer, me, Widenmann, and I believe that John Middleton went along with us with the horses on the drive to town. While we were on the way to Lincoln, a Sheriff's posse, headed by Billy Morton, rode into the ranch. They found that we were gone to Lincoln so they started after us. Some of their boys took the cattle to Seven Rivers while the rest of them came after us."

THE WEST END OF LINCOLN
Showing the rear of the Murphy Building, where Billy the Kid was confined

"We had crossed the country and was well up in the mountains when we heard them coming. We tried to get Tunstall to ride for it as we were outnumbered. He didn't want to leave his herd. He said that they wouldn't do anything, but we decided to run for it. We stood off and watched them approach the herd. They killed Tunstall in cold blood and went on into Lincoln. Afterward we rode in town and the boys went out and got Tunstall's body. None of the Murphy boys were present at the funeral of Tunstall when we buried his body behind the Tunstall store. And it was good for them that they stayed away. Tunstall was a good man. He had been good to me and treated me like a gentleman. I lost the best friend I ever had when they killed him. I swore that day that I would make them pay with their lives for this dirty deed."

"Judge Wilson, a friend of ours, swore in Dick Brewer as constable and gave him a warrant for the arrest of the murderers of Tunstall. Dick took me, Henry Brown, Fred Wayte, Charlie Bowdre, Frank McNab, and a few others to go after them. The hunt began for the murderers, who had left Lincoln for their hideout in the Seven Rivers country."

"We rode up on some of them and the fight began. Some of them got away, but we captured Billy Morton, the leader of the mob, and Baker. Both of them had been good pals of mine until I left them at Murphy's cow camp a few months before. I should have killed them the day I left there."

"We put them on horses and started for the Chisum ranch, where we stayed overnight. The next morning, we stopped at Roswell on our way to Lincoln. We knew that Murphy's boys would be waiting for us on the road to Lincoln, so we went the north road over the mountains. We stopped at Agua Negra, in the Capitans, where an argument started between one of our posse and Frank McNab. McNab had to kill one of our men during the argument. Then Morton and Baker started to run for it. I didn't want to take any chance of losing them, so I had to shoot them. We went on into Lincoln."

Brushy Bill's memories were apt to hit high spots. He returned again and again to the climactic episodes, particularly the ones in which he came near to losing his life, or in which he felt his part had been misrepresented. He was pretty clear about the next big event in the war- the killing of Sheriff William Brady- and he had reason to be, for that was the killing that brought Billy the Kid a death sentence. This is the way the story came out.

"Sheriff Brady was gunning for me with warrants for cattle stealing. He had caught us at Seven Rivers a short time before and arrested us. He took my six-shooter, a .44 single action with pearl handles that I paid twenty-five dollars for in San Antone. I thought lots of that pearl-handle .44. We got out on bond, but he said he didn't have that one six-shooter. He gave me a .44 with wooden handles. He still had the warrants and I knew he was still looking for me. He was a Murphy man and had some tough boys on his list of deputies. I didn't aim to be arrested anymore, I didn't."

"In the forenoon of April 1, Brady, his deputy, Hindman, and County Clerk Billy Matthews- I believe there was someone else, too- were coming down the street from Murphy's store to the old courthouse when we spied them. Henry Brown, John Middleton, and Fred Wayte were with me behind the adobe wall alongside of Tunstall's store. Matthews and I had a run-in a few days before, but my bullet missed him. As they passed along the wall, I leveled down on Matthews, but missed him. The other boys were firing at the same time. Brady fell dead on the spot. Hindman died soon after, but Matthews got away and ran behind an adobe wall down the street. Fred and I jumped over the wall and ran into the street where Brady was lying. I pulled my pearl-handled .44 off his body in time to catch a bullet from Matthews' rifle behind the adobe. It tore the flesh above my right hip and clipped Wayte through the leg. We got back over the wall, then rode out of Lincoln. I wasn't hurt much- never stopped riding- but Wayte was laid up for a few days. They were armed with rifles and six-shooters. They would have killed us if they had gotten the chance."

For over a century, the killing of Sheriff William Brady has been considered one of the Kid's most cowardly acts. To ambush an officer of the law and murder him in cold blood in the dusty street of the town he was sworn to protect is unforgivable in any age. Yet the paradigms and societal norms we all hold so dear didn't seem to accurately portray life in Lincoln County in the late 1870s. Far from being an agent of the law, Brady was allegedly no more than a hired enforcer for the Murphy-Dolan faction, who had co-opted the structures of society to cloak their unethical and immoral acts. Brady, for example, was alleged to have threatened to kill Tunstall, a law-abiding citizen, many times to his face in an attempt to run him out of town for his boss. This is not exactly the role of a local town Sheriff.

What's more, Brady's "posse" was the one that actually carried out his threat, and shot an unarmed and defenseless John Tunstall in cold blood. As if this were not enough, they shot his horse as well, and then posed the body with it as though Tunstall had fallen sleep with his horse.

These were clearly not ethical or moral men. Among them were many known outlaws and another well-known bully with a badge, Bob Olinger. Bob Olinger was a vain man with long, flowing hair that wore buckskins everywhere he went, as he fancied himself some kind of impressive frontier figure. He was known to carry a large bowie knife with which he would pick his teeth in an attempt to intimidate those around him. In reality, Olinger was a coward that was known to shoot men when they were at a significant disadvantage and would avenge any perceived affront against him with murder. These were the type of men Sheriff William Brady was surrounding himself with when the Regulators attacked him that day in the streets of Lincoln.

Regardless, for many years historians have wondered what in the world would have possessed the Kid to run out into the street amidst a hail of gunfire to check Brady's body. Most speculate that it was either to steal his rifle or to take the warrant he had for McSween's arrest. Neither of these seem to make much sense. For one thing, many witnesses claimed that it was Fred Wayte that took Brady's rifle. For another, even if they had found and taken the warrant, how difficult could it be for Murphy-Dolan to arrange to have a replacement made? Finally, the fact should not be overlooked that Billy already had a rifle and was in the middle of shooting it behind very good cover when he chose to jump over the wall. It makes no sense for him to run out at that point and risk his life unless he had a more significant reason.

What does make sense, however, is if, with their purpose of killing and scattering some of the Murphy men achieved, but before leaving town, Billy wanted to take a chance to finally get back his special-order pearl handled .44 pistol that had been stolen from him. According to Brushy, he paid $25 for the pistol. It just so happens that, according to James E. Serven's book *Colt Firearms* (Wolfe Publishing Company, 1954), the cost of a new Colt pistol (various new models, including the Single Action Army) remained steady at $16 each between the years 1872 and 1897. What's more, in 1872 you could add ivory grips to a derringer for $5. There is no price for pearl grips for a full-sized pistol, but one could extrapolate that $9 is within the realm of possibility, which would bring the total to $25 or very close, just as Brushy claimed.

Brushy continued, "Old Dad Peppin testified at my trial in Mesilla that I killed Brady. How did he know who killed anybody? He was the other fellow running down the street with Hindman and Matthews that day when Brady was killed. I was trying to get Matthews first. Nobody knows who killed Brady and Hindman. There was four against four. Nobody tried to find out who killed them, either."

But this was not the only gunplay in New Mexico that Spring, just three days after Brady's death, on April 4, came the fight at Blazer's Mill, in which Buckshot Roberts, a cranky but courageous old man, gave Billy the Kid and his gang more trouble than they could handle. Brushy Bill knew all about that battle, too. The shootout at Blazer's Mill has become one of the most well-known shootouts of the Wild West and the Lincoln County War. The details, according to all accounts, were that the Regulators were out in force that day and had settled in at Blazer's Mill to have some lunch. As Brushy rightly said, along with them, they had several warrants for Murphy men, and one among them was Buckshot Roberts. There is debate among historians around the nature and character of Buckshot Roberts. Some take the view that he was a broken down old man that was just in the wrong place at the wrong time and others claim he was a wily old buffalo hunter, and very deadly. Either way, Brushy was clear that as far as he was concerned he was still very able-bodied and a nothing more than a no-good bounty hunter.

"Now you take that Buckshot," Brushy said, "He was worse than any of them. He was out to get our scalps for the lousy money on our heads. He didn't fight in that cattle war. He was an outlaw before he went to that country, he was. He was a snake too, he was. But he got what was coming to him that day at Blazer's place."

"Buckshot was run out of Texas by the Rangers. He landed in Lincoln County. He came over to San Patricio, where I had a house, with Murphy's gang one time to raid us out. Then a few days before he come up to Blazer's, he stopped at my place in San Patricio and started an argument with Bowdre. I ran him off. Then he came back later as Charlie and I was leaving that night. He shot at us but we rode out of it. That's the reason I was trying so hard to kill him at Blazer's."

Whether or not what Brushy said was true, it seems as though on this occasion, Buckshot Roberts did apparently come upon the Regulators by accident. He had ridden up to mail a letter and had just secured his donkey when George Coe came around the corner. George and Buckshot were friendly with one another, and they sat for quite a while talking. This conversation was related to Walter Noble Burns in a letter from Frank Coe in detail, but the long and short of it was that Coe told him that they had warrants for his arrest, and suggested he surrender quietly.

Much to his surprise, Roberts declined. He was confident that once he surrendered that he would be killed, much like Morton and Baker, and was quite committed to taking his chances in a shootout. About that time, the rest of the Regulators came around the corner and the shooting began. It isn't definitively known who got off the first shot, but likely it was Roberts, who struck Charlie Bowdre in the gut. Likewise, Bowdre got his gun into action and put a hole right through Roberts. Bowdre's shot would prove fatal to Roberts, but not immediately, and the old man continued to fight. Miraculously, Robert's shot to Bowdre's gut was deflected by his belt buckle and Bowdre was unharmed.

Despite his mortal wound, Buckshot was game and worked the lever on his Winchester as fast as he could, sending chunks of lead towards his enemies. Everyone took cover, but would pop out from behind it from time to time to return fire. Coe mentions that at one point, when Billy the Kid stuck his head out to look, Coe yelled at him to get down and the Kid was only narrowly missed by one of Buckshot's bullets. Interestingly, due to his position when the battle started, Coe found himself on the wrong side of his friend's shooting and had to retreat into a doorway when the shooting began.

With his Winchester now empty, Roberts retreated through a doorway into a home and grabbed a Sharps rifle leaning against the wall. Although mortally wounded, he was able to run inside, slam the door, and drag a mattress across the room to lay in front of the window. He then proceeded to lay on the mattress and attempt to get a bead on the Regulators, each of which were under cover.

Regulator foreman and Deputy Constable Dick Brewer was behind a woodpile and very angry. While most of the Regulators knew that Buckshot had been hit and wanted to wait until he died, Brewer insisted they press their attack. At one point, he stuck his head up over the wood pile in an attempt to get a better view of Roberts, only to have his head blown clean off by a well-placed shot between his eyes, courtesy of Buckshot Roberts.

This ended the fight for everyone but Billy the Kid, who made his own final attempt to charge and kill Buckshot. In Brushy Bill's version he stated simply, "I'll never forget that fight at Blazer's. We had warrants for his arrest. Dick was a deputy and we were with him. He got Brewer, though. Almost got me. But Bowdre got him."

Brushy never explained what he meant that Buckshot Roberts "almost got him" but history tells us that at one point after Brewer was killed, Billy charged the building, blazing away with both six guns at Roberts. He made it to him only to knocked senseless by the barrel of Robert's empty rifle, thus ending the battle for Billy. Roberts later died from his wounds and was buried together with Dick Brewer, whom he had killed.

Chapter Three

Blood in The Streets

The next big battle for the regulators has become known as The Battle of Lincoln and was a multi-day battle that would prove to be the end of the McSween faction. On July 15th, 1878 Alexander McSween returned to Lincoln with a large number of men accompanying him. Shortly thereafter, a group of Murphy men rode into town and at some point, the two factions began exchanging gunfire and securing themselves in various defensive positions throughout the town. While the last three days were the most intense, the events leading up to those days began on July 15th. Unfortunately, this battle would prove to be the end of the struggle for the McSween faction, with the exception, of course, of Billy the Kid. It was a bloody business, and Brushy Bill Roberts described it as if every detail had been burned into his memory with a branding iron.

What's more, Brushy knew obscure details that even the most seasoned historians did not know. Details, for example, that three U.S. Army soldiers were killed during the battle. The only source for this information would have been firsthand knowledge or a careful review of Col. Dudley's court martial file, which was certainly not available to either Brushy Bill or Morrison.

Brushy continued, "John Copeland was appointed Sheriff of Lincoln County to succeed Brady. He served until he was removed by the governor. Then Dad Peppin was appointed Sheriff.

"Before he was appointed, Old Peppin worked for Coughlan, who was buying our cattle. We would take a herd of horses up to Tascosa to sell, and we drove cattle back for Coghlan at Three Rivers. Peppin skinned stolen cattle too, he did. That was rough country then. It was dog eat dog, that's all."

"Jimmy Dolan run the Murphy store in Lincoln in the Murphy building where I was in jail when I killed those two guards. They had large cattle interests and were selling to the army and the Indian agency. They would steal cattle from Chisum and we'd get them back for him."

"We were friends with Chisum until he lied to me over that cattle business. He promised to pay us boys a dollar a head to get his cattle back from Murphy. Then he didn't want to pay off. In that war, he and McSween promised to give us $500 apiece to fight for them. We'd have won that war too, if those black soldiers of Dudley's had been kept out. We had the Murphy gang whipped, we did."

"McSween had been hiding out at Chisum's ranch. They had threatened to kill him. We went over to the ranch to get him and bring him back to Lincoln. The Sheriff's posse followed us and we had a fight right there at Chisum's. We whipped them and they left. We took McSween back with us, too, we did. As we rode into Lincoln, Peppin and his posse started to fighting us. The real battle broke out a little later when we took over Montana's house across the street from the tower where Peppin's posse was holed up. Some of our boys went into Tunstall's store and the rest of us went into McSween's house next door. They had filled Murphy's building with their men. They put men on the hillside just south of town until some of our men shot them loose."

"They started firing on us as we rode in that day, so we fought back at them. On the last day, Colonel Dudley rode into town with those black soldiers. He demanded that McSween stop the fighting. We told him, 'They started it- now go and stop them, will you? As long as they shoot at us, we intend to protect ourselves."

"He told McSween that he couldn't interfere, that the Sheriff had the matter in hand. But he went and run some of our men out of town, he did. Why did he do that, if he couldn't interfere? Anyway, we didn't surrender to the mob."

"Then they set fire to the building to smoke us out. We kept fighting all that day, though. We had them whipped until the army came into town. If we could have kept them soldiers out there at Stanton, we would have whipped Peppin's posse. We didn't lose any men until that night. We had gotten a few of their men up there on the hillside."

"While the house was burning, Mrs. McSween entered Dudley's camp and begged him to stop the fighting. He said that he did not have the authority to interfere. But some of his soldiers were up on the side of that hill firing at us with the Murphy men."

"By dark the house had burned, except the kitchen, which was nearly gone. About dusk in the evening, a little after dark, we decided to make a run for it. The women had already left the house. The building was caving in from the fire."

"There was a window in the east side of the kitchen. The door opened on the northeast corner into an area way between the house and an adobe wall. There was a board fence between the house and corral, running north and south, with a gate at the northeast corner of the yard. Tunstall's store building was east of the board fence on the other side of the corral where we kept the horses. Some of the murphy men were just across the river, which run past the north of the house. The gate in the board fence opened toward Tunstall's store."

"We opened the back door and looked out just as Bob Beckwith and some of them soldiers started to come in."

"Harvey Morris, who was studying law with McSween, stepped out of the kitchen door first. I was right behind him, and Jose Chavez was behind me. Chavez was followed by McSween, Romero, and Samora. Morris was shot down in front of me. I ran through the gate with both .44's blazing, and Jose Chavez was right behind me. He and I ran toward Tunstall's store, was fired at, and then turned toward the river. A bullet went through my hat as I come out the gate. Lost my hat and one six-shooter crossing the water. We ran down the other side of the river. There was brush and undergrowth all along there."

"We all left the house together, but McSween, Samora, and Romero were driven back by the bullets when they reached the gate. They turned and ran back to the small enclosure between the house and the adobe wall, where Bob Beckwith was standing as I came through the door. I think one of my bullets killed him there in that enclosure. They started for the gate the second time but were driven back to the small enclosure where all three were killed by John Jones, John Kinney, and those soldiers of Dudley's. O'Folliard, Salazar, and the rest of our boys started through. All of them escaped except Salazar, who was cut down by the door. They thought he was dead. He crawled out that night after they left. He told me how McSween and the rest fell over there."

"I met Tom O'Folliard at Gallegos' house in San Patricio a few days afterward. Tom saw all of it. He was still in the burning house."

"We stayed at my place in San Patricio after that and tried to work on a ranch. We tried to settle down, but they wouldn't let me alone, they wouldn't. I wanted to make my home in this country, but they run me out. They made outlaws of us, that's all. We had to live some way. So, we saw to it that we did make a living."

This is an interesting part of Brushy's narrative, the claim that Billy the Kid maintained a home in San Patricio, New Mexico. It stands to reason that if Billy had a home there then there should be some record of it. The difficulty lies in the many aliases used by The Kid during this period. Census records show that in 1880 Billy the Kid, using the alias "Wm. Bonny", was staying with Charles Bowdre and his wife in Fort Sumner, NM. This census was enumerated over three days from June 17-19. Brushy stated that he would often go back and forth between Lincoln, Fort Sumner, San Patricio, and various sheep camps in the area so it is not unusual for him to be in Fort Sumner with the Bowdre family at this time.

San Patricio was only about 15 miles from Lincoln but was about 120 miles from Fort Sumner, about 2-3 days ride for a cowboy traveling under normal speeds. The San Patricio census was taken on June 16, 1880. San Patricio is, of course, where the Gallegos family lived as did the Chavez family. Both are listed on the census along with many other Hispanic families as at this time San Patricio was a Hispanic town. As a matter of fact, out of the two hundred and thirty residents recorded as living in San Patricio, there are just exactly two men with Anglo names. The first, John Newcomb, who was from Missouri, 49 years old, and living there with his wife.

The second man, Joseph S. Murphy, was single, 20 years old, and from Texas. Joseph S. Murphy lists no relatives and his occupation is supplied as a laborer. Could this single white man in an all Mexican town be another alias of Billy the Kid? If so, could he have been enumerated in the June 16th census and then arrive by July 19th in time to be recorded at Fort Sumner? Possibly, but on the June 16th census in San Patricio there is a line through Joseph S. Murphy's name. He is not deceased or he would not be listed. Perhaps he was not present? Among other questions the census asks the following: *"Is the person (on the day on the enumerator's visit) sick or temporarily disabled so as to be unable to attend to ordinary business or duties? If so, what is the sickness or disability?"*

It is interesting to note that on the day of the enumerator's visit this Joseph S. Murphy was indeed listed as "sick" or temporarily disabled. The cause of this affliction was also listed. Joseph S. Murphy was, according to the census, incapacitated by a *"gunshot wound"*. Was this an excuse used by his neighbors to account for him not being present or was The Kid really recovering from a gunshot wound in San Patricio before heading to Fort Sumner to be with the Bowdres?

Further, if this man is not Billy the Kid, then who is this twenty-year-old Joseph S. Murphy from Texas that is living alone in an all Hispanic town? He is the same age as Brushy claimed he would have been (Brushy would have turned 21 on December 31st so he would have been 20 on June 16, 1880) and the same age as Billy the Kid would have been. He is from Texas just as Brushy claimed to be, he lives totally alone, and apparently his job as a laborer exposes him to the dangers of gunshot wounds, the only one in town with such an affliction according to the census. Brushy Bill Roberts stated several times in his narrative that he "had a house" in San Patricio so it would not have been so easy to avoid being recorded on the census. After all, this was a small town of only two hundred and thirty people at the time.

No, Joseph S. Murphy sounds remarkably like an alias that would have been used by Billy, especially when one considers that "Joseph S. Murphy" could be an amalgamation of various people that "the Kid" knew, including "Joseph Antrim" and possibly even "John S. Chisum" and "Lawrence Murphy", the two prominent sides of the Lincoln Count War in 1880. Further, there are no records whatsoever of any Joseph S. Murphy as having been born in Texas in any other US Census in any other town in the country for any date. The single entry in San Patricio is the only record of this person's existence anywhere in history.

Brushy continued, "I gathered up some of the boys and hung around Fort Sumner picking up cattle which belonged to anyone who could round them up. We were accused of stealing cattle. So was Murphy and Chisum. The only difference between us and them is that they stole them wholesale and we just took them as we needed them. We thought we had a right to live, and we saw to it that we got along. Wouldn't you?"

"With Tunstall and McSween dead, Old John thought he could get out of paying us off, but he didn't, he didn't. We told him if he didn't pay us that we were going to run off enough of his cattle to pay what we thought he owed us. We cut cattle out of his herd and he didn't do anything about it. We got our share, and more too, maybe. But who knows?"

"I tried to get him to pay us. I told him the quickest way he could do it was too slow. I had my six-shooter in his ribs, and I don't know why I didn't put him in a six-foot grave. From then on Old John was our bitterest enemy."

"The country was full of bad men in those days. We were not by ourselves. The only difference was they had the law and the politicians on their side. The law was just as crooked as the rest of us."

"I didn't kill that Indian agent. I had nothing to do with it. I got blamed for it, of course. I got blamed for everything that no one else wanted. We were up there, but we did not go to steal horses like they say we did, No sir!"

CHAPTER FOUR

TO BE HANGED BY THE NECK

Brushy Bill Roberts could not talk about the events which followed the burning of the McSween's house without betraying great excitement, and sometimes shedding tears. Well, why not? Every minute was bringing him closer to the noose.

"About this time," his story went on, "the President removed the governor from office in Santa Fe. He sent General Wallace to take over as governor of the territory. Mrs. McSween and John Chisum talked with the governor about conditions in the country. It looks like things would straighten out. The governor issued a Proclamation of Amnesty to most of the people who had fought in that war. It did not apply to me. I already had indictments against me for the murder of Brady and Hindman. But I didn't kill them, I didn't. I wasn't even shooting at them. How could I kill them?"

"Most of that fall and winter we stayed around Fort Sumner and Portales. In the winter of '79 we got together with Dolan and Evans and agreed to quit fighting each other."

"When we came out of the saloon that night in Lincoln we run into Chapman, the lawyer for Mrs. McSween. Campbell and Dolan killed him in cold blood. I was standing there with them and saw who killed him."

"I heard that Governor Wallace had offered a thousand dollars for me if I would come in and testify. I wrote and told him that I would come in if he would annul those indictments against me. He wrote back that he would meet me at Squire Wilson's house in Lincoln- that house out there by the tower."

"I tied my horse up while Tom watched and went up to the back door. The governor and Wilson were alone in the house. I went in and talked for several hours. I explained that Tom and I had seen them shoot Chapman in cold-blooded murder. He wanted us to testify before the grand jury and tell them what we knowed. Also, he wanted me to testify against Colonel Dudley in his court martial trial at Stanton. I told him about things in general in this country and what started the trouble. I was not afraid to talk like the rest of them. I had the guts to help the governor out. No one else would say enough to help him."

"This happened to me one night in March. We didn't meet like they say we did in the daytime at Patron's. I had only this one meeting with Wallace until I submitted to arrest. The governor did come there after Tom and I were arrested. We were kept at Patron's that time, I think."

GOVERNOR LEW WALLACE

"He promised to pardon me if I would stand trial on my indictments in the district court in Lincoln, testify before the grand jury in the Chapman case, and testify against Dudley. I promised to do it and Tom and I left for San Patricio, where he lived with me."

"General Wallace sent Sheriff Kimbrel to San Patricio to pick us up. He let me pick the men to arrest me. Tom and I went to Lincoln with them and went to jail."

"When my case was called, Judge Leonard was not there. The court appointed Colonel Fountain to represent me. I plead not guilty to the indictments. Then we went before the grand jury that brought in the indictment against Dolan and his men for the murder of Chapman. I testified at the Dudley trail in Stanton. Then they wanted to take me to Mesilla for trail on my indictment."

"I had promised the governor that I would stand trial in Lincoln and not any place else, to which he agreed. It begun to look now like the governor could not do like he wanted. The judge was a Murphy sympathizer and a friend of Tom Catron at the head of the Santa Fe Ring. I saw that they did not intend to treat me right. I went to Kimbrel and told him to give me my scabbards and six-shooters. He said he could not blame me as it looked like I was being taken for a ride. I did ride, but not to

Mesilla. Tom and I walked out of the jail. We rode back to Fort Sumner and told them if they wanted us, to come and get us. But come a-shootin'."

GEORGE KIMBRELL

"They never arrested anyone else for the Brady murder. They never tried to arrest anyone else. They didn't do like they promised me. They pinned the whole affair on me, because they wanted to get rid of Billy the Kid. But they didn't hang me, they didn't."

There was a good deal of skirmishing after Billy the Kid walked out of the jail at Lincoln. As he increased the tempo of his activities as a cattle and horse thief, the law speeded up its efforts to catch him. Brushy Bill did not have much to say about these minor run-ins, but he did have vivid recollections of the fight at the Greathouse ranch or road house in November, 1880- possibly because he thought Billy the Kid got an especially raw deal there."

"I don't know where Greathouse's ranch was. That has been a long time to recollect, that has. But while we were there, we were surrounded by a posse. Surrounded by a posse, we was. They sent in Carlyle to get us to surrender. He had no warrant. I just told him that it amounted to mob violence, and we didn't intend to be mobbed. Not just yet, anyhow. The posse had Greathouse with them. When they commenced shooting out there, Carlyle got scared and jumped through the window. As he went out through the window, they shot him down without warning. They thought it was me making and escape, but they got fooled that time. We were going to make Carlyle ride out with us after dark. They left, and we got out that night."

"The next day they came back and burned down the house, thinking that we were on the inside. They were like rats. They burned us out of McSween's house and they were trying the same thing again. But we beat them to it again, we did."

"We went to Las Vegas, where I read that Billy the Kid had killed Carlyle. I wrote to Governor Wallace and told him that I did not kill Carlyle. That his own men killed him. But I got blamed for that killing too. Garrett told me about it later on."

Fortunately, history has preserved Billy the Kid's letter to Governor Wallace, so we have an opportunity to compare Brushy's comments in 1950 with Billy the Kid's comments from 1880 and the comparison is astounding. The Kid's letter is reproduced below in its entirety.

Fort Sumner Dec 12th 1880
Gov. Lew Wallace

Dear Sir,

I noticed in the Las Vegas Gazette a piece which stated that Billy "the Kid", the name by which I am known in the County, was the Captain of a band of outlaws who hold forth at the Portales. There is no such organization in existence. So, the gentlemen must have drawn very heavily on his imagination. My business at the White Oaks at the time I was waylaid and my horse killed was to see Judge Leonard who has my case in hand, he had written to me to come up, that he thought he could get everything straightened up. I did not find him at the Oaks. I should have gone to Lincoln if I had met with no accident. After mine and Billie Wilson's horses were killed, we both made our way to a station, forty miles from the Oaks kept by Mr. Greathouse. When I got up next morning, the house was surrounded by an outfit led by one Carlyle, who came into the house and demanded a surrender. I asked for their papers and they had none, so I concluded it accounted to nothing more than a mob and told Carlyle that he would have to stay in the house and lead the way out that night. Soon after a note was brought in stating that if Carlyle did not come out inside of five minutes they would kill the station keeper (Greathouse) who had left the house and was with them. in a short time, a shot was fired on the outside and Carlyle thinking Greathouse was killed jumped through the window, breaking the sash as he went, and was killed by his own party; they thinking it was me trying to make my escape. The party then withdrew.

They returned the next day and burned an old man named Spencer's house and Greathouse's also. I made my way to the place afoot and during my absence Deputy Sheriff Garrett, acting under Chisum's orders, went to the Portales and found nothing. On his way back he went to Mr. Yerby's ranch and took a pair of mules of mine which I had left with Mr. Bowdre, who is in charge of Mr. Yerby's cattle. He (Garrett) claimed that they were stolen and even if they were not he had a right to confiscate any outlaw's property. I have been at Sumner since I left Lincoln, making my living gambling. The mules were bought by me, the truth of which I can prove by the best citizens around Sumner. J.S. Chisum is the man who got me into trouble and was benefited thousands by it and is now doing all he can against me. There is no doubt but what there is a great deal of stealing going on in the Territory and a great deal of the property is taken across the plains as it is a good outlet. But, as far as my being at the head of a band, there is nothing of it. Several instances I have recovered stolen property when there was no chance to get an officer to do it.

One instance for Hugo Zuber, post office Puerto de Luna, another for Pablo Analla, same place. If some impartial party were to investigate this matter they would find it far different from the impression put out by Chisum and his tools.

Yours Respectfully,
William Bonney

As we can see, Brushy's testimony in 1950, although less detailed after the passing of 70 years, still exactly matched what Billy the Kid wrote in 1880. At this point it must be remembered that Brushy Bill Roberts was in 1950 simply a destitute old cowboy living in a small town in Texas. Mr. Roberts lived in poverty in a shack with his wife. It is said that the pair ate potatoes almost every day because they did not have the means to secure better meals. Local residents of Hico until this day still remember the proud old man coming to their family's back door after suppertime to receive handouts of leftover food. Even though he was old and poor, he was still proud and would not come to the front door because he did not want the town to know that, from time to time, he was basically reduced to what was in essence begging for soup.

Given this circumstance, Mr. Roberts had no opportunity to do extensive research on Billy the Kid. In 1950, there was obviously no internet, and the local small-town library in Hico, TX was not a sufficient resource to expose him to the many obscure letters and newspaper articles from the numerous small towns that would have been required for him to become a subject matter expert on all of the things he knew about Billy the Kid.

What's more, may of the details that Brushy knew in 1950 were not even discovered or widely known by experts at that time he shared them with Morrison and have only been revealed in more recent years. This makes Brushy's firsthand knowledge all the more astounding. Not only do the details of his narrative match verified sources of the Kid's writings, but in many cases, he used the exact terminology that the Kid had used.

For example, both Brushy and Billy noted the fact that Carlyle did not have a warrant and that without one their arrest would basically amount to "mob" violence.

Brushy continued, "Garrett had been a deputy under Sheriff Kimbrel. Kimbrel run for re-election. Old John Chisum, Lea, and several others put Garrett up against Kimbrel. They knew that Kimbrel was a friend of Governor Wallace and a friend of Billy the Kid. Garrett won the election."

"He had not been in the country long. He come here from Texas, where he killed a man, a partner, in a quarrel over dividing buffalo hides. We knew about it. We traveled through Texas too. Garrett had nothing when he landed in Fort Sumner. Me and my boys bought him the first pair of boots he ever owned in this country. We paid for the celebration at his first wedding in Fort Sumner. He rode with us, gambled and danced, but now he turned coat."

"He went to work for Maxwell when he landed in Fort Sumner, but he didn't last long. He bought in with Beaver Smith, who had a saloon and lunch room in Fort Sumner. The people around there had no use for him. They were all our friends."

"With this killing of Carlyle tacked on me, Garrett had another excuse to go after me, which he did. We were riding to Fort Sumner one night in a snow storm that December about eight o'clock. Garrett and his posse took over Bowdre's home and were there waiting for us to come in. O'Folliard had been living with Bowdre and his wife there. As we rode in, I took another road, thinking they might be watching for us. Tom and the boys rode up to Bowdre's and they started shooting at my boys, hitting Tom. I heard the shooting and rode in, to find the boys leaving town."

"They carried Tom inside and let him die, begging for water to drink. His cousin, Kip McKinney, one of Garrett's posse, wouldn't give Tom a drink when he was dying. Tom was a better man than McKinney. Tom's uncle on the Texas Rangers did not let him down, but the brave McKinney did it, he did. I met Cook, Tom's uncle, in Roswell in the fall of '80. He wanted to talk to Tom, but I wouldn't let him. I told him Tom was my best pal and I needed him. I wouldn't let him go yet. Later on, I wished I had."

"After a couple of days riding in the snow, we landed at the old rock house at Stinking Springs. We brought a couple of our horses inside and tied the others outside from the gable of the roof. The next morning at sunup Charlie Bowdre went out to feed the horses. When he stepped through the door opening (there wasn't any door), Garrett and his posse fired from ambush without warning, wounding Charlie seriously. He wore a large hat like mine. They thought he was me. They didn't intend to give the Kid a chance. They knew when he went down, he would take some of them with him."

HE NEVER GOT BACK TO TEXAS
Tom O'Folliard, Billy's right-hand man, killed by Garrett's posse before he could carry out his plan to leave New Mexico

"Charlie walked back in, but when he went back after them, he fell dead. We stayed in there all day, planning to ride out after dark. As we were trying to lead the other horses inside, they shot a horse and he fell over in the doorway. I had intended to ride my mare out on her side, like the Cheyenne Indians taught me in my boyhood days, but my mare wouldn't jump over the dead horse in the doorway, so we gave up the idea. I would have ridden out a-shooting if that dead horse had not fell over in the opening."

"They promised to protect us if we would surrender. We threw out our six-shooters and filed out the door. They loaded us in a wagon with Bowdre's body and took us to Fort Sumner. The next day they buried Bowdre near O'Folliard, who they killed a few days before."

In regards to this event Brushy's story matches the traditional version for the most part but offers subtle detail and nuance that one would expect from someone who was there. Details, for example, such as the fact that there was no door in the opening of the little rock house or that they tied some of their horses to the gable of the roof seem minor but challenge the notion that Brushy would have memorized the historical accounts.

As with the accounts of other contemporary witnesses, Brushy's version of events is in many ways corroborated by the historical record but also at times deviates from it or provides additional unique insights. For example, Brushy maintained that Garrett shot at Bowdre without warning, contrary to Garrett's claim that a warning was given. It stands to reason that if Brushy was a fraud then he would have made a better effort to stick close to the accepted version rather than make up his own. The fact that Brushy spoke of events firsthand and spoke from his own point of view lends tremendous credibility to his claims.

KILLED BY MISTAKE
Charles Bowdre, who fell before Garrett and his posse at the old rock house in December, 1880- shown here with his weapons and his wife

"The next day Mrs. Maxwell sent her Indian servant over to ask Pat Garrett if he would let me visit with them before taking me to Santa Fe to jail. Dave Rudabaugh was chained to me when Jim East, a friend of mine from Tascosa, Texas, and another member of the posse took us over to Maxwell's house. The Indian was wearing a scarf that she had just made from angora goat hair. I traded her my tintype picture in my shirt pocket for this scarf. I wore the scarf around my head on the trip to Las Vegas, after we left Maxwell's house."

"After we went in the house, Mrs. Maxwell asked them to cut me loose from Rudabaugh so I could go into another room with her daughter. They refused to do it. They suspected it was a trap to let me escape. I knew if they did let me in the other room, that they would go back to Garrett without me. I knew that I would find shooting irons in that room. And I knew that I would be able to use them. They knew that the handcuffs would not bother me. That's why they would not take off the leg irons. Anyway, they would not cut me loose from Dave."

DAVE RUDABAUGH

"We went back and started for Las Vegas, where we arrived a couple of days later. I almost got away from them at the jail in Las Vegas. The next day they put three of us on the train for Santa Fe, and it looked like trouble before we started out of there. I told Pat if he would give me a six-shooter that I would shoot it out with the mob and stay with him the rest of the trip."

This incident is particularly interesting as it was actually picked up by the *New York Times* and reported on December 28, 1880. That article shares some interesting details, such as the number in the pursuing posse, which Roberts describes as a "mob", and the exact dialogue between Garrett and the pursuers. What stands out, however, is the detail regarding the arming of the prisoners. Brushy claims he told Garrett "if he would give me a six-shooter that I would shoot it out with the mob and stay with him the rest of the trip". Apparently, Garrett was prepared to take him up on that offer in the event that shooting actually started.

The New York Times article reads "Somebody suggested to take the prisoners now. Stewart, of Garrett's party, said the instant the first shot was fired *he would free every man and arm him.*"

This quote is echoed in numerous first-hand accounts of this scene by multiple participants, which seems to indicate there was lots of talk that day by the participants of arming the prisoners. This begs the question, if he were not a firsthand participant, how could Roberts have possibly known there was discussion about arming the prisoners during the train standoff between a rival posse and Garrett's crew unless he was, in fact, present that day? As has been mentioned, living poor and destitute in Texas in 1950 he would not have had access to obscure details in long forgotten articles from 70 years prior. This is yet another piece of firsthand information he possessed that supports the credibility of his claim.

"At Santa Fe, we were put in jail. I wrote to Governor Wallace to come and talk to me, but he failed to do so. Sherman would not let my friends visit me in the jail, but he would let curiosity seekers in to look at me as if I was a dog. The governor had forgotten his promise to help me. They took me to Mesilla the last of March to stand trial on my indictments. We left Santa Fe on the train and wound up in Mesilla on the stage."

"In April, I pleaded to the federal indictment and it was thrown out of court. Judge Leonard represented me on this indictment. He got it thrown out by the judge. Then I was put on trial for the murder of Sheriff Brady, a territorial charge."

"Again, I was treated like a dog. They took me in court every morning chained and handcuffed. Olinger was there as a U.S. deputy marshal. He taunted and threatened me constantly. I tried for a six-shooter on one of the guards one day, but I couldn't quite reach it. I'd have killed Olinger first if I could have gotten it. They sat me up front near old Judge Bristol, who I had threatened to kill before. He was scared all the time I was in court in Lincoln and in Mesilla. He knew that he was looking for a six-foot grave if I got loose."

WESTERN OUTLAWS ARRESTED.

ALMOST A FIGHT BETWEEN OFFICERS OVER THE PRISONERS.

LAS VEGAS, New-Mexico, Dec. 28.—The notorious gang of outlaws, composed of about 25 men, who, under the leadership of "Billy the Kid," have for the past six months overrun Eastern New-Mexico, murdering and committing other deeds of outlawry, was broken up last Saturday morning by the killing of two men and the capturing of four others, including the leader. The prisoners were lodged in Las Vegas Jail, and lynching was prevented by the vigilance of the captors, Deputy Sheriff Garrett and others. Yesterday forenoon Garrett and the other captors boarded a train with the prisoners for the purpose of taking them to Santa Fé. Sheriff Romero remonstrated against taking one of the prisoners, named Rudabaugh, who killed a Las Vegas Deputy Sheriff, to Santa Fé, but to no effect. He then went to the depot with a posse of 300 men, and made a formal demand for the prisoners, but was told if he wanted the prisoners to take them. The Sheriff then stationed men at the engine to cover the engineer, and the remainder of the posse crowded about the train, the platforms of which were crowded with additional guards, pressed into service by Garrett, and nearly every window of the cars served as a port hole for rifles. Somebody suggested to take the prisoners now. Stewart, of Garrett's party, said the instant the first shot was fired he would free every man and arm him.

For a while a fight seemed imminent, when Chief Engineer Robinson appeared and demanded that the train be allowed to proceed, and the Master of Transportation said if the train was not allowed to proceed he would arm all the railroad men and take it out. Detective J. F. Morley, of the Post Office Department, jumped into the cab with a pair of six-shooters, and told the engineer to leap out. A conference had just concluded a compromise, by which it was agreed that the Sheriff and two men should go to Santa Fé with the party, and, if the Governor agreed, bring Rudabaugh back to Las Vegas. The train then proceeded.

THE NEW YORK TIMES
DECEMBER 28, 1880

The feud between Bob Olinger and Billy the Kid is well known and likewise Brushy Bill's contempt for the man was evident. One of the biggest mistakes one can make is to project on the past the worldview of the present and possibly this is a major reason for the confusion regarding the character of Billy the Kid. Although human nature does not change, the worldview and morality of any given period does.

Case in point is the view on the law and lawmen today versus in the Old West. In the Old West, many notable lawmen were involved in criminal activity both before and after being lawmen, even including such legendary men as Wyatt Earp and Bat Masterson. This is not to say that these men do not deserve worthy praise for their contributions to society or that they were not good people. The fact simply remains that at various times they were on either side of the law.

Unfortunately, at certain times in those days there are also examples where the law itself was on the wrong side of right and wrong and unfortunately at times legitimate bad men, corrupt men, or downright evil men hid behind the badge of justice. It is not true, therefore, that in every case the lawman is right and the citizen is wrong. After all, Dick Brewer was sworn in as a constable and Billy was in his posse to catch the murderers of John Tunstall. Not everyone could be on the right side of the law when there were badges on both sides of the Lincoln County War.

So, like many others Billy the Kid was himself on both sides of the law at various points in his life but that does not always mean that he was on the wrong side of right and wrong. Unfortunately for him he just happened to be on the losing side so he is almost universally condemned today as an outlaw and a "cop killer" for killing Bob Olinger, James Bell, and Sheriff William Brady. This accusation is an oversimplification of the facts. Although Brushy admitted to and regretted killing James Bell who was his friend and universally considered a good man, he maintained that he did not kill Sheriff Brady.

The killing of Bob Olinger, on the other hand, he readily admitted to and was clearly very happy about, but it was not necessarily because Billy was bloodthirsty. It is well known and documented that Bob Olinger was a cold-blooded murderer and a bully that happened to have a badge. He was known to shoot men in the back for no justifiable reason which was the case when he murdered an unarmed and cooperative Bob Jones in front of his wife and small children in 1878 while serving a small civil fine. The lead deputy on the matter, Deputy Pierce Jones, filed charges against Olinger for murder, charges that were later dismissed before the matter went to court. This is just one man of many that Olinger killed without provocation. Another may have been the unarmed John Tunstall. Olinger was in the posse that confronted and murdered Tunstall although it is unknown if he fired a shot.

In any event Bob's own mother described him thusly: *"Bob was a murderer from the cradle, and if there is a hell hereafter then he is there."* These would be strong words coming from anyone but when they come from the man's own mother perhaps that is the best indication of his character.

In this context, perhaps the actions of Billy the Kid take on a different light. As Brushy says he was railroaded and not treated fairly. The fact that he was not lynched or killed by one of the men seeking him, whether deputies or posse members, is attributed only to the fact that Billy had friends on both sides. Jim East, for example, says that after Garrett promised the Kid safety if he surrendered at Stinking Springs, Billy and his gang came out unarmed. Regardless of the Sheriff's promise, he says Barney Mason took aim and was about to shoot Billy in cold blood when Jim and another posse member stopped him. If it were not for Jim East and men like him, the Kid would no doubt have been killed by his captors long before he went to trial.

Surely these thoughts were fresh in Billy's mind as he sat in the Lincoln County jail. After all, he knew he was being guarded by one of the men that killed his boss and who would not hesitate to kill him also given the chance. Had he had he not escaped his best-case outcome would be that he himself would have been hung leaving no one left to oppose the Santa Fe Ring or to avenge his friends. Unfortunately, in the corrupt world of the old west, perhaps Billy's only chance for justice was to escape by any means necessary.

Brushy continued, "Judge Fountain was appointed to represent me on the territorial charge. He done all he could for me. I had no money. Couldn't get any. They didn't sell my mare up at Scott Moore's in Las Vegas. He was a friend of mine, but now he said I owed him money for board."

"The trial was crooked. I asked for witnesses which they could not find. They didn't want to find them. Sheriff Garrett knew where they were. Hank Brown was in Tascosa when I was on trial. Garrett knew it, too, but he didn't do anything about it. I think they turned Billy Wilson loose at Mesilla. I don't think he was tried in court, but I don't remember."

"The trial lasted about a week. They jury found me guilty of the murder of Sheriff Brady, and Judge Bristol sentenced me, on April 13, to hang on May 13 in Lincoln County. My other indictment was throwed out of court the next day."

"On April 16, they loaded me on an old Army ambulance, handcuffed, shackled, and the leg shackles chained to the back seat, and we started for Stanton. John Kinney, who fought against me in the war, sat on the back seat beside me. Billy Matthews, who had shot me and Wayte when Brady was killed, sat across and facing Kinney. Deputy U.S. Marshal Bob Olinger, my bitterest enemy, sat beside Matthews and facing me, threatening to kill me all the time on that trip to Stanton. Dave Woods and a couple other guards rode horseback, one on each side, and the other rode behind the ambulance. They told me if anyone attacked that they would kill me first and then catch the other fellows. We left Mesilla a little before midnight so no one would know where we were. As we were sleeping one night, I almost got away from Matthews, who was guarding me at the time. It took about five days to make the trip to Fort Stanton, where Garrett picked me up and took me to the jail in Lincoln."

CHAPTER FIVE

JAILBREAK

What happened in the Lincoln County jail in 1881 was still giving Brushy Bill Roberts the horrors sixty-nine years later. In August 1950, he came back to Lincoln for the first time in many decades. He was riding with Morrison, who was on his way to Carrizozo to go through the records in the county courthouse. They stopped in front of the place where Billy the Kid passed the long days and nights waiting for his death sentence to be carried out. Roberts was very uneasy and cried intermittently. He refused to get out of the car and go inside. Morrison went in alone and had a chat with Mr. Wright, who was pinch hitting for Colonel Fulton, the custodian.

That night, after Morrison had gone through the records at Carrizozo, they talked far into the small hours about what had happened in the old days, but it was not till the next morning, when they were back-trailing toward Roswell, that things began to come alive for the old man. The country had changed so much in seventy years that he had trouble locating himself, but suddenly he pointed to the mountainside on the right. "Over there," he said, "was a rock ledge that we used to ride out on and fire down into the valley. A little farther down on the other side of the road, we ought to see a cave we used to use."

Sure enough, the cave came into view. "A man could get a horse in there," he remarked.

Back in Lincoln he still refused to visit the old courthouse. But just as they reached the outskirts of town, headed for Roswell, he changed his mind. "Let's go back to that place," he said. "I might go inside if there's nobody there."

He sat in the car while Morrison reconnoitered. Mr. Wright was still the only official present, so Bill got out and came in. Mr. Wright was very courteous and showed them some of his relics. They came to a pair of leg irons of the type Billy was wearing when he escaped. Bill thought Mr.

Wright was passing them off as the genuine originals, took offense, and nearly let his tongue run away with him.

"Them are not the leg irons that Billy the Kid rode out of here with. I ought to know that Billy's leg irons were cut apart in the middle of the chain."

Then he bethought himself, turned red, counted the links in the chain to the number of fourteen, and agreed that the shackles were of the type that Billy wore.

When Mr. Wright's back was turned, he whispered to Morrison, "If you think it's safe, I would like to go up there and show you where I was locked to the floor in that room on the corner." Morrison reassured him and they mounted the stairs to the second floor.

Upstairs, Bill seemed nervous and somehow lost, as if he were trying to find a familiar landmark in a wilderness. The stairs inside were about the way they had been, but he remarked that there was no outside stairway to the balcony in the old days. The upper floor was completely changed. He explained to Morrison how it had looked in 1881.

"The stairway began on the first floor on the west side, running east into the large hall which run north and south in the building. At the east end of this hall a door opened into Garrett's office. On the east side of Garrett's office, a door opened into the room where I was confined in the northeast corner room. Across the hall from Garrett's office door was another door opening into the armory room."

He walked over to one of the eastern windows. "I was sitting right here on a soap box that morning," he said, "when Olinger loaded his shotgun with buckshot, twelve in each barrel. He snarled at me as usual and said, "Kid, do you see these buckshot I am loading into these two barrels, twelve in each barrel? Well, if you try to make a break, I'll put all twenty-four between your shoulder blades."

"I said, "Bob, you might get them before I do," and I smiled at him. Then he brought out a lariat rope and said, 'This is good enough to hang you with.' I told him a lariat rope was not fit to hang a man with."

"At noon time, as usual, Olinger went across the street with the other prisoners for lunch and left Bell there guarding me. Olinger and Bell were always on guard duty. Olinger always brought me lunch when he came back. Then Bell would go for lunch. During the week I was kept here, I was guarded constantly. They were afraid I would break jail or be rescued by my friends."

"It seemed that Bell lived in the neighborhood of White Oaks. He was a nice man. He treated me like an ordinary prisoner. But Olinger treated me like a dog."

"Olinger – wasn't nothing to him. A big bluff and a big coward. Killed all his men by shooting in the back or before they knew what was happening. He was a big fellow, too. Garrett didn't like him, either. I think the Beckwith family was related to Olinger's, but I'm not sure. Beckwiths were all right when they came to that country. Until Murphy turned them against Chisum, who helped them when they came to that country. Old John helped lots of them in that day."

"Olinger had worked for Chisum and was not liked by any of his boys. He had shot John Jones in the back in a camp on the Pecos. He murdered the Jones boy in cold blood. I promised the father that I would even the score with Olinger for this murder of his son. During my trial in Mesilla he kept taunting and teasing me. I was eager to kill him, but I did not want to kill Bell."

"The day before I got away, Sam Corbett and his wife came in to see me. Sam had hid a six-shooter in the latrine. So, the next morning I planned to wait until Olinger took the rest of the prisoners to lunch and Bell would be alone with me, when I would ask him to take me to the latrine. I expected him to take me in there and I would come out a-shooting. But I didn't need Sam's six-shooter."

"Olinger is gone to lunch. Bell and I are alone in the building. I am sitting about here on a box, handcuffed, shackled, and chained to this floor with a lock. Bell is sitting over by that window and reading a paper. I asked Bell to unlock this chain and take me to the latrine downstairs. At first, he objected; said he didn't know. Then he went into that room [Garrett's office] and got the key to unlock this chain. At this moment, I slipped my right hand from the cuff and holding them in my left, I hit him in the back of the head. He tumbled over on the floor. When he come up, he was looking down the barrel of his own six-shooter."

"I told him that I would not hurt him if he would do as I said. I told him to walk through that office and unlock the armory door as I wanted to lock him in there until I could escape. Without saying a word, he walked through the office. When he stepped into the hall, he ran for the stairway. With the fourteen-inch chain between my leg irons, I could not run, so I jumped and slid across the floor to the left toward the stairs. When he reached the third or fourth step, my left hand was nearing the stairs. I pulled the trigger and the bullet struck the wall on that side. It must have ricocheted and struck him under the arm, coming out on the other side. Bell fell down the steps, dying as he fell."

There are many versions of how Billy the Kid supposedly killed deputy Bell. One version has him getting a six-shooter from the privy outside and hiding it in his clothing until he got inside and was at the top of the interior courthouse steps. At that point, it is said that he wheeled around and confronted Bell who ran and was shot by Billy.

Other versions say that while walking up the steps Bell lagged behind which gave Billy enough time to run ahead and get a pistol from the armory which he used to shoot Bell. Still other versions say that Billy slipped his handcuffs and struck Bell in the head and either took his six-shooter or ran to the armory. There are many combinations of these events with the source of Billy's six-shooter being variously the privy, the armory, or Bell's own holster. In the end, there were only two people there inside the building that knew what happened and unfortunately deputy Bell did not survive the encounter to give his version of events.

On close inspection, Brushy Bill's version is the most credible and the one most supported by the evidence and contemporary testimony. Brushy claimed that Sam Corbett had, in fact, left a six-shooter in the privy but he did not need it. He claimed he struck Bell on the head when he bent over to unlock him from the floor (which matches the fact that deputy Bell's skull was crushed on the left-hand side) and then took his revolver. Perhaps the fact that Bell was in pain and knocked senseless contributed to his decision to run away rather than trust Billy to let him go.

Apparently, Bell almost made it. He quickly ran around the corner and down the steps before Billy, who was hindered by the chains on his feet, could shoot him. Brushy claims that since he couldn't run he dove to the left and fired as soon as the revolver was in position to shoot down the steps. In other words, Billy couldn't see Bell at that point but fired blindly in the direction Bell had gone. He actually missed which is evidenced by the bullet hole in the wall along the steps. The fact that he hit Bell and killed him with a ricochet under his left shoulder is an amazing, unfortunate, coincidence.

In this regard Brushy's account best matches the physical evidence including the hole in the wall and the location of the wound on deputy Bell, both the gunshot wound in his left side as well as his crushed skull. In fact, Brushy's account is the *only* single account that matches all of the evidence.

In addition, there is at least one contemporary witness that claims he heard from Billy firsthand the details of what occurred. This man was John P. Meadows and he was a contemporary and friend of both Billy the Kid and Pat Garrett. Meadows was interviewed in the 1930s by the *Las Cruces Sun* and shared many accounts that he claimed were shared with him directly from the Kid. In regards to this particular incident, he claimed that Bell was shot while Billy the Kid was "lying on the floor on his stomach, and shot Bell as he ran down the stairs."

Meadows also stated that Billy had struck Bell with his manacles and that the two of them wrestled on the floor at the top of the stairs before Billy came up with the revolver. Whether there was "wrestling" involved or even what exactly the use of the word may mean in this context, once again Brushy's version is the most logical and the one only that fits the evidence.

Brushy continued, "I turned and scuttled back to the office, where I picked up Olinger's shotgun where he stood it against the wall that morning. I went over to my window. When I looked out, I saw Olinger and another man coming over across the street toward the jail. Just as Olinger came across the street, he put his six-shooter into the scabbard. He probably thought that Bell had killed me in the jail. As he came near the corner of the building beneath my window, I levelled down on him, saying, "Look up, Bob. I want to shoot you in the face with your own buckshot. I don't want to shoot you in the back like you did other men, and the Jones boy." The buckshot struck him in the breast, killing him instantly. Then I fired the other twelve into him. I wanted him to get all of them like he had promised to give them to me. I wanted him to know that I was the man who was killing him."

"This was the happiest moment of my life. I promised to give him his own buckshot while he was loading the gun that morning. He shot the Jones boy in the back of the neck, killing him. He threatened to put the shot from both barrels in my back, and he would have done it if he would have had the chance. That was his way of killing other men, but he did not die that way."

"I went downstairs and out the side door at the bottom of the stairs, where Old Man Goss and someone else were standing near Bell's Body. I told Goss to cut this chain between my legs. He tried to cut it with a saw. I told him to get the axe and cut it. "And be damn careful where you hit that chain." I held a .44 on him. He cut the chain as I stood over the rock. I took and tied each end of the chain to my belt so I could straddle a horse.

Brushy's version of this story is supported by an old-time cowman named Jack Potter. Potter shared the following story, that was retold in 1955 by newspaperman Roger Thompson:

"After killing his jailers, the Kid, wearing leg irons, hobbled down the stairs and out to the shack where Old Man Goss, the cook, held sway. "Dad." the Kid said. "I've got a delicate job for you. While I squat down and put those leg irons across a piece of stove wood, I want you to cut them in two, and be careful with that ax!" The Kid held a forty-five in his hand but made no threats to the old man. The cook severed the leg irons and the Kid was on his way. Later, Dad Goss was asked why he had not hit the Kid on the head with the ax while he was squatting over the stove

wood. "Well," Dad Goss replied, "the Kid could have got me. He would have been a fraction of a second faster." The old man brightened and went on, "Furthermore, I liked the Kid. He was always bragging on my sourdough biscuits!"

This story is very similar to Brushy's version but again, Brushy's version makes more sense. For one, when the Kid broke jail at Lincoln he carried away 44-40 pistols and not 45 Colts. Secondly, it stands to reason that a rock would be a more appropriate backstop for an axe on chain than a piece of much softer wood which would give under the strike of an axe and not provide enough resistance to allow for cutting the chain. In both cases, the telling line is that the kid told Goss to "be careful with that axe!" These obscure details in Brushy's story are typical of a first-hand account as opposed to memorized historical accounts.

Brushy continued, Goss caught the horse behind the jail in the pasture. He and the Gallegos boy saddled the horse and took him to the front of the jail. I went back upstairs to this armory room and picked up a .44 Winchester belt loaded with cartridges and crossed it over my other shoulder, picking up a Winchester and two .44 single-action Colts with scabbards."

The "Gallegos Boy" Brushy mentions is Severo Gallegos and his presence and role in the escape of Billy the Kid from the Lincoln County Jail is an undisputed fact of history. Virtually every historical record of this event includes his name and actions. Also well-established is that this was not the first meeting between the two. Billy the Kid was a close friend of the Gallegos family and knew Severo well. Many years later, Severo swore an affidavit under oath regarding his affiliation with Billy the Kid which affirmed the following facts regarding their relationship:

"that Billy the Kid many times visited in the Gallegos Home; that he stayed there some times over night and that he ate many meals there; that the Kid and Florencio Chavez did much target practice at their home in San Patricio; that Billy was quick on the draw; that he fired a rifle left handed and six shooters with both hands; that he would shoot from the hip and that he was known to be a good shot. This affiant further states that Billy the Kid was a small man when he was young; that he had small feet and hands with large wrists; that he had two large teeth in the front of his mouth; that he had blue-grey eyes with small brown spots in them; that his nose was straight, high cheek bones and large ears; that he had dark hair; that he stood as straight as a whip, and rode a horse straight in the saddle. This affiant further states that he made many visits to see Billy the Kid in the Lincoln Jail; that he took berries to the jail for Billy to eat; [and] that he saw Billy escape from the Jail in April, 1881."

According to his sworn testimony it is clear that Severo Gallegos was familiar with and well-acquainted with the Kid on a personal level. Billy was part of the family, so to speak, and spent lots of time at the Gallegos home. This makes the remaining words of Severo's testimony of even greater importance to history. Again, these words are part of the public record and are just as undisputed as the fact that he was well-acquainted with Billy and on the scene the day he escaped from the Lincoln County Jail, even assisting him in his escape. Severo finishes his testimony in the following way (with a portion repeated for continuity):

"..this affiant further states that he made many visits to see Billy the Kid in the Lincoln Jail; that he took berries to the jail for Billy to eat; that he saw Billy escape from the Jail in April, 1881; that he never saw Billy the Kid again……until the first day of April, 1950; that after talking to Billy for several hours on April first, this affiant knows from conversation and looking him over, that Billy the Kid was the same person as O. L. Roberts who visited here in Ruidoso.

This affiant further states that he never believed that Billy the Kid was killed by Sheriff Pat Garrett; that he heard from time to time throughout the years that Billy the Kid was still living. This affiant further states that O. L. Roberts has the same blue-grey eyes, with brown spots in them; that his nose is straight, with high cheek bones, large ears, small feet and hands with large wrists, and he stands as straight as he stood in Lincoln County days; that he is still fast on the draw; that he talks and laughs the same, and looks the same in many ways; that he has no teeth now, and his hair is nearly gray with some dark streaks in it.

This affiant further states that he is of firm belief that Billy the Kid and O. L. Roberts are one and the same person".

How is it possible that in all of contemporary history when the tale of Billy the Kid's escape from the Lincoln County Jail is told, when Severo Gallegos is mentioned in virtually every single telling, that it is not also shared that this very same Severo Gallegos who knew the real Billy the Kid intimately *swore his oath* that Brushy Bill Roberts was Billy the Kid? This omission is inexcusable in the academic community. This testimony from Severo Gallegos establishes without question that yet another known associate (other than his childhood friend Jesse Evans) was convinced that William H. Roberts was the one and only Billy the Kid.

Morrison introduced Brushy to Severo and they spoke at length for hours. Severo was spellbound as one would imagine anyone would be to encounter their childhood hero alive and breathing almost 70 years later. Understandably Severo was also doubtful at first but after speaking to him and looking into his eyes over the course of two days he swore an oath that Brushy Bill Roberts was Billy the Kid.

Clearly, it would be one thing for an old man to make the outrageous claim he was Billy the Kid with no proof, as many old men did. These imposters are easily discredited and do not warrant serious consideration. It is quite another thing, however, when a man comes forward with photographs of himself that match the authenticated photo of the Kid, who recalls firsthand knowledge of intimate details of obscure events in the Kid's life from memory, who demonstrates that he possesses unalterable physical characteristics that perfectly match the Kid's, and who is able to obtain sworn testimony from close personal friends that were well-acquainted with the Kid that he is the same man.

This avalanche of evidence passes not just the common-sense standard, but surpasses the legal standard as well. If this evidence does not overcome the account of a few men who claimed Billy was killed because they said so, then what is the point of considering any evidence whatsoever?

Brushy continued, "As I walked out on the balcony upstairs here, everything was calm with no one trying to catch me. No one wanted to fight. I called out that if anyone was looking for a six-foot grave, that they should follow me.

"I went back downstairs and out to the front of the jail, where the horse was tied. I jumped for the saddle, but slid off the other side, hanging to the rope. The Gallegos kid went down the road and took a rope off a yoke of steers in the field and tied it to my saddle. I got on the horse and rode out of Lincoln to the west and up the canyon to the home of a friend, who cut the bolts in my leg irons. After they screwed the nuts on the bolts, they riveted over the ends of the bolts so I couldn't unscrew them with my hands."

All the while this recital was going on, the old man was in tears and greatly excited. It was as much as he could stand to be in that room. He took one last look around and headed for the stairs. Morrison loaded him into the car and they drove off.

They passed the building twice in later expeditions, but Brushy Bill would never go back inside. One time, Colonel Fulton came out to shake hands and ask him in, but once was enough; he would not get out of that car.

After leaving the building, he had an idea that he would like to see if he could retrace his escape route up the canyon, but the country had changed so much since the last time he was there (in 1892, he said) that he couldn't see anything that looked familiar. Morrison turned around and took up the route to Roswell, Bill filling in with more reminiscences as they drove.

"I turned the horse back for Lincoln and walked over the mountain. My guns began to get heavy and I hung one of them in the fork of a tree. I was headed for the house of Higinio Salazar. We had been friends for a long time. I had stayed with him and his mother before. Neither of us were married. His brother might have been married. I don't remember. I knew if I could reach his house across the mountain, he would help me as much as he could.

"Higinio was the one who escaped from the burning McSween building. He was seriously injured, but he recovered. I walked near the house and whistled several times before he came outside. He recognized me and we talked about my escape. He urged me to leave for Old Mexico. I argued that I would not leave the country until I killed Old John, Barney Mason, and Garrett. He went back in the house and brought a blanket for me. I slept in the underbrush, as I thought a posse would be looking for me and I did not expect to die alone."

"Next day he brought food to me. On the second day, he borrowed a horse and I started for Fort Sumner across the plains. I told him about hanging my pistol in the tree and he tried to find it, but never could."

"While on my way the horse broke loose and left me on foot again. I walked into Anaya's sheep camp below Fort Sumner and stayed a few days. I traveled at night and slept in the daytime. I expected Garrett down at Fort Sumner hunting for me. After dark one evening I walked to the home of Charlie Bowdre's widow, where I spent the night, and the next day or so. From here I rode back to Garcia's. I rode around Fort Sumner with some ranchers and herders for about two and a half months before I had the fight with Garrett's posse that night in July. I would not leave until I had killed Chisum, Barney Mason, and Garrett."

"It was about the middle of May, 1881, when I rode out to Old John's ranch on South Spring. I met a Mexican cowboy. I pulled down on him, telling him to go in and bring Old John out so I could talk to him in my language. He told me that Old John was not in there. I promised him that I would kill him if I find out that he is lying to me. I stayed at a camp nearby for a few days watching and waiting until I found out the Mexican was telling the truth. I left there looking for Barney Mason. He started to ride up to the camp where I was staying. When I came out, he left and mighty quick, too, he did. I could have killed him if I had known it was him."

"I sent a note to Garrett that I was waiting for him, and that he had better come a-shooting, too. They had both been good friends of mine until Chisum and others had Garrett elected Sheriff of Lincoln County. We rode and gambled together. Mason rustled cattle and horses with us after Garrett was elected. But when he started squealing to Garrett, we ran him off."

Pat Garrett in his book *The Authentic Life of Billy the Kid* just so happens to mention his last message he received from the Kid before that fateful night at Pete Maxwell's in July. Sheriff Garrett, in defense of himself for shooting Billy from concealment and in response to those who asked if he was scared, writes *"Scared? Suppose a man of the Kid's noted gentle and amicable disposition and temper had warned you that when you two met you had better "come a-shooting" ...wouldn't you be scared?"*

This reference to a warning from the Kid is an exact match to what Brushy Bill Roberts claims he sent to Garrett. Only two men would have known of a private note between themselves and in this case apparently those two men were Sheriff Pat Garrett and Brushy Bill Roberts, aka Billy the Kid. Once again, it is a simple detail buried in the historical record that adds significant credibility to the story of Brushy Bill.

Brushy continued, "I knew Celsa and Pat's wife, who were sisters to Saval Gutierrez, before Pat came to this country. Celsa was one of my sweethearts when I was in Fort Sumner. Her brother, Saval, lived in Fort Sumner. After I returned from hunting Old John, he went up to Canaditas and got Celsa for me. She wanted to go to Mexico with me, but I did not want to get married until Garrett was gone."

"While I was in Fort Sumner I stay at Gutierrez', Jesus Silva's, and Bowdre's. I also stayed at the Yerby ranch north of Fort Sumner quite a bit. We were good friends. I kept horses and mules there when Charley Bowdre worked for Yerby. He had a good-looking daughter, who was sort of a sweetheart of mine. I don't remember her name. Fort Sumner had some good-looking girls in those days."

"Most of my time was spent at the Yerby ranch after I broke jail in Lincoln. There were several cow and sheep camps on the road from Yerby's to Fort Sumner. I stopped off in most of them during the day time."

CHAPTER SIX

DEATH BY MOONLIGHT

"I rode into Fort Sumner from Yerby's a few days before Garrett and his posse rode in. When they rode in that day, I had spent the day with Garrett's brother-in-law, Saval Gutierrez. Nearly all the people in this country were my friends and they helped me. None of them liked Garrett."

"Garrett and his posse came in that night while we were at a dance. Silva saw Garrett in Fort Sumner a little while before we rode in from the dance. He knew I was staying with Gutierrez, so he went over there to warn me to leave town. Gutierrez told him we were out to a dance."

"When my partner, me, and the girls rode into town, we stopped at Jesus Silva's. Jesus told Celsa that Garrett was in town looking for the Kid. About midnight the girls left and I began asking him about Garrett. He got excited and told us to leave before Garrett found us there. I thought Garrett would go to Gutierrez', and I had better stay away that night. I told Silva that we was not going to leave until we had something to eat. He agreed to fix a meal for us."

"He was cooking the meal for us to eat when my buddy asked for fresh beef. Silva said if one of us would go over to Maxwell's and get beef, he would cook it for us. I sensed a trap, but my partner insisted that we go get the beef. He started out to Maxwell's after I refused to leave Silva's house. I thought that Garrett might still be in town, and I wanted to meet him in the daytime so I could beat him to it."

According to Brushy, he and his "partner", who told him his name was Billy Barlow, worked on the Muleshoe Ranch together. But, he said, he always suspected the young man was using an alias. Brushy said he thought that Barlow had come into the country in the winter of 1880 but that he had taken no part in the cattle war. Barlow was younger than Billy but about the same size and with similar blue eyes. "Me and Billy Barlow" Brushy said, "were as much alike as two black-eyed peas, you couldn't tell us apart."

Unlike the Kid, however, Barlow was half Mexican, wore a beard, and was dark skinned. He was also a heavy drinker and had been drinking heavily at the dance on the evening in question. Perhaps this is why he failed to heed the Kid's warning that he could be walking into a trap. Even more intriguing is the thought that perhaps this explains some of the other versions of events that have been offered regarding what exactly happened leading up to the shooting that night.

What happened next has become the Wild West's most infamous story. According to history, Billy the Kid went next door to Pete Maxwell's house to get some meat and encountered Garrett's posse on his porch. The Kid was apparently startled by the men when he came upon them and stopped abruptly, pulling a double action pistol. Deputy John Poe in his book *The Death of Billy the Kid,* published in 1933, describes what happened next from Poe's point of view.

"Probably not more than thirty seconds after Garrett had entered Maxwell's room, my attention was attracted, from where I sat in the little gateway, to a man approaching me on the inside of the fence, some forty or fifty steps away. I observed that he was only partially dressed and was both bareheaded and barefooted (or, rather, had only socks on his feet) and it seemed to me that he was fastening his trousers as he came toward me at a very brisk walk.

As Maxwell's was the one place in Fort Sumner that I had considered above suspicion, I was entirely off my guard. I thought the man approaching was either Maxwell or some guest of his. He came on until he was almost within arm's-length of where I sat before he saw me, as I was partially concealed from his view by the post of the gate.

Upon seeing me, he covered me with his six-shooter as quick as lightning, sprang onto the porch, calling out in Spanish, "Quien Es?" At the same time, he backed away from me toward the door which Garrett only a few seconds before had passed, repeating his query, "Who is it?" in Spanish several times.

At this I stood up and advanced toward him, telling him not to be alarmed, that he should not be hurt, still without the least suspicion that this was the very man we were looking for. As I moved toward him trying to reassure him, he backed up into the doorway of Maxwell's room, where he halted for a moment, his body concealed by the thick adobe wall at the side of the doorway. He put out his head and asked in Spanish for the fourth or fifth time who I was. I was within a few feet of him when he disappeared into the room.

After this, and until after the shooting, I was unable to see what took place on account of the darkness of the room, but plainly heard what was said. An instant after the man had left the door, I heard a voice inquire in a sharp tone, "Pete, who are those fellows on the outside?" An instant later a shot was fired in the room, followed immediately by what everyone within hearing distance thought were two other shots.

However, there were only two shots fired, the third report, as we learned afterward, being caused by the rebound of the second bullet, which had struck the adobe wall and rebounded against the headboard of a wooden bedstead.

I heard a groan and one or two gasps from where I stood in the doorway, as if someone were dying in the room. An instant later Garrett came out, brushing against me as he passed. He stood by me close to the wall at the side of the door and said to me, "That was the Kid that came in there onto me, and I think I have got him."

I said, "Pat, the Kid would not have come to this place; you have shot the wrong man."

Upon my saying this, Garrett seemed to be in doubt himself, but quickly spoke up and said, "I am sure it was him, for I know his voice too well to be mistaken." This remark of Garrett's relieved me of considerable apprehension, as I had felt almost certain that someone else had been killed."

Another account of the shooting was published nine days after the shooting in the July 23, 1881 issue of the *Las Cruces Sun-Times*, which tells the story the following way:

"Maxwell made no reply, and Kid then caught sight of Garrett. He did not apparently recognize the man, but pointed his revolver at him and said "Who is it? Who is it?" Garrett had not had time to draw his revolver and finding it had reached a point at which caution or delay would prove fatal, reached around and got it. Kid started back, but for some reason or other did not fire. Perhaps this was because he had no idea that Garrett was in that part of the country and suspected no harm. Whatever his reason was his delay proved fatal. With his desperate enemy's weapon aimed full at his breast at a distance of a few feet, Pat Garrett, with the quickness and precision for which he is famed; pulled down on the Kid and fired. The bullet pierced the heart and in a moment without the utterance of a word death ensued. The Sheriff fired a second shot before he had time to see the effect of the first one but in the excitement, he missed his mark. Below is given Sheriff Garrett's report is made to acting Governor Rich which contains also the verdict of the coroner's jury.

Fort Sumner, N.M. July 16, '81- To His Excellency, the Governor of New Mexico; I have honor to inform your Excellency that I have received several communications from persons in and about Fort Sumner, that William Bonny, alias the Kid, had been there, or in that vicinity for some time. In view of these reports I deemed it my duty to go there and ascertain if there was any truth in them or not, all the time doubting their accuracy; but on Monday, July 11, I left home, taking with me John W. Poe and T. D. McKinney, men in whose courage and capacity I relied implicitly, and we arrived just below Fort Sumner on Wednesday 13th.

I remained concealed near the houses, until night, and then entered the fort about midnight, and went to Mr. P. Maxwell's room. I found him in bed and had just commenced talking to him about the object of my visit at such an unusual hour, when a man entered the room in stockinged feet, with a pistol in one hand a knife in the other. He came and placed his hand on the bed just beside me, and in a low whisper, "who is it?" (and repeated the question) he asked of Mr. Maxwell. I at once recognized the man, and knew he was the Kid, and reached behind me for my pistol, feeling almost certain of receiving a hail from his at the moment of doing so, as I felt sure he had now recognized me, but fortunately he drew back from the bed and noticing my movement, and, although he had his pistol pointed at my breast, he delayed to fire, and asked in Spanish, "Quien Es?", "Quien Es?". This gave me time to bring my pistol to bear on him, and the moment I did so I pulled the trigger and he received his death wound, for the ball struck him in the left breast and pierced his heart. He never spoke but died in a minute. It was my desire to have been able to take him alive, but his coming upon me so suddenly and unexpectedly leads me to believe that he had seen me enter the room or had been informed by someone of the fact; and that he came there armed with a pistol and knife expressly to kill me if he could. Under that impression I had no alternative but to kill him or to suffer death at his hands."

It has always baffled researches why exactly the Kid would have acted so strangely on this night. The idea that he would respond to a question posed by a white person in English by saying "Quien Es?" multiple times in Spanish makes no sense.

Likewise, to stumble backwards into a darkly lit bedroom when he already had the men on the porch well covered with his pistol makes no sense. That is to say that it makes no sense, unless, of course, the person in question was not Billy the Kid at all, but rather a very drunk Billy Barlow, for whom Spanish was his primary language. Over the years there have been reports that when the Kid entered Maxwell's yard he was buttoning his trousers. This has led some to conjecture that perhaps he was coming from a romantic encounter with Pete Maxwell's sister. Another reasonable explanation, however, could be that after a night of heavy drinking Billy Barlow stopped and relieved himself in the yard outside Jesus Silva's house before coming through the gate onto Pete Maxwell's property.

This explanation would seem to not only fit all of the known facts but would also account for the behavior (and poor judgment) of the man Pat Garrett killed that evening. As with most things, the simplest answer is likely the truth, and Brushy's version of a drunk Billy Barlow sure does make a lot more sense than the story Pat Garrett attempted to sell back in 1881. It seems ridiculous today, but it likely was even more ridiculous in 1881 and perhaps this is why Garrett was refused his reward money for killing "the Kid". It would also explain why arrest warrants were later issued for the Kid in 1883 and 1885. For most people actually in the region, they had a hard time buying into the story that Garrett killed the Kid.

Brushy continued, "In a short time we heard pistol shots. I ran through the gate into Maxwell's back yard in the bright moonlight and started shooting at the shadows along the house. One of their first shots had killed my partner on the back porch. After entering the yard, their first shot struck me in the lower left jaw, taking out a tooth as it went through my mouth. As I started over the back fence, another shot struck me in the back of my left shoulder. I had emptied one of my .44's when another shot struck me across the top of my head and about an inch and a half back of the forehead and about two inches in length. This shot knocked me out and I stumbled into the gallery of an adobe behind Maxwell's yard fence."

It is interesting that Brushy mentioned that on that particular evening the yard was brightly lit. This is correct, and a fact mentioned in almost every narrative of those that were present that night. Brushy not only knew the exact layout of Fort Sumner, including the location of the houses of the various residents but even knew the quality of the moonlight on the particular evening when Garrett claimed he shot the Kid.

He goes on to say "A Mexican woman was living there and she pulled me in through the door. When I woke up, she was putting beef tallow on my head to stop the flow of blood. I told her to reload my .44's, which she did. "I started to go back out after them when Celsa came running in and said that they had killed Barlow and they were passing off his body as mine. She begged me to leave town. She said that they would not leave Maxwell's house for the night. They were afraid of being mobbed."

IT HAPPENED HERE
Pete Maxwell's House. His bedroom was at the front corner

In his book, Deputy Poe also makes it very clear that the town of Ft. Sumner was friendly to Billy and therefore hostile to the deputies. Poe wrote "We spent the remainder of the night on the Maxwell premises, keeping constantly on our guard, as we expected attack by the friends of the dead man." Fortunately for Poe, no attack came, perhaps because it spread through the town that Billy was alive after all.

As will be shown, this is one of several times Deputy Poe's version of events match perfectly with that of Brushy Bill Roberts.

Sheriff of Lincoln county.

The Kid lingered at Fort Sumner, it is claimed, because of a mutual regard existing between himself and a sister of Pete Maxwell, and also for the reason that being among friends he felt safer there than elsewere. He was allowing his hair and beard to grow and was putting his skin through a coloring process which he fondly hoped would so completely Mexicanize him as to give him a thorough disguise. Had he been left alone there is no telling what kind of an awakening he might have given the people when his plans had matured.

EXCERPT FROM THE LAS CRUCES SUN
JULY 23, 1881

The fact that Billy the Kid's body looked like a Mexican, complete with brown skin and beard was repeated by several contemporary newspapers at the time but has since been mostly disregarded by history.

The cover up of the accidental shooting of Billy Barlow is not without historical record. Early accounts of this incident corroborate Brushy's story that the man Pat Garrett shot did not match known descriptions of Billy the Kid. Several newspapers, including the *Las Cruces Sun* in Las Cruces, New Mexico printed that Billy had been living among the Mexicans and attempting to disguise himself by staining his skin brown. An article from June 19th, 1881, just five days after the shooting, reads "*Las Vegas, NM-Positive and reliable information reached this city early yesterday by a messenger in regard to the killing of the notorious "Billy, the Kid" at Fort Sumner, 129 miles distant on the Pecos River, at half-*

past 11 o'clock last Saturday morning. Billy had been stopping with the Mexicans in that vicinity, disguised as one of them, ever since his escape from the Lincoln County Jail."

Also, the account shared in the July 23, 1881 *Las Cruces Sun-Times* article is contradictory and unfortunately, that type of sensationalist journalism was common in the 1800s. Earlier parts of the article make a point to say that surely Garrett would not risk his life for a paltry $500 reward and that he was motivated only by a sense of duty. It goes on to say that Garrett intends to quit his position because he is both under paid and under-appreciated, a strange comment to be made by someone motivated solely by duty as the article claims. In any event, this is just one of many versions of the story that is fairly ubiquitous in period newspapers.

According to the article, the Kid saw Garrett enter the room and entered the room after him "expressly to kill him" but then upon entering hesitated asking "Who is it?", "Who is it?" both in English and then in Spanish before backing away and waiting patiently to be shot by Garrett, who had to retrieve his pistol from behind him. Further, the idea that Garrett was hoping to take the Kid alive, after killing both Tom O'Folliard and Charlie Bowdre from ambush, is frankly unbelievable. As we look back through the lens of history it is clear that the public face that was put on the events of July 14, 1881 was far from accurate.

The description of the Kid himself is likewise flawed. For one, the Kid carried a single action 44-40 frontier six shooter, not a double action revolver as was supposedly found in Maxwell's bedroom. He was also extremely cautious as his close friends have recounted and as his letters to Lew Wallace testify. The idea that he would walk right past two deputies on the porch and then hesitate to fire on a stranger sitting on Pete Maxwell's bed after being ambushed twice by Garrett and his posse is not credible in any way.

Billy the Kid's authenticated letters to Governor Lew Wallace show a careful, calculating man and not some Neanderthal "mouth breather" that many attempt to make him out to be. This is best shown in his letter written on March 20, 1879 which reads as follows:

Sir, I will keep the appointment I made but be sure and have men come that you can depend on I am not afraid to die like a man fighting but I would not like to be killed like a dog unarmed. Tell Kimball to let his men be placed around the house and for him to come in alone; and he can arrest us. All I am afraid of is that in the Fort we might be positioned or killed through a window at night, but you can arrange that all right. Tell the Commanding Officer to Watch Lt. Goodwin he would not hesitate to do anything. There will be danger on the road of somebody waylaying us to kill us on the road to the Fort. You will never catch those fellows on the road. Watch Fritzes, Captain Bacas ranch and the Brewery. They will either go up Seven Rivers or Jicarilla Mountains. They will stay around close until the scouts come in. Give a spy a pair of glasses and let him get on the mountain back of Fritzes and watch and if they are there, there will be provisions carried to them. It is not my place to advise you but I am anxious to have them caught and perhaps know how men hid from soldiers better than you. Please excuse me for having so much to say and still remain,

William H. Bonny

P.S. I had change of my mind. Send Kimball to Gutierrez just below San Patricio one mile, because Sanger and Ballard are or were great friends of Camuls (Campbell's). Ballard told me yesterday to leave for you were doing everything to catch me. It was a blind to get me to leave. Tell Kimball not to come before 3 o'clock for I may not be there before

To those who are not aware of these letters this perspective of the Kid shows a stark contrast to his public persona popularized by history. The facts of history are that Billy the Kid was not just a whimsical dumb kid that led a charmed life as he stumbled in and out of trouble. The "Kid" was a leader of experienced men and a solid tactician even to the point of lecturing General Lew Wallace about how to do his job, telling the general that the men after him had hidden from soldiers "better than you."

The fact that the Kid was cautious is also evidenced by his actions on the night Tom O'Folliard was killed. After a long ride, his group rode right into town but Billy himself rode around to scout the town before coming in. This level of savvy and caution had many times saved his life and it did yet again on that fateful night when he lost his right-hand man.

In this context, the comments made by Deputy John W. Poe on the night of the shooting at Pete Maxwell's house make perfect sense. As a deputy charged with finding and capturing the Kid he was well informed as to the character and nature of the man he was after. He writes in *"The Killing of Billy the Kid"* that immediately after the shooting he said "Pat, the Kid would not have come to this place, you've shot the wrong man".

The fact that Pat Garrett had, in fact, shot the wrong man for the *third* time in a row would explain a great deal as to why the events following the shooting transpired the way they did as well as why the public spin was put on the story. To this day, there does not exist a single narrative of the events of the shooting of Billy the Kid at Pete Maxwell's house that is not contradicted by other eyewitnesses, including the deputies themselves.

To believe the official version of events one would have to believe that two armed deputies, both of whom who would have their nerves on edge in a hostile town, would allow the object of their search to walk right past them on the porch with gun drawn to get the drop on their Sheriff in Maxwell's bedroom. A scenario such as this is hard to fathom.

Various other theories have been proposed and accounts put forth, all supposedly based on the testimony of the few eyewitnesses either to the public or privately to their families and friends. As previously mentioned, some say that the lad in question had his pants undone and had just come from the bedroom of Maxwell's sister. Others say that there was an alcove next to the hanging meat on the porch with a candle that was lit by "the Kid" (Barlow) and Garrett or McKinney shot him in the back while he was cutting the meat, only to find out later they had shot the wrong man. Still others say that Garrett and the deputies were hiding in Paulita Maxwell's bedroom where they had her tied up and gagged, waiting on the Kid to arrive.

The late Jack Fountain, son of Colonel Fountain (whose disappearance in the neighborhood of the White Sands is southern New Mexico's most famous murder mystery) gave C.L. Sonnichsen a new version of the shooting at Pete Maxwell's in an interview on April 15, 1944. "I rode with Pat Garrett for weeks at a time," he said, "and on one occasion he finally said, "Well, I'll tell you the whole story. After Billy got away after killing Olinger and Bell (and Olinger got what was coming to him), the county commissioners wished that job on me. I didn't want it, but that $10,000 looked good. I thought about what I knew of the Kid and his habits—heard there was to be a dance at Portales—went over. The Kid was just in off the range when we arrived and tied our horses.

He went to the house of a woman across the street and said, "I'm hungry. Can you cook something for me?" She said, "Don Pedro has just killed. You go across and cut some meat and I'll fix you a good meal." He went across, suspecting nothing. The beef was hanging in a little outer room from the vigas. There was a candle and materials for making a light in a niche in the wall. He made a light and held it up while he cut. I was in Pete's room, talking. Billy heard something and asked Pete who was there. Pete said, "Nobody." I looked out at a perfect target—Billy lighting himself up with the candle. At first, I was just going to wing him. Then I thought if he ever got to his gun it was him or me. My conscience bothers me about it now.'"

This version of events is only one of the many variations on the theme of exactly how Pat Garrett came to shoot his victim, but it is one of the few that places the body outside Maxwell's bedroom on the porch, just where Brushy claims he saw his partner lying after he heard the shots.

In any event the point remains that there is no single narrative for the events of July 14, 1881 that matches what we know about the character and actions of those involved except for Brushy Bill's. To believe Brushy's story, for example, one must accept the possibility that Pat Garrett might have accidentally killed the wrong man (he had already done this at least twice), that Billy the Kid may have been tipped off by the local townspeople that Garrett was in town (this was usually the case), that Deputy McKinney would not allow him to walk right past him with gun drawn (he would not), that Billy would have smelled a trap and not walked over to Maxwell's (which Deputy Poe agreed with), and that Pat Garrett was passing off a dead Mexican as Billy the Kid (which the Las Cruces Sun and other newspapers printed at the time).

In other words, to believe Brushy Bill's story is to believe that everyone involved that night acted in a manner that was *precisely consistent* with everything that was known about their past behaviors up to that point. In contrast, to believe the accepted version of history, which is mostly based on the word of Pat Garrett, one must believe that everyone would have acted in a manner that would have been *precisely inconsistent* and out of character for *everyone* involved, from the deputies, to Billy, to Garrett himself. To accept the historic position, therefore, is to base one's belief on one reason and one reason alone. This reason is quite simply stated "because they said so".

Brushy continued, "About three o clock in the morning Celsa brought my horse up to the adobe. I pushed my .44's into the scabbards and rode out of town with Frank Lobato. We stayed at the sheep camp the next day. Then I moved to another camp south of Fort Sumner, where I stayed until my wounds healed enough to travel."

"Around the first of August I started for El Paso, where I had lots of friends. I crossed the Rio Grande north of town and went into Sonora, Mexico, where I was acquainted with the Yaqui Indians. I lived with them nearly two years."

One of the amazing things about the comments of Brushy Bill Roberts are the small details that are woven into his story. Brushy shared many small details that at first glance may seem minor and be easily overlooked but yet fit perfectly into the historic record. Case in point is that Brushy specifically said that as he was getting ready to travel out of town with Frank Lobato around 3 AM in the morning that Celsa brought "his" horse around. This is an interesting point that raises a question that has never been answered. Namely, if Billy the Kid was killed by Pat

Garrett, then what ever happened to the Kid's horse? According to history, no one seems to know.

BILLY THE KID SLEPT HERE

Brushy Bill said that Billy was staying in one of these old barrack rooms when Garrett tracked him down. Taken from the Parade Ground, looking east

Chapter Seven

From Then Till Now

After so much gun smoke, blood, and passion, the later life of any man involved in the Lincoln County War would inevitably seem anticlimactic. And so it was with Brushy Bill Roberts. He had adventures enough, but nothing to compare with the high drama of the great cattle feud. If Brushy Bill was Billy the Kid, he gave up the role of Avenging Angel to become a bronco buster.

Just what he did after 1881, and when and where he did it, is not too easy to make out, in spite of the copious notes and bits of narrative he left behind. Bill was full of elaborations and evasions. Maybe he had reasons for leaving a crooked trail. At any rate, here is the story he told, eliminating as many of the crooks and turns as possible.

"In the fall of '82 I left Mexico and went to Grand Saline, Texas. I was dressed like an Indian and I took a job driving a salt wagon from there to Carlton, where my folks had lived. I hoped to be able to find them there. I made two trips hauling salt, but never found my folks."

"I went back to Sonora, Mexico, where I stayed until the winter of '83. At this time, I returned to Texas as the Texas Kid. I worked a short time at the Powers Cattle Company. From there I went up to Decatur, Texas, where I struck up again with Indian Jim. I had worked with Jim in No Man's Land in '75, and again in Arizona on the Gila ranch in the spring of '77."

"While on a cattle drive in Kansas City, I was arrested and held by the law as being Billy the Kid. The boys got me off, though."

"Then Indian Jim and I went to work for Tom Waggoner, at Decatur, breaking horses. Late in the winter we left for the Black Hills of Dakota. We joined the scouts, guarding the stage lines on the Idaho trail. We stayed with the scouts for about three or four years. During this time, I earned the name of Brushy Bill from riding in the brushy hills of the Dakotas."

"Oftentimes we stopped in Cold Creek, Idaho, where I joined the Missionary Baptist church. Those were tough times, but during those days

I defied any man to beat me to the draw. While working on the scout gang, I rode for Buffalo Bill on his ranch at North Platte, Nebraska. It was here where I later on rode the Black Diamond mare in the open prairie. No one else had ridden her in the open before."

"In the spring of '88 I joined the Pinkerton detectives. That fall I joined the Anti-Horse Thief Association to clear Texas of horse thieves. We rode up and down the Red River, in east Texas, and Indian Territory. We rode up the Ozark Trail in Missouri before we quit. I investigated many cases of counter branding. Several times, with some quick shooting, I shot the branding iron from the hands of the thief."

"Judge Parker, a United States judge at Fort Smith, Arkansas, asked me to go into the Ozark Mountains to pick up the many gangs of thieves operating there. He offered me twenty-five men. I refused, telling him, 'Those men know their hills and hideouts too well." I told him it would be suicide, but to wait until spring when the thieves came out of hiding with their stolen horses. It took us four years to break them up. All the offenses committed in Indian Territory were tried by Old Judge Parker at Fort Smith. I was well acquainted with him."

"Going over in the Creek Nation to Round Top Mountain, in '88, we were invited to a big dance, to which we went. We were looking for stolen horses. It was a regular outlaw dance, I'd call it. A fight started that night. Al Jennings and some others rode out. Four men were killed and seven were wounded. When the shooting started in the house, I saw I couldn't get out, so I just laid down on the floor. About the time the shooting ceased, a man came in and turned me over, saying, 'Did I get you Tony? If I knew I didn't, I'd finish you up.' I said nothing and played dead. He thought I was Tony McClure, a deputy marshal. I got up and went out of the house and started to get some water from the well, running over two wounded men. The first thing a wounded man wants is water. So, I went to the well and filled my hat with water. I began to give it to them. Jack Shaw, Tony McClure, and Ozark Jack were all shot up pretty bad. Ozark Jack is still living. I saw him about a year ago. We went down to the ravine, got our horses, and pulled back to the Chickasaw Nation."

"I joined the U. S. Marshal's force in '92. During the time I was a deputy marshal, I saw six train holdups. We saved three of them from losing any money. The Daltons held up a train in the spring of '92. I think it was in the spring. They killed a deputy who failed to put them up fast enough. One of them looked at me and said, 'We know who you are. Put 'em up or I'll kill you.' I put 'em up, too, I did."

"When this judge asked why we let them get away, I told him I knew the Daltons and I didn't want to fight them alone, either. We all put up our hands except one man, and he is buried out there, too."

"Cherokee Bill's gang held up a train. Joe Shaw's boys got one too. Joe was a good safe-cracker. They didn't get anything. Al Jennings held up a train. They didn't get much. There were four bank holdups and we saved two of them."

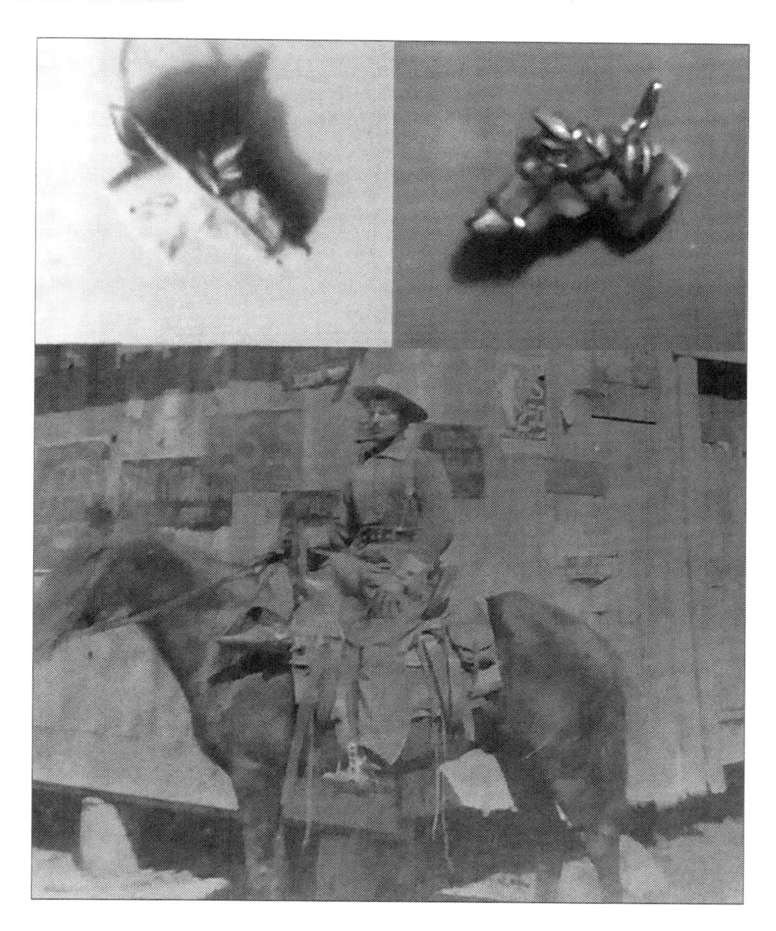

WORKING FOR THE LAW

Bill Roberts while serving on the U.S. Marshal's force, age about thirty. The small photographs are of his Anti-Horse Thief badge, made of bone laced with yellow gold wire. Note the C branded under the mane of the animals belonging to members of the Association

"I was with the bunch that took Robber's Roost. Also, I was in the bunch that captured Crazy Snake, the Indian. We chased them into the mountains, where they hid. Their boys brought food to them. A marshal named Jones roped one of the boys and hung him to a tree till he was glad to tell us where the Indians were hiding. After a brief trial, the court turned them loose."

With the exception of the testimony of Brushy's friends that claimed they served with him and some of the initial evidence Brushy provided to Morrison in the form of photographs and his Anti-Horse Thief badge, researchers have yet to find any additional hard evidence in the historical record that would verify his law enforcement service. To date, no historical reference has been found of a big outlaw dance on Round Top Mountain with many men killed (which seems strange for such a dramatic event), of a Deputy US Marshall named "Tony" (or Anthony) McClure, or of Brushy's time with the Pinkertons. However, the piece of detail he provided around capturing Crazy Snake, when investigated, does become quite interesting.

According to Mel H. Bolster in his work "*The Smoked Meat Rebellion*" (Branden Press, 1976), the posse that pursued Crazy Snake included posse men Lee Bateman of Checotah, OK; Edward Baum, City Marshal from Checotah; Herman Odom, twenty-two-year old son of the Sheriff; and Bill Carr, Deputy United States Marshal from Checotah. The band was led by Deputy Frank Jones. So, if nothing else Brushy was correct that there was a Deputy Jones involved in the event. Likewise, the obscure detail that Jones roped a man to a tree until he confessed the location of Crazy Snake is verifiable by multiple firsthand accounts.

Although there were many others involved in the campaign, Bolster's list comprises the complete list of the men who participated in the last posse that pursued Crazy Snake. If Brushy was, in fact, "with the bunch that captured Crazy Snake", then it stands to reason he meant one of the men *actually* involved in the final capture. If so, one of the aforementioned names must have been his own. This would leave only one possibility, as there is only one Deputy Marshal in the group. The remaining candidate would have to be the man known as Bill Carr.

Bill Carr was an interesting western character and had a fascinating history of his own. For one, as with other suspected aliases of William H. "Brushy Bill" Roberts, for the most part there is no record whatsoever of his birth, life, or death outside of his time with the Marshal's service and during the period that falls into the timeframe Brushy claimed he was active as a lawman. Interestingly, most of the few details of his life that do exist in the historical record fit nicely with details that Brushy Bill Roberts provided about his own life.

To begin with, "Bill" was a shortened version of Carr's full first name, which was William. His middle name is not known, but his middle initial was "H". Furthermore, he went by the nickname "Billy". While not uncommon for a man named "William" to go by the nickname "Billy", how strange is it that the man who was there with "that bunch that captured Crazy Snake" is known in the historical record, not as William H. Roberts, but as William H. Carr? Admittedly, the fact that both men have identical first names and middle initials could certainly be a coincidence, but there is more.

During the Smoked Meat Rebellion, which occurred in 1909, Bill Carr was described as being an "old deputy", which would match Brushy being approximately 50 years old at that time. Bill Carr was serving out of Checotah, OK, but his service with the marshals actually began more than twenty years earlier in Ft. Smith, Arkansas, exactly where Brushy claimed that he began his own service. Also like Brushy, Bill Carr apparently had a few extracurricular activities and breaks in his service along the way which also would allow for him to participate in some of the things Brushy had claimed to have done.

As Morrison had said, Brushy tended to jump around a bit in his story so it was not always easy to pin him down to exact beginning and end dates for his different activities. In this case, Brushy says he joined the Marshal's force in 1892, while it is said of Bill Carr that he started in 1887, so this does not at first appear to be a match. That said, Brushy did say that he had worked for the Hanging Judge Isaac Parker as a deputy in Ft. Smith before 1892, taking frequent periods of absence to ride in rodeos and pursue other activities. This was not uncommon at this time as the pay for such positions was very poor.

It is therefore not known what exactly Brushy meant when he said that he "joined the Marshal Service" in 1892 when obviously, by his own account, he clearly was active with Judge Parker prior to that time. Perhaps the only reasonable explanation could be that he joined officially full time in 1892 after working on and off some various missions and posses prior to that time. He did say, for example, that the judge offered him an assignment to go after outlaws on one occasion and he turned it down. Perhaps his role at this time as an ad hoc deputy? Another option, of course, could be that he simply made it all up and was never on the Marshall's force at all.

Regardless, both Bill Roberts and Bill Carr seem to be about the same age, with similar service records. Further, there is more information on the life and character of Bill Carr and what is known about him does seem to match many of the other details we know about the character and nature of Billy the Kid as well as things Brushy Bill shared about his own life.

For one thing, Billy Carr kept company and was friendly with a number of outlaws. Also, although well-regarded by his colleagues, Carr had a darker side and was accused at times of shooting captured criminals, which we know that Billy the Kid was known to do, at least in the case of Frank Baker and Billy Morton.

This is not to say, of course, that Carr was friendly with all outlaws. In 1894, Carr was involved in a shootout with the Doolin-Dalton gang when they attempted to rob a general store. Some accounts report that it was his own store and others say that he merely was on the scene. Like much of what is recorded in western history, accuracy in detail is often wanting, and there are discrepancies regarding Bill Carr's involvement in this incident. For example, one newspaper story relates that Carr's little boy was killed, but other sources claim he had no wife or child. Given the conflicting accounts, it seems as though perhaps the actual shopkeeper, who was not Carr, had a son on the scene that day that was killed.

Regardless, sources agree that Bill Carr was present that day and was wounded in the stomach and left for dead, but survived. He also managed to wound two of the gang. On April 20, 1895, *The New York Times* ran a feature article on Bill Carr entitled "King of the Chickasaws - Fighting Bill Carr and His Many Deeds of Daring" in which local townspeople relate stories of his exploits. In fairness, the article says many things that can only be characterized as hyperbole, such as describing Bill as "*a double-distilled rattler, a bunch of catamounts, a whole herd of Texas longhorns, and a grizzly bear all tied together with chain lightning. By profession he's a Deputy Marshal in this yer district, and he's a killer from way up near the head waters of Bitter Creek.*"

According to Brushy, he had a run in with the Doolin gang in 1892 and the meeting was not friendly. That meeting ended with Brushy's hands in the air and the Doolin's riding away victorious. It would be interesting if Brushy was then able to finally even the score a few years later in 1894. In any event, it seems that Carr was very comfortable walking a fine line between outlaw and wild west lawman. He was eventually indicted by a Grand Jury for assisting with the escape of two outlaws known as the Christian brothers and he had to sell all of his property and personal possessions to make bond. After making bond, "Billy" (as he was known) skipped town with the help of some of his lawman friends and was never heard from again in that area. Some speculated that he went to Texas while others thought he remained in Indian Territory. Even others said that they had heard he had become a Captain in the army down in Cuba, which is very interesting given what Brushy Bill would go on to share with Morrison about his own life. Aside from these unsubstantiated statements and a couple of obscure newspaper mentions, nothing more was heard about Bill Carr until he briefly reappeared on the scene during the Smoked Meat Rebellion.

On the surface, it would seem that the life and times of Bill Carr would allow for at least the possibility that he and Brushy Bill Roberts were the same person. Further, the rumors of what became of Bill Carr after his indictment are strangely similar to the life story offered by William H. "Brushy Bill" Roberts. This is not to say that at this point that it should be accepted without reservation that Brushy and Bill Carr were the same man, but it certainly would warrant additional study and consideration.

It is unfortunate that Morrison was not able to get additional details from Brushy on exactly what aliases he used and other activities participated in. We know that Brushy left out portions of his life that had no bearing on his pardon or that perhaps would reveal times when his own actions were questionable. We also know that Brushy more than likely exaggerated at times and may have told more than one story incorrectly, either on purpose or due to failing memory. This is completely understandable and in character with a man that was a notorious desperado and on the run from the law. None of this, however, precludes him from being the real Billy the Kid. If anything, it may actually reinforce his claim.

Brushy continued, "In the fall of '88 there was staged a cowboy roundup in Cheyenne. The judges wanted me to enter the contest riding a horse known as Cyclone. I didn't have the entry fee. I rode horses of every make, breed, and color on every ranch in the state till I was really saddle toughened. Then I knew I was ready for old Cyclone. So, in '89, I returned to the roundup. Tom Waggoner covered all the bets and I won the championship riding Cyclone, and Tom gave me $10,000 for winning for him. I was known as the Hugo Kid."

This episode in the life of Brushy Bill seems at first to be a trivial anecdote compared to the many amazing adventures he described. To date historical records of the event in Cheyanne have yet to be discovered but there is a contemporary record of a horse named Cyclone making the rounds in 1888.

On January 16th, 1888, the *Fort Worth Daily Gazette* published the following: "A great sweepstakes for 2-year-old horses, open to the state, will take place the first day, entrance fee of $20. The great event will be a match race between R.L. Dunman's Mark Belmont and J.J. Jackson's horse Cyclone, 445 yards, for $2200 aside. The money is now up on deposit as a forfeit, and the race has created great excitement and interest and many people are expected here."

So, it is very interesting that in the exact year that Brushy mentions there is historical evidence of a horse named Cyclone making the rounds of the horse races. Notice that it's a "great" sweepstakes open to the entire state. These types of races attracted cowboys from all around. In addition to the absolutely huge jackpot of $2200, no doubt lots of bets were placed between ranchers as well. It seems reasonable therefore that Tom Waggoner would share the profits with Brushy if he was backing him in the Cowboy Roundup race in Cheyanne.

Brushy continued, "We went to Oklahoma City for the winter. In January, 1890, Indian Jim sent me to a boxing school in Cincinnati, Ohio, where I trained. I was tired of riding outlaw horses and thought I would like to be a boxer. I was left-handed and fast, but they put me in the ring with a long-armed fellow and I decided that my arms were too short to continue boxing. I went back to Oklahoma City and rode horses again in spare time. We kept riding the anti-horse-thief trail."

"I rode Crazy Fox in Old Mexico. Crazy Fox was a buck skin with a black stripe down his back and black stripes around his legs. He weighed about a thousand pounds and was well built, about eight years old, with a ewe neck and a Roman nose, and it looked as if both his eyes came out the same place. I contested him according to Cheyenne rules. He pitched like a mountain horse, only worse while it lasted, but not so long. Pitching about three hundred yards, he broke into a run. Jim roped him, and they didn't want to pay off. They finally paid up, and we went to Fort Worth, Texas.

After that I went to Sulphur Springs, where I rode Lone Wolf in Booger Red's show. We went on to Cold Creek, Idaho, where I rode Wild Cat in the summer of '92. In the fall, I rode the Black Diamond mare at Buffalo Bill's ranch on North Platte. Then I rode Wild Hyena at Pendleton, Oregon, Smokey at the Diamond A, and Man Killer in Cheyenne."

"In 1893, my riding skill gave me a trip to the Argentine Republic. A company had shipped a large bunch of Western horses down there. The natives couldn't do anything with them. The Cattleman's Association sent me and Indian Jim there to break the horses. We left Oklahoma City about the tenth of January, 1893, and sailed to Buenos Aires. For the first few days we looked around to see the brands on the horses so we could tell where they were from. We found quite a few Wyoming horses in the herd."

"I was supposed to ride four horses a day, two in the morning and two in the afternoon. After we taught them how to ride, we showed them how to drive the horses. I would ride four one day and they would take them the next day, and so on. After we were there some six months, they suggested that we have a contest ride. We held a contest for three days, riding horses and steers, and bulldogging and roping just like we did in the United States. On the third day, I rode Zebra Dun."

"Zebra Dun was an outlaw when he was shipped there. I asked them to raise a bet and I'd ride him. I told them I was supposed to ride him anyway, but would like to have it sweetened. After I stepped off, I put a bridle on him and hopped on and rode him with a bridle. I had taught them to ride in the slick and to ride with a surcingle. Now they wanted me to ride him with a surcingle, which I did."

"Sometime in 1894 we contracted to go to the Shetland Islands to catch ponies. They were hard to rope in that brush. They would run like rabbits. We spent about three months catching some 150 head of ponies. When we came back we joined up again with the Anti-Horse Thief Association in Indian Territory. They put us on the North Canadian River."

"One morning Mountain Bill and I were riding along when a shot struck him from across the river. He fell off the horse, wounded. I drew my rifle from the scabbard. Taking my field glasses, I spied a Creek Indian across the river. I fired four shots. He never showed up any more. I put Bill on his horse and took him to a cow ranch some ten miles away. We shipped him to Ardmore, where he died from the wound. I wrote to his sister in Arizona and his brother-in-law came and got his belongings. I made a report of all this and they signed me up with a fellow named Boyles."

"In the fall of '94 I went back on the marshal force and served three more years. I would take off a couple of months each year and ride with Buffalo Bill's and Pawnee Bill's Wild West shows."

"In '95 I struck out for El Paso, where I run into a bunch of cowboys with whom I was acquainted. They said it was a good time to put up a ranch in Old Mexico, as Old Diaz had offered good terms on the grazing land. By paying a small fee, you could graze all the land you needed. It looked like a good proposition. Ten of us agreed to put up a ranch over there, with not more than ten shares to each man. We bought about a thousand cattle and fifty pony mares. We fixed up everything and appointed a boss. I decided to put Jim in my place and I went back to Indian Territory. Late in the fall I went back to Mexico, arriving about Christmas at the ranch. I was still called Hugo Kid here. We ranched through the years of '96 and '97, raising mules and steel-dust horses."

"In the spring of '98 Roosevelt called for volunteers for his regiment of Rough Riders. Jim and I were in Claremore about this time, so we went to Muskogee and enlisted."

"They transferred us to San Antonio, where we stayed about three weeks before we started for Cuba. We went through Mobile, Alabama, where they gave us a midnight supper. It was not long until we landed in

Cuba. A lieutenant by the name of Cook stepped up to me and said, "Ain't this the Texas Kid?" I told him it was, and he said, "You'd make a good scout. You were good in Indian Territory scouting horse thieves. We will take you and the Cherokee Indian for scouts."

"They put from one to fifteen on a scout gang and they would hunt the enemy out and report back to headquarters. I told Jim that we had put ourselves up as another target. I followed that about two months, seeing scouts shot on every side of me. Jim and I always made it out."

"They shipped lots of Western ponies down there, and there were lots of them that the boys couldn't ride. Cook told them he could get them a man that could ride them. So, they sent for me and the Indian to come down to the corral. I saddled up one and kicked him out like I'd always rode. They said they would give me a job riding them. I told them I wanted Jim for my helper. I thought this was better than being shot from ambush."

"In a little while I had charge of these horses. Some of the officers didn't like this and I told them to take off their stripes, which they did, and we proved our manhood. In about four days I whipped two of them, but still held my job. The officers treated lots of the boys very mean."

"During a battle one day there were four officers shot in the back. They thought that some of us and the Cherokee Indian did it, which they tried to prove in court-martial, but failed. When our time was out they gave us a bobtailed discharge. I didn't think I was entitled to it, because they did not prove anything on me."

"We mustered out, coming back to the U. S. Jim and I went back to Mexico on the ranch."

This is the extent of the detail Brushy provided to Morrison regarding his service in the Spanish American War, but it is enough. His claim to be a Rough Rider during the Cuba campaign is often ridiculed by historians. No record, it has been said, has ever been found to validate such a claim.

Actually, as shown below, the historical record is very clear that William H. Roberts did in fact serve with the Rough Riders as found in the following document in the National Archives:

U.S., Buffalo Soldiers,
Returns From Regular Army Cavalry Regiments, 1866-1916

Name: William H. Roberts
Regiment: United States Tenth Cavalry
Regiment Return Date: Aug 1898
Officer or Enlisted: Enlisted
Rank: Private
Company Letter: D
Action Date: 26 Aug 1898
Action Place: Montauk Point, New York

Roll number: 99
Archive Publication Number: M744

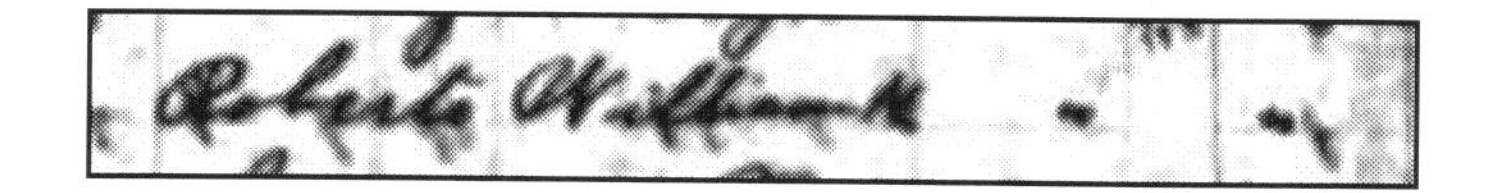

ROSTER REGISTER ENTRY SHOWING WILLIAM H. ROBERTS

This entry would seem to conclusively prove that Brushy is telling the truth about his military service. There is very little information, however, on this William H. Roberts so it is difficult to corroborate this name to Brushy Bill. There is one mention in an early New York Times article that references a "Dr." William H. Roberts "who served with the Rough Riders" but does not elaborate in any way. In those days, many men would claim to have been members of armies or regiments that they did not actually serve in so it could be possible that this "Dr." Roberts was making such a claim. After all, would it stand to reason that a doctor would hold the rank of private? Also, would it stand to reason that a white man would be assigned to a company of Buffalo soldiers? Either way, the record exists and shows William H. Roberts present in the muster rolls.

But what if the William H. Roberts listed in the roles was not Brushy? Would this necessarily discount his claim and preclude his service? It has already been established that his practice was to use multiple aliases over time. Is it reasonable then to consider the possibility that he would have used an alias during his army service? This line of thinking leads to some very interesting results.

Immediately prior to his service in the Rough Riders Brushy claims to have been serving as a deputy U.S. Marshal under the "Hanging Judge" Isaac Parker in Oklahoma Territory. He claimed that Judge Parker and he were very close and that the Judge would personally send him on assignments. His claim of being a lawman was supported by physical evidence and many witnesses. Even most detractors of Mr. Roberts concede that he was in fact a lawman of some type, if not a Marshal then at least a member of the "Anti-Horse Thief Association", considered by some a quasi-law enforcement organization or vigilante group, but referenced by others as a legitimate effort. In any event, Brushy had in his possession artifacts and photos to verify his service.

What is not known, however, is the alias that he would have used during this period, although as has been shown it is within the realm of possibility that he may have used the name William H. "Billy" Carr, whose life and service as a deputy marshal seems to fit Brushy's narrative pretty well. Unfortunately, records and photographs of deputies are extremely scarce as opposed to Sheriffs and Town Marshals. All that is known definitively at present is limited to what Brushy shared during his interviews with Morrison.

In addition to the alias "Billy Carr", the possibility has already been raised that in 1880 a twenty-year-old Brushy may have been using the alias "Joseph S. Murphy" in San Patricio, so perhaps it would be worthwhile to search for this name in the historical record, not just in regards to his time as a deputy, but in the rolls of the Rough Riders as well. This search leads to an interesting result. While there is no listing of a "Joseph S. Murphy" listed among the Rough Riders, there is a "William S. Murphy" listed as a Rough Rider and the details of his service are astounding.

Brushy claimed that during his service he was first a scout and then assigned to break horses. He said that eventually he was put in charge of all the horses which led to jealousy and conflict with certain officers. Amazingly, William S. Murphy was not only a private and the man in charge of breaking horses for the Army, but he was referred to as "The Judge" because immediately prior to joining the regiment it was thought that he was a judge in Oklahoma, Indian Territory…exactly where Brushy claimed to be serving under Judge Parker. William S. Murphy was also the private chosen by the men to present Roosevelt with Frederic Remington's famous "Bronc Buster" statue, a copy of which sits in the Oval Office of the White House today.

Whether this man actually made the claim that he was a judge or whether the men called him that because he was affiliated with a judge is unknown. Nicknames are notoriously vague and often taken up with little question and any blanks filled in by conjecture. This was especially true in the old west where the lack of specificity in historical records is notoriously poor. For example, the contemporary record concerning William S. Murphy is contradictory with it being said of him variously that he was a lawyer, Justice of the Peace, and Judge.

In his book "*Frederic Remington and the West*" Ben Merchant Vorpahl writes in regards to the presentation ceremony that "A trooper named William Murphy who had been a *Justice of the Peace* in Indian Territory, made a brief, emotional speech."

On the other hand, contemporary newspaper accounts, the *Chicago Tribune* for one, referred to Murphy as a lawyer in an article titled "Roosevelt Given a Present" printed on September 14, 1898. It states: "Camp Wikoff, Sept. 13.-Roosevelt's Rough Riders presented to Colonel Roosevelt today a bronze replica of Remington's "Bucking Bronco."

Private William S. Murphy of Troop M, *an Indian Territory lawyer*, made the speech."

It is interesting to note that despite the ubiquitous naming of Mr. Murphy in association with this event and his obvious prominence among the troops, there is *no record whatsoever* of any William S. Murphy in Indian Territory before or after the war, either as a Justice of the Peace, Judge, Lawyer, or plain citizen. In fact, there is no record of him whatsoever outside of his relation to the Rough Riders. Once again, just as with Joseph S. Murphy in San Patricio and with Deputy William H. Carr in Indian Territory, it is as though he never existed aside from the specific point in time where his presence is recorded exactly where William Henry Roberts claimed his would be.

But there is considerably more in the record concerning this William S. Murphy. For one, he was also a private, like Brushy Bill claimed. He was also involved in, and apparently in charge of, handling the horses for the army and there is considerable documentation about his service.

Brushy had stated, "They shipped lots of Western ponies down there, and there were lots of them that the boys couldn't ride. Cook told them he could get them a man that could ride them. So, they sent for me and the Indian to come down to the corral. I saddled up one and kicked him out like I'd always rode. They said they would give me a job riding them. I told them I wanted Jim for my helper. I thought this was better than being shot from ambush."

"In a little while I had charge of these horses. Some of the officers didn't like this and I told them to take off their stripes, which they did, and we proved our manhood. In about four days I whipped two of them, but still held my job. The officers treated lots of the boys very mean."

It is clear from Brushy's statement that his job was not one that officers felt suitable for a mere private, yet he claims he had the job regardless. Now compare his comments to those made by fellow Rough Rider Lt. Tom Hall in his book "*The Fun and Fighting Rough Riders*" published in 1899.

Hall states, "The horses for the regiment were purchased before the arrival of the horse equipment. They were all Western horses, most of them broncos although a few were of mixed blood—half thoroughbreds. (As a matter of fact, the bronco is of mixed blood himself.) Troopers were sent from our camp to Fort Sam Houston several times a day to ride or drive the accepted horses to our picket lines. As most of these horses were practically unbroken, the men were constantly performing feats of horsemanship that were truly remarkable."

He goes on to say, "By a peculiar arrangement the regiment did possess some very fine horses, however, of a bluer blood. Many of the

Eastern men brought or bought their own horses, valued up in the hundreds, and sold them to the government at the rates that were being paid by the purchasing board for Western horses, with the agreement, of course, that these horses should be assigned to them. By such an arrangement a private *(a man of considerable notoriety)* came to ride the finest horse in the regiment."

While not claiming specifically that said private was in charge of all of the horse breaking, Hall does validate that there was a private responsible for breaking horses and that he rode the finest horse in the regiment, something one could understand that could lead to resentment from those of supposedly higher status due to their rank. Furthermore, Hall makes a point to note that this was no ordinary private but one "of considerable notoriety". This is an odd comment and one that unfortunately he did not elaborate on. Regardless, for Hall to make this comment is remarkable, especially given that it is the only one of its kind that he makes regarding an enlisted man in his entire book.

Unfortunately, Hall does not name this trooper but there are references to someone that appears to be the same person in other contemporary accounts where his name is revealed as William S. Murphy. The following scene is recorded in *The Story of the Rough Riders* by Edward Marshal regarding the presentation to Roosevelt of Frederick Remington's famous "Bronco Buster" statue.

"It was all over before one o'clock; at that hour, a committee of embarrassed troopers waited upon Colonel Roosevelt at his tent and asked him if he minded stepping over to a rough pine table, which stood unsteadily on uneven ground. His command was informally drawn up in a square of where this table formed the center. Upon the table was a curious something, full of knobs and bunches and covered by a horse blanket. Lieutenant-Colonel Brodie happened along just then, and taking Roosevelt by the arm, conducted him to a place in front of the table. Up to this time Roosevelt had not known what was coming.

The breathless silence which pervaded the place and the curious expectant manner of his troopers warned him now that something pleasant was likely to presently occur. His face, already tanned to a deep dark brown, took on the ruddy hue of a Cuban veteran's blush, and he stood there awkwardly, not knowing what to do. There was a pause while he looked about at the men who followed him so bravely at Guasimas and San Juan. He saw that in the eyes of some of them the tears were beginning to start, and while he waited, his own were dimmed with moisture.

From the ranks of M Troop stepped William S. Murphy, who, although he was a private in the regiment, had been a judge in the Indian Territory at the time of his enlistment, and was known as one of the most eloquent men in that part of the West. He took off his campaign hat and presented the colonel with Frederick Remington's famous "Bronco Buster." Murphy had prepared an elaborate speech, which would have done honor to the Indian Territory courts, but he couldn't speak it, and if he had, most of the men in the regiment would not have heard it."

Now why would a common trooper, a private from M troop, present the "Bronc Buster" statue to Roosevelt? Some could argue that it was merely due to him being considered "one of the most eloquent men in the West" and not that he had anything to do with handling horses, but this is not the case. According to Vorpahl, Private Murphy didn't say much of anything which doesn't exactly resonate with what one would expect the "most eloquent man in the west" to say. Even Marshal has to explain away Murphy's silence by saying that he prepared an "elaborate" speech but ended up not being able to speak it. And, he says, no one would have heard it if he did. In the end, this attribute of eloquence given to Murphy seems to be simply an attempt to fill in the gaps to make a better story than an actual characteristic of the man.

Marshal's book also states: *"Just before the regiment departed for the concentration camp at Tampa, the gathering and shipping of the livestock afforded much pleasure and instruction to the men. That any of the men who entered the corrals lived to go afterwards to Cuba was not the fault of the merry mustangs who plunged therein. "Judge" Murphy was the sergeant of the guard. His heart had been broken by the work of getting the horses out. He had been at it for twenty hours, and war seemed cruel to him. That was when he learned to love Captain Capron. He was between two plunging brutes in the middle of the corral, finding it difficult to keep awake, even in such distressing circumstances. Captain Capron, long and big, climbed over the surrounding fence and said: "Go up and go to sleep on one of those boxes. I'll do your work for you. I don't want to kill my men — yet."*

Clearly then, Murphy had been working at the job of getting horses mustered out for more than 24 hours at a time at one point. This speaks to someone who is active in mustering them out for the whole regiment and obviously not just for his own use. This would seem to fit the narrative that, if he and Brushy were one and the same, that he was talented and active in the handling of horses. It would also explain why he would be chosen to present the "Bronc Buster" statue to Roosevelt.

What does not seem to fit at first glance, however, is the chronology of how Brushy explains his rise to being in charge of the horses. Brushy stated that he was at first a scout and then rose to head bronc buster. How then would he be handling horses prior to shipping out to Cuba? Under closer inspection his statements are found to not be necessarily mutually exclusive of each other. Anyone who has been involved in large scale logistics knows that they are constantly evolving situations. It is very reasonable to think that while in camp Brushy could have been utilized to help handle horses and then once on the ground in Cuba he was assigned to be a scout.

Later, when a need arose for someone to handle the horses, his skill with horses could have been remembered resulting in his being assigned once again to bronco busting. This would explain why, if he was one of the few scouts that was able to avoid getting killed on his missions as he claimed, that they would be willing to donate him to the horse breaking effort. His skill had already been demonstrated.

It therefore makes logical sense that all of the above is true. Brushy assisted with other duties, including mustering out the horses in camp, before he became a scout. He then later returned to working with horses, eventually rising to be in charge of the effort. This would also explain why this lowly private, who was the head of the bronc busting effort, would be the one to present Remington's "Bronc Buster" statue to Roosevelt.

Unfortunately, there are not any individual photos attributed to be of William S. Murphy but in Theodore Roosevelt's 1899 book: "*The Rough Riders*" there is a group photo of "Five Bronc Busters" and one of these men, the man 4th from the left, looks surprisingly like Brushy.

FIVE BRONC BUSTERS

Note "arrow straight" posture, the sloped shoulders, the similar mustache, the tilted head, the long fingers, and the facial features of the rider 4th from the left, a close match to Brushy Bill Roberts.

The presence of this photo provides opportunity to conduct analysis verses known photos of not just William Henry Roberts but to the tintype of Billy the Kid as well. After all, both are full body shots of the men. Upon close examination, there is in fact a match in body type, posture, tilt of the head, arm length, foot placement and facial structure between the two men. Even though the tintype would have been taken when Billy was just over twenty years old and the bronc buster photo when he was thirty-nine years old, they are remarkably similar.

As can be seen when scaled correctly (heels on the ground), the two men are the same height and possess similar dimensions, although the Rough Rider looks to have slightly more muscle on him than the Kid, which would make sense since he would have been a full-grown man by this time. The apparent discrepancy in the length of his right arm is explained by the younger Billy's arm resting behind his pistol.

An even more obvious comparison results from looking at photos of Brushy versus a close up of the Trooper in the photo and various photos of Brushy throughout his adult life. The trooper's mustache, nose, eyebrows, chin, hairline, ears, and other features are a close match to Brushy Bill.

The notations on this photo are likewise interesting, one of which identifies the man on the right side of Brushy in the photo (Brushy's left hand side) as a Cherokee Indian. If true, this would match Brushy's claim that he brought Indian Jim, who was a Cherokee Indian, with him to do the work of breaking horses.

But there is more. This photo in Roosevelt's book is actually only one of two similar photos taken at approximately the same time on the same day that show some of the bronc busting Rough Riders. Both photos were taken at the end of the war in Montauk, NY during the mustering out process. The second photo depicts a different group of bronc busters but one of the men, the man who resembles Brushy, is also present in this photograph. He is the only man present in both photographs.

This begs the question, "Why would only one man be present in both photographs?" Perhaps it is because he was indeed in charge of the effort and it was therefore appropriate for him to pose with both groups of men that helped him. The presence of a second photograph provides another opportunity to evaluate the man in question that appears to be Brushy Bill Roberts.

The subjects of these photos are clearly visible but unfortunately the names given for them in the historical records are uncertain. The archival description of the first photo has "probably" in front of each man's name, clearly indicating their identities are unknown. The notations for the second photo list some of the same names, although the men in the two different photos are obviously not the same people. For example, the 2nd man from the left in the first photo, who is wearing suspenders, is listed with the same name as the 1st man from the left in the second photo, who is clearly a different person.

SIX BRONC BUSTERS

In this photo, the man who resembles Brushy is standing at the far-right end. It would seem reasonable, if in fact he were in charge of the horse breaking effort, that he would pose with both groups of bronc busters.

Likewise, the short man in the first photograph (1st from left) is identified as the same man who has different features and is much taller than him that appears 2nd from left in the second photograph. Finally, the man who resembles Brushy is given different names in both photographs, although again they are clearly the same person

THE REAL WILLIAM D. WOOD?

Both men in the above comparison are listed as "William D. Wood" in the archival record despite having different features, different insignia, being dressed differently, and one man having a mustache.

TWO BRUSHYS

The man shown above is dressed identically in both photographs with the exception of the scarf which he has removed in the photograph on the left. With the scarf removed his "USV" lapel pin is shown which represents "U.S. Volunteers", also supporting Brushy's claim that he enlisted as a volunteer.

THREE BRUSHYS

A closer view of both photos with the photo of a 27-year-old Brushy in the middle for contrast and comparison. The photo on the right is a much clearer one and better reveals his features. Aside from the fact that he is frowning, it is obvious that the three photos show the same man.

Any doubt that may remain that the man that resembles Brushy is the same man in both Rough Rider photos is immediately resolved when taking a close-up view of the man's hands.

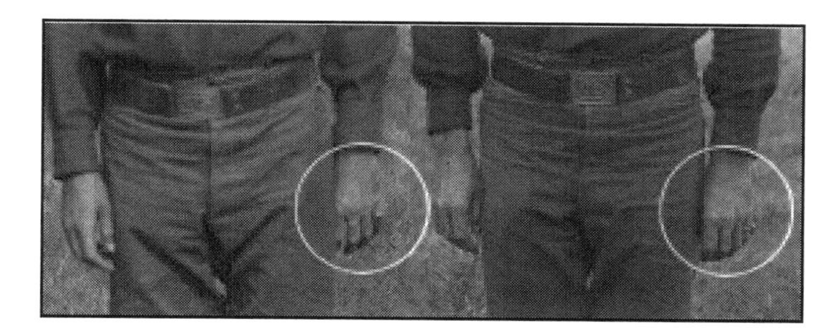

As shown above, in addition to facial features, both men have identical hands and are also wearing the exact same "gambler's ring" on the left pinky finger of the left hand. Far more interesting, however, is the fact that one of the more unique features of Billy the Kid was that he, like this man, also wore a "gambler's ring" on the left pinky finger of his left hand.

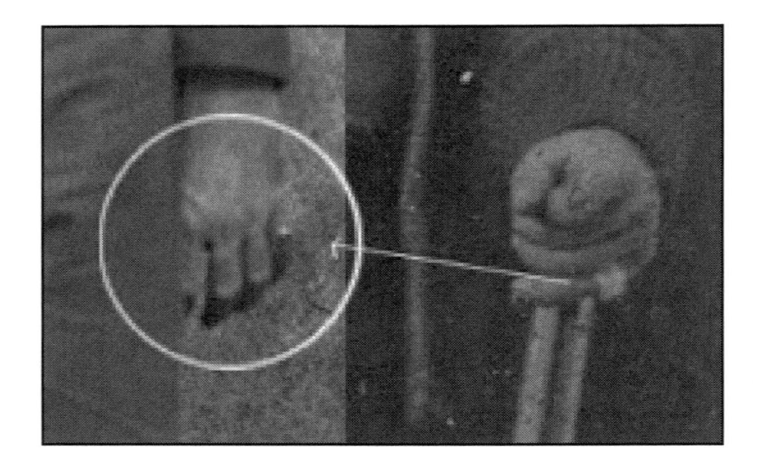

THE GAMBLER'S RING
The pinky ring was considered flashy even by Wild West standards and not every gambler wore one. It is highly unusual that an enlisted man on active duty would wear jewelry of this type. Show above is the "Gambler's Ring" of the Rough Rider compared to the "Gambler's Ring" of Billy the Kid in the famous tintype.

What are the chances that in 1949, more than fifty years after the Spanish-American War, and almost seventy years after the supposed death of Billy the Kid, that an impoverished old man living in a shack in Hico, TX could invent a life story that would be supported by an obscure photo of a man that closely resembled him, whose peculiar military service matched his own claim of being a life-long bronco buster, who had a Cherokee Indian companion that also participated in said service just as he claimed, whose used a first name and middle initial (just as Billy the Kid did with his other aliases "William H. Bonney" and "William H. Antrim") and who wore a "gambler's ring" on his left pinky finger, exactly like Billy the Kid?

The chances seem astronomical, although we know that coincidences do happen—no matter how improbable. The *likelihood*, however, that all of the supporting evidence for William H. Roberts is coincidental is extremely low. This is especially true because the evidence on the other side of history, the side that claims that Pat Garett *did* kill Billy the Kid, has absolutely no evidence other than verbal hearsay and contradictory eyewitness accounts. In contrast, the testimony of William H. "Brushy Bill" Roberts, with its own witnesses and all of its supporting evidence in the historical record, stands far above accepted history in that regard.

But Brushy had more to say about his military service. He claimed that he enlisted in the Rough Riders in Muskogee, OK and then transferred to San Antonio Texas. M Troop just happened to be one of the Indian Territory troops, including the Oklahomans which sure enough were sent to be briefly trained in San Antonio, Texas. Brushy claimed that they were trained in San Antonio for three weeks and according to records the troops stayed in San Antonio exactly nineteen days, or the almost exactly three weeks, just as Brushy claimed.

Brushy then says he went through Mobile, AL on his way to Cuba as part of the rough riders. As it so happens, *The Encyclopedia of the Spanish-American and Philippine-American Wars, Volume 1* edited by Spencer Tucker says on p. 94 that there were three main embarkation points in the Eastern US; Tampa, FL, Mobile, AL and New Orleans, LA. In addition, many of the troops would travel by train from Mobile and New Orleans to Tampa and then depart from there.

But there is additional support for Brushy's story in Hall's book. Brushy mentioned that during his period as a Rough Rider that some of the officers were shot in the back and that their own enlisted men were suspected. He states that an inquiry was held but charges dismissed. Hall, too, mentions a similar incident in his book, he states "In fact one officer came back from his troop to protest that some other troop of "ours" was firing on his from the rear. It was explained to him that there was no troop which could fire on him from the rear as all were at that time on the line."

Hall goes on to say that the shooting was later attributed to guerilla snipers and not to the other Rough Riders. This simple statement from Hall's first-hand account dovetails perfectly with the comments of Roberts. Clearly there were officers during the Rough Rider campaign that suspected their own soldiers of firing at them from the rear. Given their resentment of Brushy's status as the horse handler, his notorious reputation, and the jealousy and friction between he and some officers it would make sense that he would have been a prime suspect in this incident. It would further make sense that he would be cleared because there were other officers, Hall included, that held the position that the firing was from the enemy and not their own men.

What is interesting is that Brushy links this incident to the fact that he received a "bobtailed" discharge but what is more likely is that it was a result of jealousy for him, being a private, having the opportunity to participate in the prestigious activities he participated in. A "bobtailed" discharge is a type of discharge that is an act of spite by the discharging officer. It occurs when the bottom portion of the discharge certificate, the portion that provides information on the soldier's character, is cut off making it appear that he was dishonorably discharged and the soldier cut it off to hide the fact. In the case of Brushy Bill this would make total sense. Brushy had earned an honorable discharge but the discharging officer apparently could not stand to show him that respect, so he cut off the paper above the character line.

Clearly someone who received a dishonorable discharge would not be permitted to present the enlisted men's gift to Colonel Roosevelt. However, if in fact Brushy was held in high regard by the men but was held in contempt by certain jealous and spiteful officers, it would make sense that they would take one final petty jab at the lowly private to show their contempt…one that could easily be defended as a cutting mistake if they were ever to be called on it.

The bottom line is that every new piece of evidence that is discovered over time supports Brushy's story rather than detracts from it. Whether he used his real name of William Henry Roberts or the alias William S. Murphy the fact remains that he knew numerous detailed insights into the history and activities of the Rough Riders, information that was only known by those who participated firsthand at the time.

Following the Rough Riders Brushy says he returned to his ranch in Old Mexico.

He states "In June, 1899, Old Diaz seized everything. They would not let us ship or drive our cattle out of there. They sent soldiers down to drive our stuff off. We asked for thirty-days grace. We thought we might get some help from the U.S. If not, we could get some ammunition.

"About fifty soldiers came there to round up our cattle and horses. We sent an interpreter down to talk to them. They said it was Diaz' orders. We had thirty-six cowboys. We fired into them with .30-30 rifles and picked them off like blackbirds."

The detail Brushy offers regarding his conflict with the Mexican Army is telling. The .30 caliber Winchester Center Fire or "WCF", later referred to as ".30-.30", was introduced late in the year in 1895 and represented a significant leap forward in ballistics technology over earlier munitions. It was a dedicated rifle cartridge, rather than another version of ammunition that was able to be used interchangeably in both pistols and rifles up until that time.

The previous cartridge of choice for cowboys had been the Winchester .44 WCF, also known as the .44-40 cartridge. This cartridge featured a .44 caliber bullet with 40 grains of powder. It was a powerful round, one that could send a chunk of lead the size of a man's finger through a four-inch pine board at 1200 feet per second. It delivered over 600-foot pounds of pressure on impact. Brushy had mentioned that he previously preferred this cartridge because when he shot a man he "wanted him to stay down" and this was not an uninformed comment.

The .30-30, however, even though it was only a .30 caliber bullet with 30 grains of powder, could travel at 2,398 feet per second and delivered over 1900-foot pounds of power to its target, which was a significant advancement over the .44-40, both in regards to range as well as accuracy. Further, the Winchester rifles of this era were the first *lever action* repeating rifles that gave a much faster rate of fire than the single action weapons used by the Mexican army. It is quite reasonable, therefore, for Brushy to mention that with .30-30s he and his men were able to pick the Mexican soldiers off "like blackbirds". To anyone of his time, the mention of the .30-30 would be understood as making it far more likely for thirty-six cowboys to defeat fifty opposing soldiers at a distance as he claimed.

This is not to say that there were not present during this time longer range single shot rifles with ammunition that could have been better suited to shooting at a distance, it is merely to say that Brushy's comment would add meaningful clarification to the fighting men of his era.

He continued, "The fourth morning when we got up, we were surrounded by almost two thousand soldiers. I climbed up on the barn and tacked up a red blanket."

"Each man packed his horse like he was going off for a ride. We agreed to fire into them in the weakest spot, then make our getaway if we could. We fought for twelve days, living on wild game and trying to escape into the U. S. On the thirteenth morning, we crossed the Rio Grande below Del Rio. I had a cousin there on the Ranger force. He helped us with food. I was supposed to be worth about thirty thousand dollars, but came out with one horse and saddle."

"In the spring of 1902, I started a Wild West show which I operated until 1904. Then I went to Canton, in Van Zandt County. From Canton, I went into Indian Territory, trading horses and cattle."

It is important to remember here that Brushy stated that during this period he primarily used the alias "Texas Kid" and was recognized by that name by one of the Rough Rider officers. This alias was a familiar one to Brushy and the one by which he had been known since he was a young boy, during his time with Belle Starr and from time to time throughout his adult life. He had used many aliases off and on from his birth but claimed he went back to using the name "Texas Kid" during the period from roughly 1892 until 1900 or so. It would seem then that if such a personality like Billy the Kid were to use an alias that there should be some contemporary record of a man by that name.

Fortunately, like many of Brushy's other claims, contemporary records do exist of a man in New Mexico going by the moniker of the "Texas Kid" during the period William Roberts claimed he was known by that name.

The following article was published in the *Fort Worth Gazette* on April 21, 1895 and was titled "Bad Men with Records". After describing several other notable "bad men" the writer comes to the "Texas Kid". What follows is the remainder of his article in its entirety.

TEXAS KID WAS A COOL ONE

From the beginning to the end Dan Scott was a type of the man who, twenty years ago, was handy with a gun. In later times, the man called "The Texas Kid" was another. True, he was not so cowardly, and he was far more interesting. But he was not a chivalric gentleman, nor a model of Christian forbearance. Furthermore, he was not handsome. But that is another matter.

In Albuquerque, New Mexico, one day, at a horse auction, a newspaper man named Rhoades, who was visiting a rancher friend in the vicinity, felt himself severely jostled in the crowd, and the next moment his hat was knocked off. As soon as he could free himself he turned about, and saw a youngish, towheaded fellow, who albino eyes seemed hopelessly weak under the glaring sunlight and who was laughing at him. It was clear that he had knocked off the hat.

Rhoades approached him in a temper of either peace or war, and asked urbanely if the act was intentional. "Not at all," said the insignificant youth, still laughing. And there was the end of their quarrel.

Late that afternoon Rhoades was standing by his mustang, ready to start home, when a commotion in the saloon across the street aroused him.

A man came running out crying: "Texas Kid has killed Johnny Summers!"

And behind him strolled, very deliberately, that same weak-eyed young man who commanded the alarmist to make less noise, accenting his wishes by shooting the herald in the leg.

There was another answering shot from across the street. The city marshal was on hand. In a very prompt and orderly manner, the Texas Kid disabled the marshal's pistol arm, and then pulled down the rim of his hat, for the light was troubling him.

Then the crowd came from the saloon, some shooting, some declaring they would shoot and all very much excited. The Kid sheltered himself between a wagon and dispersed them, paying occasional attention to gentlemen in the flank and rear who were annoying him.

But he seemed to catch some hint of a rising unpopularity, and so turned and trotted—not too hastily—across the street. He had a pistol in each hand and Rhoades tried to get out of his way.

"I want to borrow your pony," said the Kid, and taking two or three running steps, he leaped into the saddle and ambled awkwardly away.

There was a posse out after him in no time, and how he ever managed to escape was more than Rhoades could understand. One cinch strap was still unfastened, and they found a saddle blanket about a mile from town. If he had been a prudent man he might have had most of New Mexico and Arizona for a habitat, but he was not.

"He filled up on unripe whisky at Deming, was arrested and brought back to Albuquerque for trial. There he escaped, and appearing at the ranch of Rhoade's friend, asked for shelter. The farmer had small choice, and he took it. In the morning, the Kid gave him $40, and told him to go to town and buy two good revolvers, and a quantity of cartridges, centre fire and long.

When the rancher came back he found the Kid examining with much interest the somewhat damaged works of a Waltham watch. "What have you been doing?" demanded the host. "A man never knows when he will need the mainspring of a watch." Replied his guest, removing his left boot and pointing out where he had bestowed that flexible wand of steel, round and round the leg, beneath the lining. The heavy gold case he had hung back on the nail where he had found it, for he was an honest man.

They ran him out of Texarkana in an attempt to capture him, but he stole a saddle horse of a contractor along the railroad and went gaily into Las Vegas, where he consorted with a woman of the town—to his undoing; for they took his weapons away and imprisoned him. He lay there for two weeks, resting and writing poetry for the Vegas Herald, and then one night he sawed his way to liberty with his mainspring, took his revolver from the Sheriff's office, and a couple of horses from a livery stable, whose title was in litigation, and was next seen in Trinidad, far away from danger.

How many men he had shot, more or less seriously, or dangerously, rather—he never did anything serious in his life—I do not know. In that Bradstreet of blood, current on the border, I have heard him quoted variously at from five to twenty-five, but the exact number was something he probably could not have told himself.

And whether he is dead, or whether he still troubles those sunlit plains—I do not know. I only know that the Texas Kid is a man of note in the country.

This article contains a number of interesting references that would seem to match what is known about Billy the Kid. For one, the youth described in the article has a very strange sense of humor. His personality seems to combine an equal measure of humor and cockiness along with humility, frontier morals, and a deadly cool demeanor in combat. These are strange combinations of personality traits that are ascribed to both Billy and the "Texas Kid". On the one hand, he is deferential and polite, almost clumsy and "tow-headed" (which, among other meanings, can refer to "tousled" hair and not necessarily "blonde" hair) but on the other hand he is a stone cold blooded killer that keeps his head when greatly outnumbered by the townspeople bent on ending his life.

The article also references the Texas Kid's "albino" eyes. It is well known that Billy had clear blue eyes as a prominent feature. Eyes, by the way, that exactly match those of Brushy Bill Roberts down to the "little brown specs in them". Whether the story teller in the article meant "clear blue" by "albino" is debatable but certainly the Texas Kid shared notable eyes as a feature just like Billy the Kid.

PHOTO OF BILLY THE KID
This photo was provided by the Jones Family. Could these be the "Albino Eyes" of the Texas Kid?

Part of the charm of Billy the Kid to the masses has always been that deep down he was somehow a "good guy", a type of western "Robin Hood" that broke the law at times but perhaps only in a way that furthered his own sense of justice.

Apparently, the Texas Kid that was spoken of in the newspaper also had his own sense of fairness and, even after killing a man and shooting it out with the townspeople, he was not a thief to rob a man's pony without cause. It is a known fact that Billy the Kid rustled quite a few cattle, but according to Roberts it was only because he was stealing them *back* from rustlers under orders from his boss, to get what was coming to him after being double-crossed on a deal, or to make a living instead of starving when times were lean. Even when Billy the Kid killed Bell and Olinger in his escape from the Lincoln County Jail, he eventually turned the horse he had stolen loose and sent him back to Lincoln.

Another similarity between Billy the Kid and The Texas Kid in the story are the number of men they were each supposed to have killed- ranging from five to twenty-five, but obviously this is anecdotal. Still, one has to wonder, why five to twenty-five? Why not five to ten, or ten to twenty? What was the math used that brings historians to five to twenty-five men killed for Billy the Kid and what was the math that brought the newspaper man from 1895 to exactly the same range?

It's an interesting question but one that may or may not add any value to Brushy Bill's claims. In fact, none of the similarities between the "Texas Kid" in the article and the real Billy the Kid definitively prove that they were the same person, or even that the events described in the article even happened in the manner claimed by the article's author. They do, however, show that there was an actual "bad man" known as the "Texas Kid" that was described in very similar terms as Billy the Kid, and that he was active during the period Brushy claimed to be active under that very name.

This, however, is not the only historical evidence of a man that goes by the moniker of the "Texas Kid". There are in fact, other references to men of this name. We should be reminded, however, that the mere historical mention of a specific name would only have value if it somehow linked that name with the person in question, like in the story above. After all, don't many men have similar nicknames such as "shorty", "slim", or "Tex"? How then could one be certain that a historical reference refers to the proper person? The answer lies in the specific details on the reference. Time, place, characteristics, and associations must all match. References must therefore be considered in context and it can often be frustrating when searching history to support or prove things without cross referencing historical records.

Fortunately, however, there is ample evidence in history to support Mr. Robert's claims. For example, Brushy stated that over the years he was well acquainted and friendly with a veritable "Who's Who" list of Wild West celebrities, from Belle Starr to Jesse James to Buffalo Bill Cody to Tom Waggoner. In fact, he claimed he knew Buffalo Bill so well that he rode in his famous Wild West Show over several summers and even spent a lot of time at his personal ranch breaking horses.

He further claims that Buffalo Bill's Wild West show wasn't the only time he performed. Brushy says from the spring of 1902 until 1904 he spent some time doing his own Wild West Show. During that period, he says he used the name "Texas Kid" which was also the same name he had used throughout his life and the reason he was selected as a government scout when riding with Teddy Roosevelt's Rough Riders. Lastly, although he claims he was not *born* in New York City, he claimed that he did eventually visit the city as a grown man.

It is interesting, therefore, that in the New York Times on March 10, 1901 features the following PLAYBILL which mentions a performance by a man using the name "Texas Kid" at Huber's Fourteenth Street Museum. The listing reads *"Dick Parr and Texas Kid, Government Scouts, with all of their Wild West apparatus"*.

Huber's Fourteenth Street Museum offers many novel features, among the principal ones being Olga, the snake charmer; Dick Parr and Texas Kid, Government scouts, with all their wild West apparatus; Col. Paul Henry, American giant, and the re-engagement of Mlle. Vallecita, who enters a steel cage in which are three lions. There will be two companies in the theatre, one of vaudeville and the other the play "Rip Van Winkle," presented by the Burke company.

PLAYBILL NOTICE FROM THE MARCH 10, 1901 ISSUE OF THE NEW YORK TIMES.

This event was also advertised in by Huber's in the same issue:

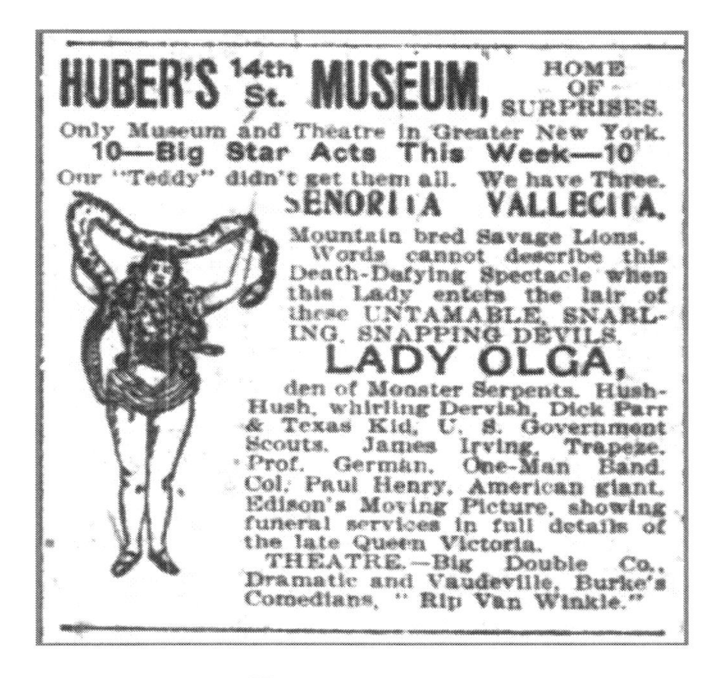

HUBER'S 14TH STREET ADVERTISEMENT

The presence of this PLAYBILL and corresponding advertisement is an amazing corroboration to Brushy Bill's account. It undeniably establishes the presence of a performer known as the Texas Kid in the Spring of 1901 who was formerly a government scout that was conducting a Wild West Show...exactly when Brushy claimed to be doing exactly that under that exact name.

Even more amazing is that this "Texas Kid" was touring with a man by the name of Dick Parr.

Dick Parr is not a recognizable name in modern America today but at the time he was one of the most famous scouts in American history. He had served among other things as "Chief of Scouts" for General Sheridan during his Western Campaign and also for the 7th Calvary under Hancock. He later served on General George Custer's personal staff. In addition to his army service he had lived more than 22 years with hostile Indians. His skill as a scout was perhaps equal to or greater than Buffalo Bill himself. In fact, Buffalo Bill hired him as his own "Chief of Scouts" and held him in extremely high regard. Clearly this "Texas Kid" kept some pretty auspicious company and was quite notable himself to share equal billing with someone like Dick Parr on the PLAYBILL announcement.

Granted, at the time Huber's 14th St. Museum was considered a bit of a dive in a seedy part of town and the attractions there were not exactly Broadway, however, it was also a known venue and the place where Harry Houdini made his debut. Brushy never claimed that Wild West Shows made him rich, but the idea that he did what he could to get by and moved from town to town and job to job as needed fits his narrative perfectly.

The reality of it all is that this short mention in an obscure PLAYBILL is a smoking gun in Brushy's favor and establishes a direct link to Buffalo Bill Cody and his Wild West Show. It is yet another contemporary historical record that supports the claims made in 1949 of a destitute old cowboy living in a trailer in Hico, Texas.

This record positively and definitively establishes a link between the "Texas Kid" and the claims made by Brushy Bill Roberts. There is no one else that has ever presented themselves to history and claimed the name "Texas Kid" except William Henry Roberts. According to Roberts, the Texas Kid was in fact a government scout, he did indeed know those close to Buffalo Bill Cody, and he had his own Wild West Show apart from Buffalo Bill's.

The fact that "The Texas Kid" is mentioned at all in the record is amazing and speaks to the level of respect that Roberts carried with the peers of his day. Dick Parr was a bonafide hero and Army veteran. He was regarded as a top expert during a time in American history when the country was filled with outlaws, apaches, and settlers-each of whom were men of extraordinary skill themselves. But then, the man who was variously known as Billy the Kid, Kid Antrim, Texas Kid, Kid Hugo and Brushy Bill Roberts was equally accomplished himself. One could fairly say that he was more than a hero in the eyes of those that knew him. Billy was a true friend and loyal companion that in the passing of time became a legend. It is unfortunate that history has cast him as an outlaw. As he said "I never robbed no stagecoaches" and he was both a soldier and a lawman during his adult life, committed to doing right. It was only during his youth and early twenties that he crossed the line into illegal behavior, and typically then only in extenuating circumstances.

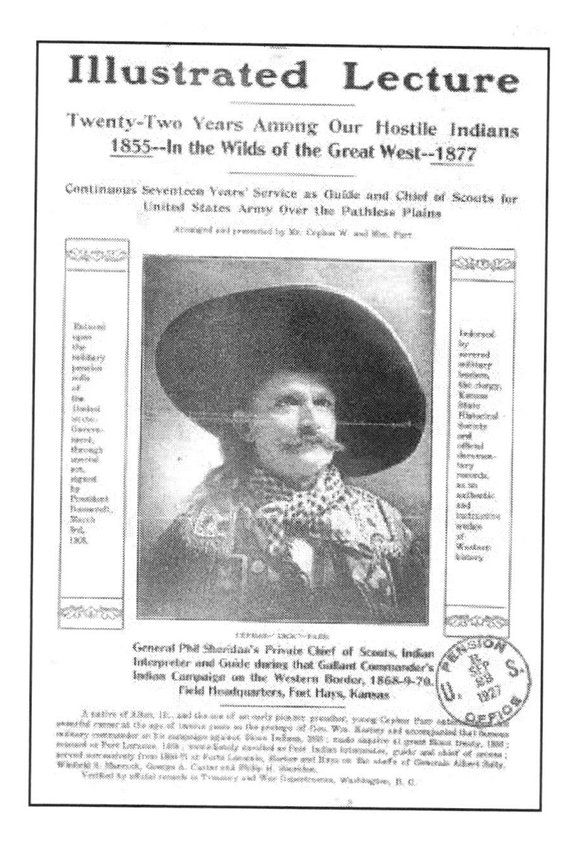

ADVERTISEMENT FOR A LECTURE BY DICK PARR

Brushy continued, "I went back to Mexico about 1907 and three of us started another ranch known as the Three Bar. In 1910 the revolution came along, and we had to start fighting again. We joined with Carranza's men, and later with Pancho Villa. I was captain of 1o6 men, all mounted on steel dust horses from our ranch. Our steel dust horses could outdistance the Spanish ponies of the Federals. We left Mexico in 1914, coming across the border at Brownsville, Texas. The Mexican revolution broke us up. We lost everything we had, about $200,000 between the three of us.

"In 1912, I met Mollie Brown of Coleman, Texas, and we were married. She was a member of the old Brown family, of Brownwood, Texas. We went back to east Texas and then into Oklahoma, in the trading business again. Later on, I had a ranch in Arkansas, near Oklahoma. I kept on riding bucking horses and doing about anything I could find to do. I worked in the oil fields of Oklahoma. When oil was struck in east Texas,

I went to Gladewater. I worked for the city of Gladewater as a plainclothesman. I aided Green, the Chief of Police. It was here that I took part in breaking up a gang of bank robbers holed up in the Sabine River bottom.

"Molly died in 1919. I married Louticia Ballard in 1925, with whom I lived until her death in 1944. Then I married Melinda Allison, in November, 1944."

That brought Brushy Bill up to date. He had little to be proud of at the end. He was old and poor, and just another old character to most people. He had memories, but he couldn't talk about the ones that meant most to him—not until he decided to "come out," and then they were beginning to fade.

He commented to Morrison on the difficulty of bringing those far-off events into focus:

"Sixty-nine years is a long time to recollect some of those things. I never forgot some. I'll never forget that trial at Mesilla . . . the fight at Blazer's. He was pouring it on us. Got Brewer too…almost got me . . . McSween's house burning . . . my jail break when I killed them two guards . . . that fight with Garrett's posse at that rock house on Christmas. The reason I can't forget about some of those times is that I was fighting for my life. You wouldn't forget about them either, would you?

"All these years I have been running and hiding when I knew I wasn't wrong. But I had to hide. Been thinking about it more since I don't have long here anymore. I want to get straightened out before I die, I do. I've been a good useful citizen and I think I deserve a break. If we have to go to court, I can still tell 'em a few things. That Ring bunch was terrible. I'm not afraid to talk if you don't let them lock me up.

"Sixty-nine years is a long time to recollect, my friend."

STILL ABOVE GROUND IN 1950?
Brushy Bill Roberts beside the grave of Billy the Kid. Snapshot taken July 6, 1950, at Fort Sumner, New Mexico

THE TINTYPE AND DELUVINA'S SCARF

Billy traded the tintype for the multicolored angora wool scarf woven by Deluvina Maxwell and wore it about his head on his way to jail

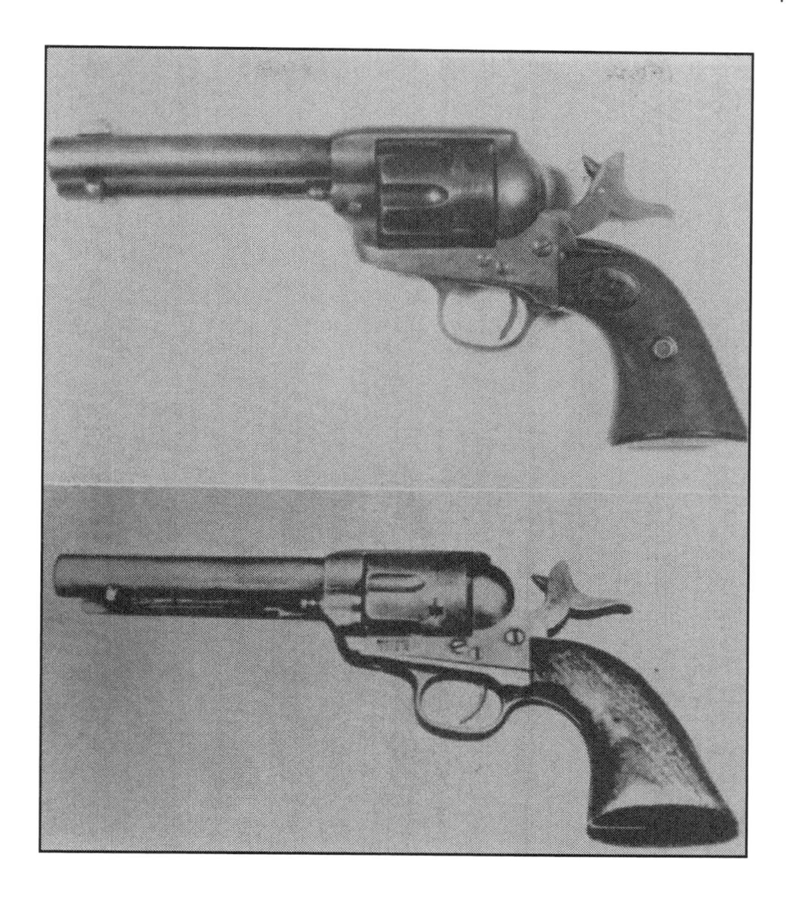

TWO .44'S

At the top is the six-shooter carried by Bill Roberts from the nineties until his death- a Colt's single-action Frontier Model, serial number 176903. At the bottom is the weapon taken from Billy the Kid when he surrendered to Garrett- a Colt's single-action Frontier Model, serial number 0361, made in 1874. These revolvers were chambered to fire ammunition that would also fit popular rifles of the day

THE OLD COURTHOUSE
Taken about 1884
The man on the extreme left is John W. Poe

A STUDY IN EARS

Brushy Bill Roberts at fourteen [inset] (photography made at Fort Smith, Arkansas); at seventeen [top, left] (taken, according to his story, at Dodge City with the Jones brothers); at twenty-seven [lower left] (crayon portrait made at Butte, Montana); at fifty-five [top right] (Brownville, Texas); and at eighty-five [lower right] (Hamilton, Texas). Note the protruding left ear

CHAPTER EIGHT

THE TANGLED WEB

Brushy Bill was a hard man to back track. He had wandered over many lands, had used a dozen aliases, and had covered his trail wherever he could. He had, in fact, spent seventy years making it hard to believe that he could be anybody but Brushy Bill Roberts.

There is some reason to believe that he spent much of his mature life impersonating one of his own relatives. This was the real Ollie Roberts, a cousin, who was born in 1879, ran away from home, and was killed in Indian Territory around 1910 in a difficulty about some stolen horses.

As Brushy Bill told it, he and his side-kick, Indian Jim, were scouting for stolen stock one time and reached a community named Shakerag. Here they expected to pick up some contraband horses. The deputy Sheriff at this place reported that he had killed two men who were in possession of the animals, and they all went out to bury the bodies.

The deputy searched the dead men, appropriated their money and personal effects, and was going on with the burying when Bill recognized one of the victims as his cousin Ollie. He looked under the mane of one of the horses and found the brand of the Anti-Horse Thief Association, realized that his cousin was working for the law, and stopped the proceedings at once. "We know this man," he said to the deputy. "He ain't no horse thief."

Using his leverage as an officer, he took over his cousin's belongings, intending to return them to the man's family. He probably hung onto them, however, for when he finally located the survivors at Sulphur Springs, Texas, they took him for the runaway boy and he let them think he was. The dead man's mother took Brushy Bill to her bosom as a long-lost son, and members of the family through the years called him Ollie and supposed he was the son of the woman who claimed him.

Naturally, this led some of the family that had only known Brushy as Ollie to doubt Brushy's claim of being Billy the Kid when he revealed himself in 1950. Interestingly, however, this was not true for everyone in the family and some apparently knew all along that Brushy Bill Roberts was not the man they had known years earlier as Oliver Pleasant Roberts. Ollie's brother-in-law, for example, once told his wife quite directly "that's not your brother", but this was a time when the younger generation did not speak out of turn to elders, and apparently the family chose to humor the matriarch in her decision to accept Brushy as her now fully-grown boy rather than to make a fuss about it.

In more recent years, however, some descendants of Ollie's extended family who never actually met him at all have gone to great lengths to attempt to use the life of Oliver Roberts to prove that William Henry Roberts was not Billy the Kid. The obvious issue with this approach is that no one has ever alleged that Oliver Roberts was Billy the Kid. Oliver Roberts was in fact a real person, but he was not William Henry Roberts. Brushy Bill merely said that very late in life he assumed Oliver's identity.

According to both his family and also numerous historical records, Oliver Roberts was a simple farmer his entire life. Brushy Bill, however, had gunshot wounds and knife wounds as well as photos and artifacts that show that he had led the life of an adventurer and not that of a farmer. Furthermore, according to Brushy, he did not assume his cousin's identity until much later in life, which matches sudden deviations in the historical record around 1910. To assert the fact that Oliver Roberts was born in 1879, therefore, has no bearing whatsoever on the birth date of William Henry Roberts, as all of Oliver Robert's historical records would have still applied to him until his death in approximately 1909 or 1910.

Wayne Land, of the Brushy Bill Roberts Forum, makes the following observation: *"In the 1910 census, Brushy (after assuming Oliver's identity) reports for the first time that he* (Oliver Roberts) *was born in Texas after reporting in every other census he was born in Arkansas. He also reports his parents were both born in Kentucky. Yet, if he was really Oliver Pleasant Roberts, he knew he was born in Arkansas, his father was born in Texas, and his mother in Arkansas. This was almost 40 years before he revealed himself to be Billy the Kid. In later census years, he went back to reporting his parents as born in Texas and Arkansas, yet he continued to say "he" was born in Texas. Why would he do that? Remember, in 1948 he told Morrison his parents were born in Kentucky."*

While there are certainly a lot of unanswered questions around the details and timing of how Brushy used his many aliases, the facts are that Brushy's assertion that he took Oliver's identity around 1910 is not without support in the historical record. What's more, he actually has more evidence on his side than his detractors do in this regard. If, in fact, Brushy Bill Roberts *was* Billy the Kid *and* he was successful in assuming the identity of a dead man, one must admit this would have been a brilliant move to conceal his identity. Further, the fact that there is evidence that some of Ollie's immediate family *did* believe that he was Billy the Kid is interesting as well.

But ultimately it is how all of the pieces of Brushy's story fit together that makes his story so compelling. If, in fact, he *was* Oliver Pleasant Roberts, then why are there anomalies in his historical record? Also, why was he so resentful over the years of being accused of being Billy the Kid? For example, he once wrote to Morrison about an Oklahoma woman who wanted to write him up: "She said she had three affidavits that people knew me in 1887...These men said I was Billie the Kid. I told her she thinks she caught a sucker, but she ain't caught one yet! I ain't putting out nothing...I don't like for other people to meddle with my business." Based on what we now know about the lengths he went to conceal his past, not wanting people meddling in his business is an understatement.

Not only was Brushy "putting out nothing" as he put it, he apparently attempted to manufacture a story that would definitively *preclude* him from being the Kid. For example, one popular dodge that he would often use to throw people off was to leverage his youthful appearance. Many times, when someone would accuse him of being the Kid, Brushy would say "The Kid would have to be 90 years old by now! Do I look like I'm 90 years old to you?".

At first, Brushy tried this familiar routine with Morrison during their initial correspondence, where he flatly denied that he was Billy the Kid. But, despite Brushy's many deceptions, Morrison was masterful in breaking the ice and gaining Brushy's trust. He used his work on the Maxwell land grant and his own knowledge of history to gain his confidence. Finally, when he felt the time was right, Morrison wrote that he had affidavits in his files from people swearing that Brushy was Billy the Kid, and that if that were true, he could help him. He promised the strictest confidence if Brushy would be willing to confide in him.

Brushy's response was to argue with him and try to persuade him that he was not the Kid. In one instance, he said bluntly "You can just forget about me being Billie the Kid" and moved on to discuss other matters. He was very aware of the death sentence over his head, and did not want to risk coming out and being held to account for the crimes he was convicted of seventy years earlier.

However, as Morrison persisted over time, Brushy would hint that he had more to say, but that he would not put it in writing; the two would have to meet face to face if Morrison wanted to know more. One reason for this, in addition to not wanting to be hanged, was that he was very determined that his wife not find out about the things he had done many years earlier, and at the time she just so happened to be writing his letters for him.

It is worthy to point out at this point that, yes, Mr. Roberts could read and write, both in English and in Spanish. The legibility of his text had certainly declined over time, and Morrison could not always make out his scrawl, but Brushy had numerous notebooks where he had made attempts at writing his story and there are extant letters today that he personally sent to friends. That said, by the time he met Morrison, he had not written regularly in almost thirty years, and his wife had taken to writing his correspondence on his behalf.

This is no doubt one of the major reasons he did not want to put anything about being Billy the Kid in writing to Morrison, although as mentioned, he also did not want to provide evidence that could hang him, either. This concern is reflected in a letter from June 23, 1949 where he writes to Morrison "Don't fool with Billie the Kid unless everything is clear that nothing is against him." Despite his obvious concerns, however, it was obvious that deep down he wanted to come clean and so he tried to provide enough to convince Morrison to come visit him. At one point, Brushy wrote Morrison that "The Kid could slip handcuffs as fast as you could put them on and he had a bullet scar on top of his head from front to back from the night Garrett shot Barlow." A few sentences later, Brushy states "I can slip handcuffs and I have a scar on my head from front to back also."

Although no doubt trying to lay false scents at times, what's interesting is that during their correspondence Brushy was always consistent with certain details like, for example, that Garrett killed Billy Barlow and not the Kid. He likewise maintained from the beginning that the Kid had shot it out with the posse in Maxwell's yard, received a head wound, and that a Mexican woman treated Billy with beef tallow. What's more, he added certain tidbits around Billy the Kid's life, like the fact that Billy was *right* handed, contrary to popular belief at the time. This was enough to get Morrison to meet with him face to face where, after he wife left the house, he finally did confess to being the Kid.

It was at this early meeting where Brushy shared many of the details of his life story with Morrison, but it was early in their relationship and Brushy was hesitant. He often had his doubts about going through with the pardon at all, and he hated to own up to a good many things he supposedly had done. At times under questioning, he would grow red in the face and object violently: "Now you're trying to get me to admit I did that, and I won't do it. I won't admit it!"

Morrison would fuss back at him, "Do you want me to take this case or not? If you don't I'll take my hat and walk right out of that door. How do you expect me to do anything for you if you won't talk?"

And the old man would look sheepish and try to be frank.

Morrison got some of it on his tape recorder, and more of it in his notes, but he had to be careful. The sight of pencil and paper made Roberts uneasy, and sometimes he would shut up like a clam when Morrison began to scribble. When he did get strung out he told whatever came into his head, seldom following a straight line of narrative. At one point, however, Bill talked at some length about the people who knew, or had known, who he was, and about the trouble he had in keeping under cover.

Buffalo Bill, he said, had been acquainted with Wild Henry Roberts and was aware of the identity of Henry's son. Pawnee Bill was another who knew, and there is some evidence to support this contention. In 1938, the newspapers picked up a story from the Associated Press that Pawnee Bill and a group of friends were laying plans to visit the Southwest in search of Billy the Kid, whom they believed to be still alive.

Tom Waggoner, who backed Brushy Bill as a bronc rider at Cheyenne in 1889, knew whom he was backing, according to Brushy Bill.

Judge Parker, of Fort Smith, Arkansas, told Bill he knew who he was when he came up for appointment as Deputy United States Marshal, and at first said he would have no goddam outlaws working for him. However, he changed his mind.

Brushy went on to tell about a good many more: "A lot of dead men in those days showed up in Old Mexico later on. They would leave Texas for New Mexico. Then from here they would go to Old Mexico or California. A lot of them never left New Mexico because they never got caught. Longwell went to El Paso and opened up a stable. I saw lots of him after I went into Old Mexico. He knew Garrett did not kill me. He knew George Cole, who I stayed with sometimes in El Paso after that killing in Fort Sumner. They knew Tex Moore, too.

Tex worked for Chisum but he was not in that war. Tex knows who I am too, he does. John Selman knew Garrett didn't kill me. saw Selman at Cole's saloon in El Paso in the 90's. He was afraid to say anything, though. He followed me outside and we talked. He had no use for Garrett. Almost killed Garrett in the Panhandle before the Lincoln County War. He said Garrett killed a man that did not need killing. I had helped Selman when he needed help and he was ready to help me now. But I wasn't ready to come out yet."

"I started to come clean when that revolution broke out there in Old Mexico. I talked to a lawyer in El Paso about it, but I lost everything in that Mexican war. Come out with one horse and riding rig. Didn't intend to make myself known after that. They would not have let me alone if I'd come out that time. I didn't want no more trouble, so I just lived Brushy Bill, that's all."

"I got around and talked to some of the boys until I got too old to run around. I was accused of being Billy the Kid from Montana to Missouri, but I denied it, saying I never knew Billy the Kid, that I was too young. I looked younger than I really was all through my lifetime. Then again, I had to tell some of them, 'If you know who I am, you will keep your mouth shut.' These little feet, little hands with large wrists, standing so straight, talking and laughing all the time, would give me away when I was around anyone who had known Billy the Kid."

"There have been lots of them said they knew Billy the Kid, but they didn't, they didn't. They just thought they had known him. There were lots of them looking for Billy the Kid until he showed up. Then they changed their minds. Captain Hughes and Captain McDonald were my friends. They didn't know I was the Kid. That was before their time. They thought Garrett had killed the Kid. It made me mad, it did. I told Captain Hughes Garrett didn't kill him—that I had seen him in South America in '93."

"I saw Brown in '82, but he didn't want anyone to know about it. Brown and Jesse Evans knew that Garrett didn't kill the Kid. I helped Jesse with money after I was on the marshal force. Tom Pickett too. I run into Tom in Arizona. I don't remember where, but Jim and I were on the trail of a man. We went through New Mexico about '92 after a man. That is when I talked to George Coe over there. He was scared to death when I walked up to talk to him. He told me to get out of the country, that a lot of my enemies were still around. He had left the country at the time I was supposed to be killed, but he was told I was killed by Garrett. I saw him again sometime in the early 1900's. He knew I was ranching in Old Mexico too."

"I was in Albuquerque and Santa Fe in the late 90s and 1900s early. I came to El Paso all through the years. I never saw Rudabaugh after that war in Mexico. I saw Pickett, though, after that. Yes, quite a while after that."

Morrison was quite diligent in his notes and very thorough, but Brushy's evasiveness was a real challenge. Although his hesitancy to "shoot straight" in the beginning and his fear of providing incriminating evidence is understandable, it certainly didn't help given the timetable both were facing and it unquestionably slowed Morrison down in obtaining the whole picture. There is no question in this author's mind that, given enough time, Morrison would have eventually been able to deal fully with any inconsistencies in Brushy's story and get to the full truth. After all, he was a professional probate investigator and extremely thorough. But, for the time being, his focus was by necessity on gathering the evidence for a pardon that he would need and so he did the best he could with the time…and the client…that he had.

Following their face to face meeting, Morrison began to diligently work on assembling the evidence for Roberts' pardon and the two continued their writing, being careful not to reveal what they were doing to Brushy's wife. When referring to Billy the Kid in their correspondence, the two would continue to refer to Brushy's "half-brother" instead of Brushy himself. Somewhat humorous is that often in the same letter they would refer to "your case" or what "you" did, despite the fact they were supposedly referencing the half-brother. They continued this practice when referring to Joe Hines as Jesse Evans, and at one point Brushy refers to "Joe's half-brother Jesse". There is no question in the context that there never really was a half-brother, and the dialogue reinforces to this author that Joe Hines was, in fact, Jessie Evans.

The correspondence between the two was a fascinating dance and Morrison played his part perfectly, being direct when he should be direct, and being deferential when he needed to be deferential. Brushy wanted badly to trust someone, but could not find anyone trustworthy until Morrison came along, and even that took time. The relationship between the two became a very real and personal attempt to secure a pardon for Brushy, and there is absolutely no evidence whatsoever in any of their correspondence that there was an attempt to perpetrate fraud on the world or gain financially from the exercise.

In this sense history has done a tremendous disservice to William Vincent Morrison, who was a man of supreme ethics and a man committed to only presenting facts that would stand in a court of law. He was a consummate professional, that followed procedure and protocol to the letter. He was also immensely knowledgeable of the law and thorough in all of his work. Many have attempted to criticize this man over the years, but in examining both what is available in his archives and what was said of him by his peers at the time, it is without question that he was a man of utmost character that was widely respected.

Brushy, on the other hand, acted quite a bit like someone with a shady past that he was trying to hide. We know, for example, that Brushy lied in the beginning, and probably a lot. How then could any human being take him seriously when he claimed to be Billy the Kid? The answer lies in context. If Brushy really was Billy the Kid and running from the law for 70 years, with no intention of revealing himself, then of course he is going to lie when he is confronted.

When it came time to "come clean", however, in order to achieve a pardon, then it is reasonable to assume he was shooting straight with

Morrison, at least in matters relative to the pardon. We would not, for example, expect him to further implicate himself in other crimes. Every other aspect of his pardon request makes sense; his request for privacy and no publicity, his request to not reveal his past misdeeds to his wife, his bitterness or Lew Wallace reneging on his promise, his sympathy for his murdered friends, and his sense of urgency due to his advancing age.

But we must understand the logistics involved in the mad rush against the clock that Morrison faced in preparing a pardon petition for a ninety-year-old man in a pre-internet and pre-email world. In addition to interviewing Brushy and gaining his trust, Morrison had to gather all of the hard evidence required to convince the governor that Roberts was Billy the Kid. He kept diligent notes when he could and especially on matters relative to the pardon, but much of the time they spent together was when Morrison was driving, thus preventing him from capturing Brushy's every word on certain subjects.

And yet herein does lie a certain dilemma. We no longer know precisely which sources Morrison drew upon when he compiled *Alias Billy the Kid* after Brushy's death. Morrison himself wrote that Brushy's story "had to be assembled from various interviews where he added details about this or that episode." This was no easy task, and no doubt value judgements had to be made with the material he possessed at hand.

One of Morrison's available sources was a series of paper-covered composition books—the kind schoolboys use for their class exercises—and a couple of loose-leaf notebooks. One of the latter was dated 1925. In these hand-written texts, Brushy attempted to tell his story the way he wanted it told. He started over two or three times and told the tale approximately the same way in each case.

When reading Brushy's account of his life in these notebooks, one fact hit Morrison between the eyes at once: there was not one single reference to Lincoln County, Billy the Kid, Pat Garrett, or anything else that might have connected Brushy Bill Roberts with the cattle troubles in New Mexico. In fact, the author never places himself closer to the Ruidoso country than the Diamond A ranch, many miles to the west.

This is almost enough to make a skeptic laugh Brushy Bill out of court. But then comes the thought that the complete omission of all such detail might be highly significant. Brushy Bill certainly knew plenty about New Mexico troubles and the people who fought in them. He must have been on the inside somehow; Why should he have passed this chapter over completely unless he had something to conceal?

It is certainly easy today to look backwards with hindsight and criticize how Brushy's story evolved or to wish that the relaying of his story was a "clean" affair, but the reality is that it was a dynamic process with many factors at play. The bottom line is that in November 1950, all of Morrison's energy was appropriately dedicated to obtaining the meeting with Governor Mabry and obtaining a pardon so that Brushy could die as a free man. Morrison knew there was a lot of incidental details to straighten out with Brushy, and he planned to go over all of it with him as soon as Governor Mabry acted favorably on the application for pardon. Unfortunately, the whole show went to pieces when Brushy suffered a devastating stroke in the Governor's mansion and when Mabry refused to act.

It is very interesting, however, and very consistent with their motives, that once the meeting with the Governor was complete and Brushy returned home, all pretense was dropped in their correspondence. Morrison advised Brushy that he could go ahead and own up to being the Kid if he wanted to, and that he would provide legal defense if litigation arose. All reference to the mysterious half-brother immediately vanishes in their correspondence. The dialogue was direct at that point, with Morrison referring to Brushy as Billy the Kid, and even encouraging him to not be too hard on himself for the things he had done in New Mexico. Brushy was ill, and very near death, and Morrison did what he could to lift his spirits.

Brushy wanted very badly to take the time to write down what actually happened and straighten out all of the facts he had misrepresented in his previous interviews before he died, but would do nothing without Morrison's permission. One opportunity, Brushy suggested, was to hire a local woman to take down his story at the rate of $.50 per hour. Morrison encouraged him to have his wife write down everything for him and mentioned that he would come visit again very soon and tape record everything that Brushy wanted to say. Audio tape, he believed, would be more credible than second hand notes anyway.

GOVERNOR THOMAS J. MABRY

Sadly, Brushy was closer to death than anyone knew. His doctor advised him to "stay in bed and keep quiet or you will be dead" and, for the most part, Brushy complied. However, this did not stop a constant stream of reporters from harassing him at his home and even attempting to guilt him into an interview by saying he was being disloyal to his own local community by refusing an interview when so many other papers had already run the story about his meeting with the governor. Brushy's nerves were already shot at this point, but he kept his promise and would not share a word. Meanwhile, he continued to write to Morrison for comfort and advice.

For his part, although publicly professional and careful not to criticize the Governor's official action, Morrison was privately incensed. He promised Brushy that he would insure that the scene with Mabry would never be repeated and that they would get another hearing with the next Governor when he took office on January 1st. He was determined to redouble his efforts and gather more evidence than ever before.

He told Brushy he wanted Brushy to mail him the buck teeth that were in Brushy's trunk so that he could have dentures made to their exact specifications to the effect that he would have them during the next interview. He further wanted to have Brushy's mouth X-Rayed to provide conclusive proof from dental experts that Brushy Bill Roberts did, in fact, have Buck teeth and that the ones that were present in his trunk actually came from his mouth.

Morrison would leave no stone unturned and assured Brushy that there would be no more shows or betrayals. The next time they went before a governor, they would have even more indisputable evidence that Brushy was the Kid. Unfortunately, this was never to be. Shortly after Christmas Day in 1950, Brushy Bill Roberts passed away.

Stunned, Morrison was stopped in his tracks. He had significant legal evidence and was personally convinced that Brushy was the Kid. He also had many confirmations of the same from many acquaintances of the Kid, including such notorious old timers as the outlaw Al Jennings, but he would never again have further opportunity to question Brushy Bill Roberts about the specific details of his story as he had planned to do.

Any chance at a pardon while the old man was living was now out of the question. Any chance for additional affidavits from those that knew the Kid were now eliminated, as the old man was no longer available to meet them face to face. What's more, Morrison would not have an opportunity to allow Brushy to "come clean" and clarify any intentional misrepresentations from their first meeting or their earlier correspondence when they were dancing around the subject with each other to gain mutual trust.

Nevertheless, Morrison still loyalty to Brushy and felt obligated to tell his story. He diligently compiled his notes, transcribed his audio tapes, and continued to write to Brushy's acquaintances to obtain additional facts. Roberts' wife was supportive and provided access to Brushy's notebooks that Morrison had previously reviewed briefly during their meeting, but that the old man would not allow him to examine carefully at the time.

What stood out right away was that three of these notebooks had disappeared. Morrison and Mrs. Roberts looked for those books and could not find them. Morrison thought that Brushy destroyed them just before he left for his disastrous interview with the governor in Santa Fe, thinking they might be incriminating evidence if he should be arrested and sent to jail, as he feared he might be.

After some time, he enlisted the aid of renown folklorist and academic C.L. Sonnichsen, who came alongside to assist with putting the information into book form. Finally, in 1955, *Alias Billy the Kid* was published by the University of New Mexico Press. The book only survived one printing, and was mostly ignored at the time of publication. It did, of course, receive high praise from President Harry S. Truman, who described it as the "most satisfactory arrangement with supporting evidence I have seen", but in the main the book was dismissed.

But Morrison was not deterred. During his interviews of Brushy he had come upon information on Pancho Villa, whom Brushy claimed to have known well. The fact that Morrison was fluent in Spanish allowed him to conduct primary research in that language, and he made many trips to Mexico. In the late 1950s, Morrison completed his manuscript, titled *The Real Pancho Villa*, and began submitting it to publishing houses. Sadly, for history, no one at the time was willing to publish the material. Over the next decade, Morrison struggled with health issues. He continued his research, and maintained his belief that Brushy Bill Roberts was Billy the Kid, but finally, on August 30, 1977, Morrison himself passed away at 70 years old.

Thus, the subject waned over the years and much of the original research was lost. According to some reports, Morrison's original files were lost in a Kansas City house fire many years after the book was published in 1955. Archive searches for copies of these documents have so far been mostly fruitless, and so for the most part those that follow in Morrison's footsteps are left in many cases with only what was recorded in *Alias Billy the Kid*. That said, there have been some additional tidbits gleaned over the years from various archive searches and fragments of files in private collections which have been very helpful.

The careful reader will note that in many cases this author has preserved Morrison's words from his original work. This is intentional as the intent is to come alongside of the original story and add further context or evidences, for or against, given the benefit of modern research methods and technology. It is not an attempt for this author to claim Morrison's work as his own. Modern researchers today owe a significant debt of gratitude to Morrison and Sonnichsen, and we stand on their shoulders with our efforts. It is appropriate, therefore, to allow them to continue to tell their story directly to a new generation to the extent possible.

But, at this time, it is unclear exactly what sources Morrison drew upon for which items of fact he presented in *Alias Billy the Kid*. If, in writing that work, he returned to some of the details from Brushy's pre-discovery personal notebooks to fill in any blanks, then it is possible he inadvertently used some information that was intentionally changed by Brushy to obscure his trail before he was discovered and before he decided to come clean.

This appears to be the case with his genealogy as in one of his final letters to Morrison *after* the meeting with Governor Mabry, Brushy hints that he wants to tell the truth about how he got the name "Bonney", which seems strange considering he already mentioned that his acquiring that name was a consequence of being adopted by his Aunt Katherine Bonney. However, in his final letter, being very near death and apparently not wanting to wait any longer to reveal his secret, he reveals to Morrison that Bonney was a wholly fabricated alias given to him by Belle Starr in the Spring of 1874.

This is an amazing revelation that, if true, would solve the genealogical problem that has vexed historians for over a hundred years. There are no marriage records that exist for Catherine McCarty to anyone named Bonney, yet we know that Billy lived with Catherine as her "son". The only answer, historians claim, is that she must have been married prior to coming to the USA. However, if, in fact, William Henry Roberts' mother was Mary Adeline Dunn, and if, in fact, Catherine McCarty/Antrim was William Henry Robert's Aunt, then this explanation for the origin of the surname Bonney for Billy the Kid would be the missing link to explain the total lack of genealogical information on the Bonney family in relation to the Kid.

But none of the inconsistencies of Brushy's early story or the challenges faced by Morrison by Brushy's sudden passing need hinder a full and thorough investigations of the claims made by William Henry Roberts. Rather, each claim may be considered independently and together in order to test their veracity. As shall be shown, in the vast majority of cases not only was Mr. Roberts correct, but the author has identified individuals doing the things Mr. Roberts claims to have done in the exact place and time that he claimed to have done them, and with names that are strikingly similar to one another. What's more, although in every case these individuals are known men, they exist only in these times and places Mr. Roberts described, and there is no record of them outside of the periods they appear doing what Mr. Roberts claimed he had done. This is very peculiar, and may support the idea that these men were actually one man using different aliases, and it is very possible that man was William H. Roberts.

But still problematic for some is the fact that Brushy Bill was outed to Morrison by a man named J. Frank Dalton, who in 1948 declared to the world that he was the famous outlaw Jesse James. Many of those that have doubted Brushy's story over the years have attempted to claim that Brushy was seeking attention or hoping to become famous, although the fact of the matter is that the *exact opposite* is true. For one, Morrison had to find Brushy, and when he did, he denied at first that he was "the Kid." Brushy had told no one that he was Billy the Kid, and wanted no one to know.

One thing that must be remembered about this is that Morrison began working with Brushy in 1949 when Dalton was already making national headlines. *The Lawton Constitution* on May 19, 1948 had already shocked the world with the headline **"JESSE JAMES IS ALIVE!"** If Brushy wanted publicity, he had every opportunity to get it then. However, on every occasion, even though he was secretly working with Morrison to prove he was Billy the Kid, he told no one else his story and refused the spotlight.

Why then would Brushy support J. Frank Dalton? There could be a number of answers to this, including that the whole affair could be one elaborate hoax. If this were the case, however, one would expect the two men to publicly support one another to strengthen one another's claims. After all, as mentioned, Dalton was already national news at the time and he was also the one who had outed Brushy Bill as Billy the Kid to Morrison. He could have certainly mentioned that Brushy was Billy the Kid in the many interviews he had at the time, especially when he had Brushy standing right there next to him.

But this was not what happened. Despite all of the buzz and publicity around Dalton from 1948-1950 and the added publicity and credibility that Brushy could have received from aligning himself with him, Brushy wanted none of it. He was certainly working hard behind the scenes with Morrison to assemble evidence for his legal brief, but apparently his focus seems to have been on genuinely getting his pardon so he could die a free man and not on getting attention for this claim.

What most people do not know is that at this time Dalton had outed Brushy to another man, who was very interested in telling Brushy's story. This man was named Orvus Lee Howk and he was from Billings, Montana. Howk would go on to write several books over the years and would attempt to claim that he was J. Frank Dalton's grandson "Jesse Lee James" aka "The Hawk", which was obviously not true. What's interesting in reading the books penned by Howk is that they contain obvious "snake oil salesman" characteristics, like folksy wisdom combined with fanciful claims that are easily disproven and sharp criticisms of straw men.

Ironically, Howk's real job was as a used auto and trailer salesman and one can only wonder if he practiced the same ethics in that profession as he did in his writing. Regardless, it was the position of Morrison and Roberts that Howk was a charlatan and a fraud. Prior to his contact with Morrison, Brushy entertained correspondence with Howk as a favor to Dalton and shared some photos of some old timers, but he did not tell him his own identity. For his trouble, Howk thanked him by stealing his photos and then claiming someone else had taken them. Shortly thereafter, Brushy's "good friend" J. Frank Dalton spilled the beans to Howk regarding his identity as Billy the Kid, which Brushy vehemently denied.

Howk continued to try to get in on the story with Brushy and even attempted to get Brushy to leave Morrison and sign a contract allowing him to write his story, but Howk had lied many times to Brushy previously and had proven himself untrustworthy. Morrison, with his unquestionable ethics, identified Howk as a fraud immediately and insisted that they not work with him. Brushy had already given Morrison power of attorney to represent him, and Morrison demanded that Brushy do things properly or he would drop his case. Roberts correctly chose to stick with Morrison. Neither of them would confirm to Howk that Brushy Bill Roberts was, in fact, Billy the Kid.

Brushy's connection with Dalton and Howk's scheme, therefore, is very slim. He did claim that he knew Dalton and he probably did, but he was not involved in the Howk plot to gain notoriety for Dalton as the famous Jesse James. Brushy *had* made one appearance for Dalton in the early stages of writing to Morrison and before he fully came clean about his own history which is a favorite point of detractors against him. There is no question that it would have been better for his legacy had this not occurred, but some sources say he was paid $100 for the trouble, which would have provided more than enough incentive for a poor old cowboy to make the claim he made on Dalton's behalf, especially if Dalton had been calling himself "Jesse James" for many years and Brushy knew him by that name.

While this may demonstrate bad judgement on Brushy's part, it really is a minor anecdote in a much larger case. In fact, Brushy shared with Morrison privately that he did not even know "Col. James E. Davis" who appeared with him at Dalton's birthday and that he doubted he was who he said he was. He surmised that it was possible he was Jim Burr, but was not sure. The fact is that in the old west many men threw around names casually, and there were many men that used the same alias. In the case of Dalton's claim to be the famous Jesse James it must be asked, "Which one?"

In any event, the facts are that even though Brushy Bill Roberts had some history with Dalton, he was not deeply or actively involved with either Orvus Lee Howk or J. Frank Dalton and their activities in 1950. Anecdotally, neither was Joe Hines, who likewise stayed away from the whole mess. For his part, Morrison was very clear that he had interviewed Dalton on several occasions and had found him to be non-credible. Unfortunately, this is one of the few areas that Brushy was never able to straighten out before he passed away. One may only assume that, if he was covering for Dalton out of friendship or because he was paid, he would have eventually "come clean" with Morrison about it, but sadly we will likely now never know.

Of course, it is possible that Brushy really did know J. Frank Dalton as "Jesse James". Certainly, there were a lot of old timers at the time that claimed to know him as James and testified as such. For Brushy to make such a claim could simply mean that he thought it was true because it was, that he was lying out of loyalty or for payment, or even that Dalton had Brushy fooled, but none of these possibilities have any bearing on whether or not Brushy was "the Kid."

But, perhaps there is yet another possible reason why Brushy may have supported Dalton's claim. Perhaps Brushy, with a death sentence hanging over him, wanted to know what would happen if a notorious wild west outlaw came out of hiding and faced the world? If this was the case, certainly the situation with J. Frank Dalton would have given him some comfort that he would not be arrested and hanged, as the old man had for the most part gone completely unmolested.

Regardless of whether or not J. Frank Dalton was the real Jesse James, and it is the position of this author that he was not, Brushy claimed that he did know the *actual* Jesse James when he was Billy the Kid, which is yet another point detractors hold against him. Billy the Kid, they claim, never knew Jesse James. There has been much discussion between historians over the years as to whether or not this is true, with the consensus being that the two never met. According to Brushy, however, Billy the Kid not only met Jesse James, but the two were well-acquainted.

In this case, Brushy had details, and those details fit with obscure historical records. For example, Brushy even went so far as to claim that Jesse had come to Lincoln County under an alias at times. Opinions among historians may vary, but there was at least one notable figure who happened to agree with Brushy Bill, and that person is none other than Confederate General and New Mexico Governor Lew Wallace, who is quoted as saying the following in the June 29,1902 issue of *The New York Sun Times*: "Shortly before I became Governor of New Mexico, Chapman, a young attorney at Lincoln, had been murdered. Half a dozen men were arrested, accused of the crime. Among them was Jesse James."

This is interesting as it is not the only contemporary mention of Jesse James being with or around Billy the Kid in the southwest, yet some choose to continue to claim he never traveled there. Another contemporary story was published in the book *A Frontier* Doctor by Dr. Henry F. Hoyt. Doctor Hoyt claimed that on July 26, 1879 he had dinner with the Kid and Jesse James in the old Adobe hotel in Las Vegas, NM.

At the time, he claims that Billy introduced Jesse as his friend from Missouri, Mr. Howard, but Hoyt later discovered his true identity of Jesse James. Regardless, whether or not one accepts Brushy Bill's claim of being Billy the Kid, it would seem that attacking his credibility on the "wild claim" that he said Billy the Kid knew Jesse James would not be a worthy point of attack on his veracity. After all, once again real history seems to be on the side of Brushy Bill Roberts when it comes to this point.

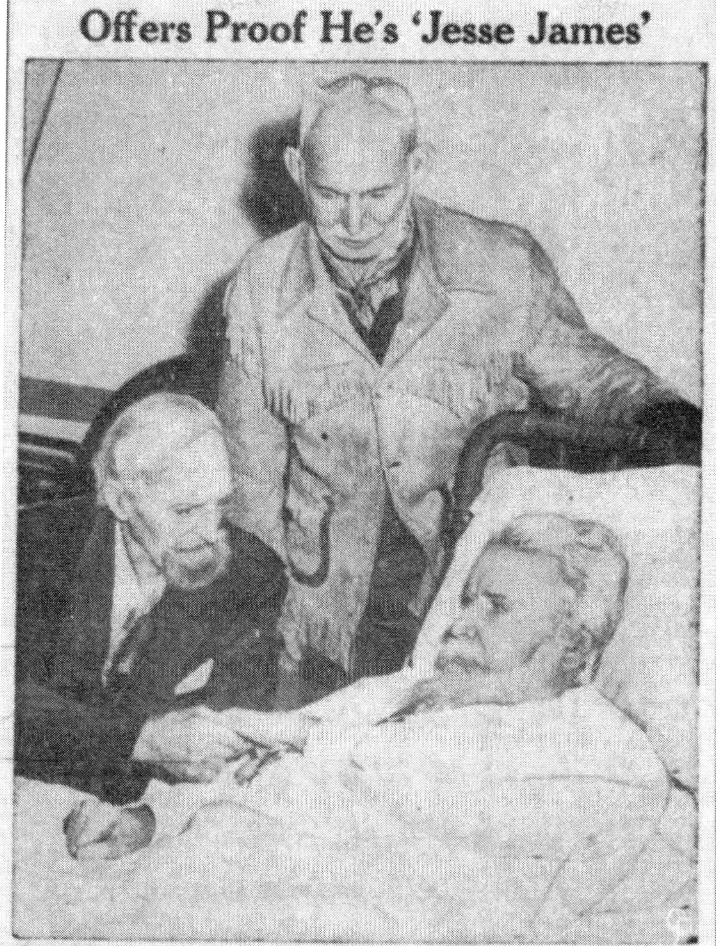

Offers Proof He's 'Jesse James'

Insisting that "history is incorrect in its report that I died on the 3rd of April, 1882, at the gun of Bob Ford," 102-year-old J. Frank Dalton, alias Jesse James, is pictured in his bed at a New York hotel. His visitors, Col. James R. Davis (left), 109, and Brushy Bill Roberts, 90, say they can prove "without a doubt" that he's the real "Jesse."

The Pottstown Mercury, January 12, 1950

CHAPTER NINE

BE HE ALIVE OR BE HE DEAD

The most ticklish part of Brushy Bill's case was the process of locating and interviewing old-timers who could and would say yes or no to his claim. The whole thing was complicated by the fact that Billy the Kid had become a legend, even in the minds of those who had known him. Stories about the Kid's death or survival had been current for so long and had been argued over so often that practically all interested persons had their minds already made up. Some were ready to maintain with firmness, and even with fury, that Billy was absolutely dead and positively buried. A much smaller group was unalterably convinced that this was not so, and they knew it.

Strangely enough, the ones who had the most deeply rooted doubts about Billy's demise were not necessarily outsiders who had steeped themselves in *The Saga of Billy the Kid*. They were likely to be real old-timers, or people who had known the Lincoln country for a long time.

The rumor that Billy had survived was current at the time of his supposed demise and apparently even the law believed this to be true because arrest warrants were issued for "Billy the Kid" in 1882 and in 1885, well after it was widely reported that he was supposedly killed.

Mrs. J. H. Wood, whose husband was a rancher and blacksmith at Seven Rivers, maintained to the day of her death that Billy ate dinner at her house three days after he was supposed to have been killed.' And there were others.

Among the letters which Morrison received when he announced in the newspapers that he wished to make contact with people who had known Billy the Kid, was one from Mrs. W. W. Carson, of San Angelo, Texas, dated November 29, 1950. "I lived in the Penasco country for 2 years, she wrote, "from October, 1887, to October, 1889. It was rumored then that 'Billie' was in hiding in the mountains there. In the spring of '88 or '89, I was returning to my school on Lower Peliasco, riding horseback. Couldn't get my pony to get into the water to cross the river. After quite a while of useless attempt, a young man suddenly appeared from nowhere and asked if he could assist me. He led the horse or pony across the wide expanse of that river. When I described, him to many of the old timers they all said 'it was Billie the Kid—He was supposed to have been dead a few years previous but those in the Peliasco region did not believe him to be dead. I recall that he was very kind to a young scared girl school teacher and was a perfect gentleman."

Similar testimony came from Arthur Hyde, of the Veterans' Hospital at Whipple, Arizona. He told of a visit he paid, in 1914, to Mr. Goforth, a relative who had lived since 1900 at the head of the Mimbres River. Goforth sent him to an old-timer named Thompson, late of the Sacramento country, when the subject of Billy the Kid came up. Thompson was convinced that Garrett and Billy had cooked up a scheme to make it look as if Garrett had lived up to his campaign promises—which included getting rid of the Kid. A Mexican boy turned up who looked something like Billy and could be used as a substitute.

"Garrett told the young Mexican to go to the Maxwell house where he would meet a rancher who might give him a job. The rest of the episode went off just as it had been written over time and again. They had a quiet burial on the grounds lest some of his followers might cause trouble and the casket was not opened at the burial. Mr. Thompson told us he had heard that Billy went to the state of Chihuahua, Mexico, and went into ranching. As it happened, I got "T.B." in the service and was sent to the old army hospital at Fort Bayard, near Silver City, New Mexico, for treatment. After I got discharged early in 1920 I spent the next four years rambling around in the Mogollons and the Black Range. I met up with several old-timers who told me just about the same story. Among them was a Mr. J.E. George (now dead) at Mule Creek and a Bill Jones, also dead, at Reserve, New Mexico. They all told me it was just a case of dirty-rotten politics, and Billy just happened to serve their purpose. They didn't seem to consider the killing of the innocent Mexican of any importance. Judging from what they told me it was common knowledge among those who were on the inside at the time."

The undercurrents of gossip which carried rumors such as these sometimes allowed a piece of conversational driftwood to come to the surface. Over and over again, as the years went by, the newspapers would discover that Billy was rumored to be alive, would print a story about it, and then run for cover as attackers and defenders closed in from all sides.

One such tidbit appeared in the El Paso Herald for June 23, 1926. Someone had heard something at Alamogordo, New Mexico:

"The story that Billy the Kid was not killed by Pat Garrett in 1881, but that he was seen as late as 1910, did not come as a complete surprise in this section for old men in the Lincoln vicinity have never conceded the Kid's death. George Coe, of Glencoe, a side partner of Billy the Kid and one of the two survivors of the Kid's faction has declared many times that he did not believe that the Kid was killed.

"C. C. McNatt, of Alamogordo, was in the vicinity of Lincoln when the Kid was supposed to have been killed, and he recalls that the settlers there at the time doubted the story of the Kid's death. Many believed it was a frame-up between those who wanted the reward, and Billy, who had served his purpose in breaking up the cattle ring and was willing to leave."

So, it went. Billy's ghost walked again—in 1937 when Pawnee Bill and some of his friends advertised an intention to search for Billy the Kid somewhere in the Southwest—again in 1948 when an old prospector named Manuel Taylor told a strange tale to Mr. L. S. Cardwell, of Las Cruces. Mrs. Cardwell was a special writer for the El Paso Times, and sent the story in.

"I knew Billy the Kid well when he was at Silver City," Taylor declared. "We used to run horse races together. In fact, another young fellow and myself once pried the bars off the chimney top at the old adobe jail so that Billy could climb out.

"The man killed at Maxwell's was a young cattle detective who had come in from the East and expected to make some easy money capturing cattle rustlers and "got his" by mistake....

"I was in Guadalajara, Mexico, in 1914 where I met the Kid. The recognition was mutual and we had a few drinks together for old time's sake. He has married there and has a family.

Cardwell stopped off at Hillsboro, New Mexico, and "took the trouble to inquire regarding Manuel Taylor and was told that he was well known there and was known to be truthful and trustworthy."

A good running summary of the ebb and flow of the underground currents is provided by John J. Clancy, now of Neihart, Montana, but for many years a resident of eastern New Mexico: "In passing, I might say that in the 1930's there arose a big controversy over whether the Kid had really been killed by Garrett or not. Some fellow up and said he had seen the Kid somewhere in California running some kind of restaurant. Another said he had seen him in Old Mexico. Somebody over in Mora County, a close Anglo-American friend of the Kid's, claimed he had seen the Kid a couple of weeks after he was alleged to have been killed, over in his country. Then the late Jim Abercrombie, daring adventurer in his own right, late pioneer merchant of Anton Chico, N. M., claimed he had seen the Kid, had been with him after his alleged 'taking hence' at Fort Sumner, N. M., by Pat Garrett. The story went around with the usual heated pros and cons back and forth, but finally petered out. Even Burns, author of the Saga of the

Kid, came to the rescue with a rather high-falutin' comeback. The latest revival of this claim was a couple of months ago when someone claimed that the real Kid was up to then living at Duncan, Arizona; that he was an old man, of course, quite pleasant of character and talked of things quite intelligently. This summer, when I was at Santa Rosa, NM, a telegraph operator named Thomas told me casually that he knew this "Kid man and confirmed quite well what I had already heard about him."

OLD FORT SUMNER
Company Quarters from the Old Sutler's Store

Such stories, of course, establish nothing more than the fact that many people chose to believe the old folk story that keeps every outlaw hero alive—a story which would naturally retain its vitality in a region where even the school children are said to cherish the old partisanships.

But it is harder to get around the fact that some of Billy's very closest friends are reported, on good authority, to have doubted the fact of his death. Higinio Salazar was mentioned in 1933 as one who had his doubts. Newspaper stories involving George Coe have already been mentioned, though in fairness it should be admitted that George accepted the usual version of the Kid's death in his autobiography *Frontier Fighter*, and many of his friends and relatives insist that the book expresses his real opinion. His cousin, Frank Coe, seems to have had a strong feeling that the Kid might still be above ground. Frank's daughter, Mrs. Helena LeMay, told Morrison that he always investigated reports that Billy was alive. Once he heard that his old friend was living in California. He took the family with him and went out to see about it. He left them in the car while he paid a visit to the claimant, who was living in a shack on the outskirts of a California town. He came back disappointed, and with tears in his eyes, saying that the man was an impostor.

With this background of contention and counter-contention, Morrison had his difficulties when it came time to gather testimony which would establish the identity of his man. After so many false alarms, people were mighty touchy—afraid of making themselves ridiculous—afraid of causing trouble and argument in their communities. Nevertheless, the job had to be done, and during the month of April, 1950, Morrison and Brushy Bill went on pilgrimage to interview as many old settlers as possible.

One of their best prospects was Severo Gallegos, of Ruidoso, New Mexico. He was the boy who was playing marbles under the tree in Lincoln while Billy the Kid shot Bell and Olinger, and who got the outlaw a rope just before he rode away. This is Morrison's account of the conversations with Mr. Gallegos:

"Upon arriving in Ruidoso, I visited with Mr. Gallegos. While talking to him, I told him that I had an old friend in my room that I would like him to meet. At my room, I introduced my friend as William H. Bonney. Mr. Gallegos seemed spellbound as he looked at and talked to Billy. They talked about happenings there during the days of Billy the Kid. After several hours of visiting, he was still somewhat skeptical, but thought it might be Billy the Kid. He would not commit himself without some more positive identification.

"I took him home late that night. He wanted to talk to him the next morning before we left Ruidoso.

"The next morning, I arrived at the Gallegos home late. He was waiting to talk to me. His first remark was: 'Your man talks like Billy; he looks like Billy; he has small hands and large wrists, small feet, large ears, stands and walks like Billy; but he is not old enough to be Billy the Kid.'

"I told him that I would not take him back just out of curiosity, but if he thought he might be able to identify my friend, I would let them visit again. I knew Billy was peculiar, and that he wanted no publicity.

"Mr. Gallegos said, 'If I could look into his eyes, I could tell for sure if he was really Billy. Billy had small brown spots in the blue of his eyes. If your man has these same kind of spots, I will say that he is Billy the Kid.'

"I was very familiar with my man, but I had never noticed the spots in his eyes. I thought it only fair that Mr. Gallegos have another chance to view Billy and find out for himself whether or not he was really Billy the Kid.

"When we arrived at my room, I stepped inside and asked Billy to open the Venetian blind and stand in the light of the window so that Mr. Gallegos would have an opportunity to see for himself in daylight. Billy stepped up as directed. Mr. Gallegos looked very carefully, then remarked: 'That is Billy the Kid, all right. Only Billy has eyes like that. I am ready to swear that this man is Billy the Kid.'

"An affidavit of identification was executed before a notary public."

Morrison and Brushy Bill went back to El Paso, where there were more old-timers to see. Luis Martinez, of Parral, Mexico, and Hernando Chavez, of Torreon, stated that to their knowledge Billy the Kid had lived in Mexico after his supposed death. "We were told," said Chavez, "that Billy the Kid fought with Carranza and Pancho Villa during the Revolution."

After that they went calling on one of Billy the Kid's old acquaintances—Mrs. Martile Able, widow of John Able. Both she and her husband had been Billy's friends.

Mrs. Able was eighty-nine years old at the time of the interview, and bedfast, but she was sure. To an El Paso reporter she delivered herself as follows:

"I knew him the moment I saw him. He is alive. Others have tried to impersonate him, but the man I talked to in July was the real Billy. A long time ago a man was brought before me as Billy the Kid, but he wasn't. He was a faker."

"But I recognized this Billy because I know him well.

"I had not seen Billy since before Pat Garrett claimed he shot him."

"When Billy's lawyer, William V. Morrison, of St. Louis, brought Billy to the home of my grandson in the Lower Valley, he asked Billy, 'Do you know this lady?'"

"And Billy said, 'Sure, that's John Able's wife."

"Would a faker know my husband, John, or remember me?"

"Many times, Billy would come to our house when he was on the dodge. My husband would give him horses and would be on the lookout while Billy was eating."

"When he came to see me he still had his gun and pocket-knife that he always carried. I would never forget them because I saw them many times.'"

Mrs. Able did not hesitate to sign an affidavit that Brushy Bill Roberts was Billy the Kid.

On July 2, Morrison and Bill started on a final jaunt through the Lincoln country. Their first stop was Carlsbad, where they had arranged to meet Sam Jones and his older brother, William Jones. Sam was living in Carlsbad, but Bill was still operating on the old ranch in Rocky Arroyo—the same ranch Billy the Kid had stumbled into when he lost his horse in the Guadalupe Mountains in 1877. They were brothers of John and Jim Jones, who worked with the Kid at Chisum's ranch and fought in the cattle war.

The three old men had a long talk together and Morrison was certain that they would help his cause along with the affidavits he wanted, but he was disappointed. William Shafer, Bill Jones' grandson, wrote on July 9, 1950: "I am sorry, but Mr. Jones does not feel that he can sign your affidavits that your man is Billy the Kid. He gave no conclusive proof of this at the time we met him. It seems to me that if he were Billy the Kid, he would not need affidavits to prove his contention. He would just be Billy the Kid."

Sam Jones wrote, "Received your letter, and am sorry but feel that I can't sign the affidavit. I'm old and I just don't feel like being obligated so."

They had better luck at Carrizozo, where they stopped the day after visiting the Jones brothers. They went to see Jose B. Montoya, who had previously told Morrison that he had seen Billy the Kid at a bullfight in Juarez in 1902. He knew it was Billy, he said, because he had been a schoolboy in Lincoln during the time that Billy was there. His people lived on a ranch in the Capitan Mountains, and Billy sometimes stayed there. After the escape from the Lincoln jail, Montoya did not see the Kid again until 1902, when he ran into him in Juarez. "He was wearing a large hat and a buckskin jacket. Alfred Green and I were there. Both of us knew Billy. Alfred was older and he really knew Billy well. He was talking to a couple of Mexican officers. We looked for him after the bullfight but couldn't locate him."

Morrison introduced Brushy Bill to Montoya, and they talked for a while. Finally, Montoya said, "By golly, that's Billy and I am ready to swear that it is him." They looked up a notary and he signed an affidavit.

The next stop was Hot Springs, now Truth or Consequences, where Morrison took up the trail of Manuel Taylor—the same Manuel Taylor who had told his tale to L. A. Cardwell, in 1948. Senator Burton Roach had once employed him and was able to pass on the disappointing intelligence that Manuel was dead."

They went on to Albuquerque and Santa Fe. In neither town where they able to find anyone who had actually known Billy the Kid, but they had some interesting conversations. As they passed the Governor's Palace in Santa Fe, Bill remarked, "Now right here is where I crossed the street on the way back to the jail down there (pointing westward). I was handcuffed and leg ironed always. Sometimes they would bring me up here at noon time and keep me here all afternoon so people could come and make fun of me. I had to hobble over stones down there to the adobe jail. Those leg irons and chains would get heavy before I got there. They walked me every place.

"I spent some bad times in this old town, and some good ones too. Used to have big affairs here—dances....

"Here is where the governor double-crossed me, too. He wouldn't come down to the jail here and talk to me. He was glad to come down to Patron's when I was locked up in Lincoln that time, because he needed my help then. But he forgot how I helped him and wouldn't come down here to talk to me. He thought I was helpless and they were going to hang me.

"That governor didn't treat me right, he didn't. This governor here now ought to help me, since the other one promised to pardon me, don't you think so?"

Morrison thought so.

They went on to Las Vegas—where nobody was left who knew Billy—and on to Fort Sumner, where Brushy Bill boarded the train for Texas.

So, it went, with success and failure intermingled. Bill had said Tex Moore, the cowboy artist at Wichita Falls, knew who he was and would testify. Morrison wrote just after Mr. Moore fell into his last illness, and was never able to arrange an interview. But DeWitt Travis, a Longview, Texas, oil man, wrote that he had known Bill from his own boyhood and had always been certain that he was Billy the Kid. He signed an affidavit and wrote to Morrison:

"My father, Elbert Travis, and Brushy Bill's father served together under Quantrill during the Civil War. My mother, Martha Ann Patterson, and Brushy Bill's mother were girlhood friends—in fact, friends through life. With this background, I have known Brushy Bill intimately all my life."

Of all of the witnesses that signed sworn affidavits, Mr. Travis was the only one that was born after Billy the Kid was supposedly killed by Pat Garrett in 1881. It should be noted that Mr. Travis also was one of the men who supported, and was quite close with, J. Frank Dalton, who claimed to be Jesse James. In fact, E. Dewitt Travis went so far as to financially support Dalton and handle his financial affairs. This relationship could be either quite problematic or quite helpful, depending on one's view of whether or not one believes that Dalton was Jesse James.

In any event, it must be said that Travis was indeed a successful businessman and a prominent member in Gladewater, TX social circles. Period newspapers list his many oil transactions and his wife's presence at social events. On one occasion, he is even listed as a groomsman for a local man named Dudley Vincent. One thing is for certain, Mr. Travis was certainly a known commodity when he came out to support Brushy Bill and a reputable citizen with roots and prominence in his local community, one that likely would not want to risk his reputation on a fraud.

That is not to say that all of the press on Mr. Travis, however, was positive. Apparently on a couple of instances in the 1930s, Mr. Travis was accused of violating certain regulatory policies in his oil business. On one occasion being accused of polluting a stream and on another of "over production and using a bypass." Then there was the time Mr. Travis lost control of his automobile and ran head on into a truck, injuring two men in the other vehicle as well as himself. No one, fortunately, was seriously injured. None of these occurrences, however, appears to have any particular bearing on Mr. Travis' credibility. It stands to reason that someone who was prominent in the oil business would, at one time or another, face some form of regulatory exposure and certainly being involved in a car accident is not uncommon.

Nevertheless, Mr. Travis' life and the details of what he actually said about Brushy are available for scrutiny, and historical records do show that Mr. Travis' father, Elbert Travis, was born on January 20, 1847 and did in fact serve in the civil war as a member of Company E of the 3rd Mississippi Calvary Reserves. Sure enough, there is a James Roberts in the same regiment. However, Brushy had stated that his father had served under "Ross", which would have been Confederate General Lawrence Sullivan "Sul" Ross, who led various regiments from Texas, not Mississippi.

Sul Ross was a famous Texas soldier who had earlier in his career led a successful attack on a Comanche village only to discover that one of the captured squaws had blue eyes. Ross remembered the 1836 Ft. Parker Massacre and the subsequent search for survivors following that event. Sure enough, Ross had discovered Cynthia Ann Parker, a survivor of the massacre who had been living with Indians as though she were one of them. Her son, Quanah Parker, became a famous Comanche chief in his own right.

During the Civil War, Ross had a number of important assignments with the army and, while it is true that General Ross led Texas troops, on several occasions those troops were joined with units from other states, including the 3rd Mississippi Calvary. In July 1863, the Sixth Texas Calvary was merged with the 1st Mississippi Calvary to form a new regiment with Ross in command. Given these circumstances, it is quite possible that Brushy Bill's father, James Roberts, did in fact serve with Elbert Travis, Sr., and that they served under Ross.

Morrison had the opportunity to interview DeWitt Travis and he gave detailed answers to Morrison's questions, for instance, one about Billy the Kid's teeth—those famous teeth. On January 23, 1951, he wrote:

DeWitt Travis could give circumstantial answers to Morrison's questions, for instance, one about Billy the Kid's teeth—those famous teeth. On January 23, 1951, he wrote:

"About Bill's teeth—the two eye teeth were so very big until they looked like tusks—when he lost several of his under or lower teeth, they bothered him an awful lot so he had a Dr. Cruz in Gladewater take them out—Dr. Cruz died about six years ago.

Taking Bill's teeth out made him a lot harder to identify. Bill was a better-looking man after his teeth were taken out than he was before—for they really ruined his looks."

Scraps of information accumulated to bolster Morrison's conviction that he was on the right track. He interviewed one pioneer woman, whose name he promised not to mention, at San Patricio, New Mexico. Among the questions he put to her, writing them down since she was too deaf to hear, was one asking if Billy had ever owned a house in San Patricio. Brushy Bill had said he did. The books make him out a homeless drifter. The old lady swung her hand out toward the hills across the way and said, "Yes he did. Right over there where that road is now. He used to live over there when he was in town."

Even Brushy Bill's wife, though she was supposed to have been kept in ignorance, contributed a touching little interview which Morrison captured on a tape recorder.

"Of course, you didn't know that he was actually Billy the Kid," Morrison said to her, and in her small, timid voice, she answered:

"No, I didn't. He never did tell me. But I suspicioned it, though."

"But he told you when he came back from Santa Fe?"

"Yes, he told me then. And one day we was there a-talkin' and I wrote you a letter and he said, "my half-brother," and I said, "Now Bill," I says, "now you know good and well it ain't," and I says, "now don't, don't story to me," I says. "I know you're Billy the Kid." And he looked at me and laughed and he said, 'No, that's my half-brother." I says, 'Well, now I can read between lines, I know you're Billy the Kid." I says, 'That's all right if you are. It don't make me any difference. . ."

"And I says, No, I ain't quittin' you. I'll live with you until you die or until I die." I said, "I'll never quit you as long as I live. I love you with all my heart. And he cried and grabbed me around the neck, and he says, "love you too, honey." And so, he got all right—got over it."

Chapter Ten

In Black and White

In 1881, Billy the Kid was condemned to hang by the neck until he was dead. In 1949 —supposing he were still alive—he was still under sentence.

As Billy Roberts' representative, Morrison had some strenuous investigating to do before he could risk announcing his client as Billy the Kid. First, he had to show that Billy the Kid was legally dead in order to have the death certificate set aside. Then he needed to assemble certified copies of all the indictments and other documents bearing on Billy's conviction so that proper steps might be taken to remove him from jeopardy.

It was a big job. For two years Morrison traveled, took notes, collected affidavits, gathered certified copies of legal instruments, and conducted an ever-widening correspondence. He did it at his own expense, for Brushy Bill had no money, because he was convinced of the soundness of his contentions. Paying little attention to rumor, hearsay, and legend, he concentrated on what had been set down in black and white regarding the windup of the Kid's career.

As the process went on, he found more and more indication that Billy the Kid's story had not been well and truly told. There were confusions, ambiguities, and out-and-out lies to be cleared up. He came to the conclusion that Billy was not always as bad as he had been represented to be, that, in some cases, he was more sinned against than sinning, and that he had grounds for asking that the noose be taken from around his neck.

He found that the very beginning of the Kid's career as a killer had, in all probability, been misrepresented. Old residents of Silver City have declared again and again that the story of his first murder—in defense of his "mother's" honor—is fictitious. They agree that he left home because he was put in jail for petty theft."

Likewise, a number of the black marks chalked up against Billy in Lincoln County were not deserved. The killing of Buckshot Roberts at

Blazer's Mill, on April 4, 1878, was one such case. Pat Garrett credits Billy with giving Buckshot a "mortal wound," and he was actually under federal indictment for this crime when he went on trial at Mesilla in 1881. He was not acquitted, however, as Garrett says. The indictment was thrown out of court.

The death of Joe Bernstein, clerk at the Mescalero Indian Agency, also was wrongfully laid at Billy's door. Pat Garrett and others say that Billy fired the shot which killed him, but later historians, including Garrett's editor, place the blame elsewhere.

Jim Carlyle's demise presents another case in which Billy's guilt is more than doubtful. The Authentic Life merely states that the volley which killed Carlyle when he crashed through Greathouse's window came from "within the house." Walter Noble Burns goes all the way and says that Billy "sent a bullet through him." Billy's letter to the governor protesting that the posse surrounding the house was responsible for Carlyle's death has already been noted. It should be added that Morrison found no record in the courts of New Mexico charging Billy the Kid with this crime.

What happened to Billy after the law finally caught up with him needs also to be re-examined—and the records are there to show that he got something less than justice.

He went on trial for his life on April 8, 1881, in the old adobe building on the southeast corner of the plaza at Mesilla, considering himself the victim of a frame-up. He was firmly convinced, in the first place, that he had been deserted, without adequate cause, by Governor Wallace. He had made a bargain and had lived up to it, as he thought, to the letter—had submitted to nominal arrest, had testified at two trials, and had declared himself ready, in April, 1879, to answer at Lincoln for the murder of Sheriff Brady.

But then the deal began to come queer. District Attorney W. L. Rynerson had introduced a motion for change of venue to Dona Ana County. Billy, thinking he was being railroaded (as he probably was), had walked out of the jail and gone about his business. The business happened to be stealing livestock, and the law eventually caught up with him. He was taken first to Santa Fe and then to Mesilla to stand trial under the original indictment for the killing of Brady. This was the charge which Governor Wallace had urged him to face—and for which he had promised Billy a pardon in case things went wrong. Governor Wallace might have argued that since Billy had walked away from the Lincoln Jail, the agreement had been nullified. Billy's answer would have been that the original agreement did not include trail anywhere outside Lincoln County, and he had not left the game until he found that the rules were being changed.

At any rate, his first grievance was against the court and its officials, all of whom were more or less under the thumb of the Santa Fe Ring-the unsavory rulers of New Mexico. Judge Warren Bristol and District Attorney Rynerson had been friendly with the Murphy faction in the Lincoln troubles, and were, therefore, on good terms with the Ring. Both had been political opponents of Governor Wallace and friends of Governor Axtell, deposed by President Hayes.

The newspapers were against Billy too. The power of the Ring extended throughout the territory, and made itself felt in the editorial comments of many of the country weeklies.

S. H. Newman, editor of the *Las Cruces Semi-Weekly*, commented before the trial began:

"We expect every day to hear of the Kid's escape. He is a notoriously dangerous character, has on several occasions escaped justice where escape appeared even more improbable than now, and has made his brag that he only wants to get free in order to kill three men—one of them being Governor Wallace. Should he break jail now, there is no doubt that he would immediately proceed to execute his threat."

Billy was quoted as saying, in regard to this statement:

"Newman gave me a rough deal; has created prejudice against me, and is trying to incite a mob to lynch me. He sent me a paper which shows it. I think it a dirty, mean advantage to take of me, considering my situation and knowing I could not defend myself by word or act. But I suppose he thought he would give me a kick downhill."

The trial itself gave Billy his most profound grievance. He thought it was rigged from start to finish. After he had entered a plea of not guilty to the charge of killing Brady, the first witnesses were called. They included his bitterest enemies—such men as J. B. Matthews, J. J. Dolan, Bonny (for Bonifacio) Baca, George W. Peppin, and Bob Olinger. His friends, whose testimony might have cleared him, could not be located. Among these were Henry Brown, Robert McCormick, Ike Stockton, and Robert Widenmann. Widenmann in particular should have been there, for he was behind the adobe wall with Billy when Brady was shot, though he took no part in the action. Billy thought the authorities had made no real effort to pick up witnesses for the defense.

Only circumstantial evidence was introduced. None of the witnesses testified that the Kid had shot at Brady, or had hit Brady. All that was definitely established was the fact that four men had walked down the street in Lincoln on the morning of April 1, 1878—that two of them, both officers of the law, had been killed by shots fired by several men (exact number unknown) concealed behind an adobe wall near Tunstall's store—that the shooting had been done through holes in the aforementioned wall so that no one on the other side could identify positively the person or persons who fired the fatal shots—and that several men had appeared from behind the wall after the shooting was over.

It appeared furthermore that, although three men had been indicted for the murder, only one had been apprehended and that little if any effort had been made to catch the others.

The evidence, such as it was, being all in, the judge gave his charge to the jury. He instructed them to bring in a verdict of murder in the first degree or to declare the prisoner not guilty.

He then continued:

"In this case in order to justify you in finding this defendant guilty of murder in the first degree under the peculiar circumstances as presented by the indictment and the evidence you should be satisfied and believe from the evidence to the exclusion of every reasonable doubt of the truth of several propositions:

1st- That the defendant either inflicted one or more of the fatal wounds causing Brady's death or that he was present at the time and place of the killing and encouraged—incited—aided in—abetted-advised or commanded such killing.

2nd- That such killing was without justification or excuse.

3rd- That such killing of Brady was caused by inflicting upon his body a fatal gunshot wound.

4th- That such fatal wound was either inflicted by the defendant from a premeditated design to effect Brady's death or that he was present at the time and place of the killing of Brady and from a premeditated design to effect his death he then and there encouraged —incited—aided in—abetted—advised or commanded such killing.

If he was so present—encouraging—inciting—aiding in—abetting-advising or commanding the killing of Brady he is as guilty as though he fired the fatal shot."

Billy thought this was carrying things pretty far, considering the fact that none of the witnesses had seen him do the thing he was charged with, whatever it was, exactly, and whatever the "peculiar circumstances" mentioned by the judge might have been (the indictment is missing from the file).

He expressed his views to a reporter for the Mesilla News who interviewed him after sentence was passed and asked if he expected the governor to pardon him:

Considering the active part Wallace took on our side and the friendly relations that existed between him and me, I think he ought to pardon me. Don't know that he will do it. When I was arrested for that murder, he let me out and gave me the freedom of the town and let me go about with my arms. When I got ready to go, I left. Think it hard that I should be the only one to suffer the extreme penalties of the law.

After the trial came the death sentence, the long ride back to Lincoln, the killing of Bell and Olinger, and the famous escape. Pat Garrett surrendered the now useless death warrant to the Secretary of State, at Santa Fe, on June 3, 1881, and no subsequent warrant was issued, so that Pat had no papers for the apprehension of the Kid on the night of July 14, 1881, when scene was played at Fort Sumner, though, of course, as an officer he had the right to pick up a condemned criminal anywhere he found him.

And this brings us to what can be found in black and white about the events which followed the shooting in Pete Maxwell's house. At once we encounter a most peculiar fact: THERE IS NO ACTUAL LEGAL PROOF OF THE DEATH OF BILLY THE KID.

A coroner's jury assembled and made a report—in fact two coroner's juries assembled and reported. But neither of these bodies made the proceedings a matter of official record. It will be said that the keeping of legal records in those days was notoriously lax—and anyone who knows even a little about such matters will agree. But records were being kept in San Miguel County at this time. A legally constituted justice of the peace presided over the inquest and should have made an entry in his books. He made no such entry.

And that was not all. Garrett was Sheriff of Lincoln County and had stepped out of his own bailiwick when he entered San Miguel County. It was his duty to turn over an apprehended criminal to the Sheriff of that county, whose name was Hilario Romero. Apparently, he did not take the matter up with Romero, either before or after the killing, but went ahead and ran his own show.

Undoubtedly, he had good reason for proceeding as he did.

There was a smoldering feud between Garrett and his men on the one hand and Romero and his men on the other. Romero had ignored Pat on one occasion when he wished to turn over some prisoners, and then, belatedly, had sent a posse which tried to take Deputy Barney Mason along to jail. Pat had won a pistol fight with a member of the gang and had refused to let one of the Romeros arrest him. Under these circumstances, there was not much point in asking for co-operation from the officers of the law in San Miguel County.

But irregular as Sheriff Garrett's proceedings may have been up to this point, they were impeccable compared to what followed. Mr. A. P. Anaya, former member of the legislature, now dead, described the inquest, or inquests, to George Fitzpatrick, editor of the New Mexico Magazine. "Mr. Anaya told me that he and a friend were called as members of the coroner's jury the night the Kid was killed," writes Mr. Fitzpatrick, "and that this jury wrote out a verdict stating simply that the Kid had come to his death as result of a wound from a gun in the hands of Pat Garrett, officer. Anaya claimed that this verdict was lost and that Garrett had Manuel Abreu write a more flowery one for filing. New signatures other than Anaya's and his friends appear on the semi-official verdict. Anaya claimed Milnor Rudolph, who signed as "presidente" of the jury, was not a member of the original jury which viewed the body.

Anaya wrote Fitzpatrick on April 2, 1936:

"Yo he dicho tocante al Ditamen del Jurado Coronario que el ditamen que el Mismo Patt. escrivio y nosotros lo Firmamos no esta en Registro. el Patt Perdio ese papel y Luego Don Manuel Abreu le escribio uno en espanol. en Donde Puso al Mine Rudolfo Presidente, eso yo he dicho que no es verdad y pruevo eso."

Again, on February 5, 1936, he wrote in English:

". . . there has been many things said in the other stories that are nothing but falsehoods, there are many things said that are just like the report that Pat Garret gave the court, he lost the report that we the coroner jury gave him and he got Mr. Manuel Abreu to write him another one..."

What happened to the second purported death certificate? Garrett stated in his report to the governor that he filed it with the district attorney of the first judicial district. This should have meant that it was deposited in Las Vegas, the county seat of San Miguel County; but no such document could be found there. Records of this kind turn up in odd places, however, and one could not say the certificate had disappeared without checking every likely or unlikely place.

In handling Brushy Bill Roberts' case, Morrison had to find that death certificate if it was still in existence. Without some record that would stand up in a court of law, his man was not legally dead. If he could not be proved to be legally dead, there was no point in going to court to have the death record set aside, and proceedings would have to be taken up at some other point.

Morrison made diligent search, in person and by letter. He could find no evidence that Billy the Kid's death had ever been legally recorded anywhere in New Mexico.

In any event, as soon as might well be after the coroner's jury had acted, Garrett's attorney, Charles W. Green, applied for the governor's reward. He submitted a copy, plainly labeled as such, of the paper signed by Milnor Rudolph and his jurymen. This copy, together with the application for the reward money, was filed in the office of the secretary of the territory on July 20, 1881. Then another curious thing happened. Acting Governor W. G. Ritch would not validate Garrett's claim and refused to approve payment. As a result, Pat Garrett never collected the $500 offered by Governor Wallace for the apprehension of the Kid.

Ritch's ostensible reason for turning down Pat's application was strange and wonderful also. He interpreted Governor Wallace's offer as an unofficial and private act, and issued a statement which concluded: "In addition we will add as a fact that there was no record whatever, either in this office or at the Secretary's office of there having been a reward offered as set forth by the Attorney General, nor was there any record on file in said offices of a corresponding reward in any form."

This is truly amazing. For Acting Governor Ritch was secretary of state at the time Governor Wallace offered his reward, and he recorded Wallace's offer over his own signature in the same book which contains Garrett's letter of application. The entry begins:

"NOW THEREFORE, I, Lewis Wallace, Governor of the Territory; by virtue of the power and authority vested in me by law and believing the end of justice will be best served thereby, do hereby offer a reward of five hundred dollars ($500.00) for the apprehension and arrest of said William Bonney, alias "Kid" and for his delivery to the Sheriff of Lincoln County at the County Seat of said county.

The proclamation is signed "Lewis Wallace, Governor.

By the Governor.

[Signed] W. G. Ritch."

Why did Ritch side-step payment of the reward by asserting the absence of a record which he had made himself? At this late date, the question can probably be answered only by conjecture. The newspaper notices of the governor's offer, one of which Garrett referred to in his application, were not in proper legal form and could have been interpreted as extra-official on Wallace's part; but it was simply not true that there was no record of "a corresponding reward in any form."

One possible explanation would be Ritch's knowledge of the shaky character of the purported death certificate—a document which cannot now be, and perhaps never could have been, produced. It is conceivable also that the solution lies somewhere among the murky undercurrents of territorial politics.

And with that thought we are back with the Santa Fe Ring again. Charles W. Greene, Garrett's lawyer, was editor of the Santa Fe New Mexican and an important Ring man. Ritch, of course, was a friend of Governor Wallace and in opposition to the Ring. For some reason, Wallace's wing of the state government, including Ritch and the attorney general (who advised against paying the reward), did not want Garrett to get his money.

The members of the Ring, all of whom had been Murphy-Dolan sympathizers and opposed to McSween and Billy the Kid, were, naturally, on the other side of the fence. That may explain, at least partly, why Charles W. Greene asked the legislature to do what Ritch would not or could not do. A bill was introduced to afford Garrett "relief." On the list of committeemen charged with considering this bill appears the name of W. T. Thornton, law partner of T. B. Catron—and T. B. Catron was the Big Man of the Santa Fe Ring. The legislature, of course, was heavily loaded with Ring supporters and henchmen. It was no trouble to get an act passed giving Garrett the money the governor had promised to pay.

It is interesting to note that the act credits Garrett with killing William Bonney "on or about the month of August, 1881," which adds to the complications by disposing of Billy a month later than the date given in the purported coroner's verdict. None of the gentlemen involved had any notion that their acts would be scrutinized so carefully almost seventy years later, or that a man named Brushy Bill Roberts would be frustrated by their lack of care and method.

All this confusion added up, in Morrison's view, to a series of doubts—doubts about Billy's guilt; doubts about the justice of his sentence; doubts about the governor's right to withhold a pardon; doubts about the actual circumstances of Billy's death and burial. The only way to get it all cleared up was to go to law about it. A pardon from the governor was to be the first step. After that the man who said he was Billy the Kid hoped to have his day in court in order that his representatives could produce whatever was down in black and white for or against him. It all came to nothing, for Brushy Bill Roberts was called to appear before a tribunal much higher than the courts of New Mexico

A Comparison of the Famous Billy The Kid Tintype and Photos of William H. Roberts

Tintype of Billy The Kid- The Only Authenticated Photograph Known to Exist Prior to 1950

Anyone who has ever seen a photo of Billy the Kid has seen the famous tintype of Billy with his rumpled hat, six-shooter revolver, Winchester rifle, and legendary buck teeth. In fact, this has historically been the only authenticated photo of Billy known to exist. What most people do not realize, however, is that the photo is actually a mirror image.

Upon close examination, this becomes obvious due to the presence of the Winchester rifle loading chamber on the left side of the rifle. In reality, all Winchester loading gates are on the right side of the rifle receiver. This detail becomes very important when comparing the photo of a 27-year-old Brushy Bill Roberts with the photo of the 21-year-old Billy the Kid.

As you will see, the faces of the two men are absolutely identical.

Upon careful examination of a high-resolution image of the famous tintype the following becomes evident:

- Billy is posing with his mouth open
- Billy's head is slightly tilted backwards and to the left
- Billy is slightly squinting

Upon examination of the 27-year-old Brushy Bill photo it is evident that:

- His eyes are wide open
- His head is straight up and down
- His mouth is closed

Despite these differences, when overlaid upon one another it becomes strikingly obvious that these two men are exactly the same person.

PHOTOGRAPHIC OVERLAY OF BRUSHY ON BILLY

From left to right: Eyes, Most of face except mouth and cheeks, whole face, untouched Billy the Kid

PHOTOGRAPHIC OVERLAY OF BRUSHY ON BILLY 2

This version is even more dramatic. From left to right: Complete overlay with one line removed, left half Brushy/ right half Billy, right half Brushy/ left half Billy, complete overlay. When properly compared to the correct orientation of the original tintype rather than a mirror image and carefully evaluated these photos show conclusively that William Henry Roberts and William Bonny, alias Kid, alias William Antrim are the same man. The features of Roberts are quite literally an exact match including a sloping right eyebrow, an angular crooked left eyebrow, high cheekbones, mustache pattern, eye spacing and size, jawline, hairline and ears. The only difference between the two photos is that in the tintype Billy is squinting so his eyelids cover the top halves of his famous eyes. Were he to have opened his eyes, the match would be obvious, even without the overlay.

A PAGE FROM AN INTERVIEW WITH BRUSHY BILL ROBERTS, JUNE 16, 1949, AT HAMILTON, TEXAS

Captain Hughes and Captain McDonald were my friends. They didn't know I was the Kid. That was before their time. They thought Garrett had killed the Kid. It made me mad, it did. Captain Hughes later committed suicide in El Paso. I told him Garrett didn't kill the Kid, that I had seen him in South America in '93 after that shooting scrape.

I saw Brown in '82 but he didn't want anyone to know about it. Brown and Jesse Evans knew that Garrett didn't kill the Kid. I helped Jesse with money after I was on the Marshal force. Tom Pickett too. I run into Tom in Arizona. I don't remember where, but Jim and I were on the trail of a man. That is when I talked to George Coe over there. He was scared to death when I walked up to talk to him. He told me to get out of the country, that a lot of my enemies were still around. He had left the country at the time I was supposed to be killed, but he was told I was killed by Garrett. I saw him again sometime in the early 1900's. He knew I was ranching in Old Mexico, too. I was in Albuquerque and Santa Fe in the late 90's and 1900's, early. I came to El Paso all through the years. I never saw Rudabaugh after that war in Mexico. I saw Pickett, though, after that. Yes, quite a while after that.

That is a long time to recollect, my friend. I'll never forget that trial in Dona Ana, the fight at Blazer's. He was pouring it on us. Got Brewer, too. Almost got me. Also, McSween's house burning, my jail break when I killed them two guards, that fight with Garrett's posse at that rock house in the Panhandle. I worked up there at times on some of those large cattle companies. I knew Bausman and another fellow. Jim East, I knew him too. He was a friend of mine. He knew Barney Mason and I were gunning for each other. Jim was all right. Garrett was all right, but some of his posse were no good. You mention some names I can't recall just now. They are in those books you saw, I guess. I gave you a list of some of those men, I did. The reason I can't forget about some of those times is that I was fighting for my life. You wouldn't forget them either, would you?

All these years I have been running and hiding when I knew I wasn't wrong. But I had to hide. Been thinking about it more since I don't have long here anymore. I want to get straightened out before I die, I do. I've been a good useful citizen and I think I deserve a break. If we have to go into court, I can still tell 'em a few things. That Ring bunch was terrible. I'm not afraid to talk if you don't let them lock me up.

That governor over there didn't do right. He made promises; then he failed to do as he said he would. I done everything I promised him to do. Now I think this governor ought to go through with the deal they made to me. I didn't have to testify against Evans and I shouldn't a done it. I helped him in '79, after that, when he couldn't help himself. He wasn't no worse than the rest of them. They were all more or less in the same boat. That Catron bunch was to blame. Not the men working for them. Don't you think so? It was just dog eat dog, that's all. I had the guts to help the Governor out. No one else would say enough to help him. I don't think I was treated right. No, no, I wasn't. Now you take that Buckshot. He was worse than any of them. He was out to get our scalp for the lousy money on our heads. He didn't fight in that cattle war. He was an outlaw before he went to that country, he was. He was a snake, he was. But he got what was coming to him that day at Blazer's place. He got Brewer, though. I hope this governor comes through on that agreement they made with me up yonder. If we have to go to court, go ahead. I talked that other time and I can do it again if I have to.

EPILOGUE

The world of Billy the Kid was one of bad men, gunslingers, corrupt lawmen, corrupt politicians, and thieves. It is incomprehensible that any of them would consider for a moment that modern men more than a century later would be diligently studying their lives. More likely, they took life one day at a time. After all, this was a period when the average life span was roughly 37 years old and daily life was by today's standards very primitive and extremely local.

Is it so strange to think then that perhaps Billy the Kid survived? Is it so strange to consider that a local Sheriff who was elected by the corrupt members of the Catron gang, out of his jurisdiction and eager for a reward, would falsify a coroner's jury rather than face a trial for murder after ambushing and killing yet another wrong victim in his attempt to get Billy the Kid?

When the circumstances are considered it is not so strange at all. There is no doubt the legend of the man who was known as "The Kid" has grown to the point that it has become the stuff of fantasy and not history. Likewise, accepted history, so called, records innumerable stories of those that claimed to know and speak for him but whose testimonies are full of contradictions and exaggerations. Billy the Kid was not a comic book hero. He was a young man of his time and, although there is no doubt that the real Billy the Kid was a notable individual, in the end he was as human and real as the rest of us.

This has not stopped the men of his era, and after, from playing on the human desire of the masses to hear innumerable stories of daring and adventure, even if it means inventing them and turning the real life "Billy the Kid" into a character from a dime store novel. Had Billy really been killed by Pat Garret that night in Pete Maxwell's bedroom perhaps this would have been appropriate; had William H. Roberts not revealed himself perhaps it would have been justifiable; but once Mr. Roberts came forward, with proof and witnesses to demonstrate that he was the real Billy the Kid, it should have been the duty of every honest historian to dig into his claims.

Regardless of how history has chosen, thus far, to characterize him, there is no doubt that William Henry Roberts was the same man known as

William H. Bonney, Billy the Kid, The Texas Kid, Kid Hugo, and who knows how many other aliases. He simply knew too much and had too much evidence to support his claim, both then in 1950 and now in the modern era. Even his reason for coming forward is unique and understandable. In the end, the evidence for Brushy is far too great for a reasonable person to deny.

Sadly, there was only one, the Harvard educated C.L. Sonnichen who seriously entertained Brushy's claims and he was ridiculed for it. Along with Dr. Sonnichen, William V. Morrison also sought for the truth but was ostracized and criticized as well.

Today, however, we have new evidence and historical record that verify the most mundane aspects of Brushy's story. In addition, we have modern photographic software that can compare with the authenticated images of the Kid with startling results. When these critical proofs are added to the already extensive burden of evidence that Sonnichen, Morrison, and Roberts presented there can be no doubt that William H. Roberts was the one and only Billy the Kid and no one else even comes close to filling his shoes.

To a seeker of the truth it is fascinating to know the real story of Billy the Kid. A man who had some amazing exploits, but was also just a man. He married, he stayed in touch with his close friends, and he even did chores for his wife just like the rest of us. He had said he never wanted to die by the gun and that he was not born to hang, and he was right. Regardless of all the naysayers and men who tried their best to cause it to be otherwise, Billy died a free man.

It has been said that the living write history and not the dead. But when one comes back from the dead, so to speak, that which was forever lost to history is recovered. This is the case with Billy the Kid. He did indeed return from the dead and he shared his story with all of us. In many ways, his story is a story of redemption. Although he had many regrets along the way, he defied the efforts of some to make him into an outlaw and rewrite history in their favor. In the end he survived, lived to a ripe old age, and even got a chance to tell his story to the world, a story that finds new evidence and support with every passing year as more and more people begin to dig for the truth.

Rest in Peace, Brushy, and thank you for straightening out this mess once and for all.

Daniel A. Edwards

APPENDICES

The following pages contain transcripts of legal documents, letters, and other papers bearing on the career of Billy the Kid in New Mexico. They establish many pertinent facts about what actually happened at the end of Billy's career as an outlaw.

To show what may be deduced from these records, take the application for change of venue (Appendix B). District Attorney Rynerson filed the motion—not Billy himself, as is sometimes stated. It is not improbable, therefore, that Billy walked out of the Lincoln jail because he thought he was being railroaded, just as Brushy Bill Roberts said.

Appendix A

Governor Wallace's Proclamation of Amnesty

15 November, 1878
Proclamation of Amnesty for Lincoln County Disorders
356
Proclamation by the Governor

For the information of the people of the United States, and of the citizens of the Territory of New Mexico in Especial, the undersigned announces that the disorders lately prevalent in Lincoln County in said Territory have been happily brought to an end. Persons having business and property interests therein, and who are themselves peaceably disposed, may go to and from that County without hindrance or molestation. Individuals resident there, but who have been driven away or who from choice sought safety elsewhere, are invited to return, under assurance that ample measures have been taken and are now and will be continued in force, to make them secure in person and property.

And that the people of Lincoln County may be helped more speedily to the management of their own affairs, as contemplated by law, and induce them to lay aside forever the divisions and feuds which by National Notoriety, have been so prejudicial to their locality and the whole Territory, the undersigned by virtue of authority in him vested, further proclaims a general Pardon for misdemeanors and offenses committed in the said County of Lincoln against the laws of the said Territory, in connection with the aforesaid disorders, between the first day of February, Eighteen hundred and Seventy Eight and the date of this Proclamation.

And it is expressly understood that the foregoing Pardon is upon the conditions and limitations following: It shall not apply except to officers of the United States Army stationed in the said County during the said disorders, and to persons who, at the time of commission of the offense or misdemeanor of which they may be accused, were with good intent, resident citizens of the said Territory, and who love hereafter kept the peace and conducted themselves in all respects as become good citizens. Neither shall it be pleaded by any bar of conviction under indictment now found or returned for any such crimes or misdemeanors, nor operate the release of any party undergoing pains and penalties consequent upon sentence heretofore had for any crime or misdemeanor.

In Witness Whereof I have hereunto set my hand and caused the Seal of the Territory of New Mexico to be affixed.

[Seal]

Done at the City of Santa Fe this the thirteenth day of November A. D. Eighteen hundred and Seventy-Eight.

By the Governor
W. G. RITCH, *Secretary*

LEWIS WALLACE
Governor of New Mexico

Entered of record November 15th A. D. 1878
W. G. RITCH, *Secretary*

(Copy certified by Alicia Romero, Secretary of State, Aug. 21, 1950)

Appendix B

The Change of Venue

1. Rynerson's Motion
2. The Supporting Affidavit
3. Change of Venue Granted

APPENDIX B:1

RYNERSON'S MOTION

The District Court of the Third Judicial District of County of
Lincoln, Territory of New Mexico, at the April A.D. 1879 Term Thereof
Cause No. 244 - Murder
(532. Dona Ana County.)
The Territory of New Mexico
vs
John Middleton
Henry Brown and
William Bonny alias Kid
alias William Antrim

Now comes the said Territory by her attorney W. L. Rynerson, District Attorney of the said Third Judicial District and moves the Court to change the Venue in the above entitled Cause as to the said defendant William Bonny alias "Kid" alias William Antrim for reasons set forth in the following affidavit.

W. L. RYNERSON
District Attorney
Territory of New Mexico, County of Lincoln

W.L. Rynerson district attorney for the Third Judicial District of the said territory of New Mexico, being first duly sworn deposes and says that justice cannot be done the said Territory on the Trial of said defendant in the said County of Lincoln for the reason that jurors in attendance and liable to be summoned for the Trial of said defendant from partisanship in the troubles existing in the said county have so prejudiced the said Jurors that they cannot fairly and impartially try the said defendant and for the further reason that the said Jurors and witnesses in said Cause are so intimidated by lawless men in said Lincoln County, that the said Jurors and Witnesses cannot fearlessly perform their respective duties at said Trial in said Lincoln County.

W. L. RYNERSON

Sworn to and subscribed before me in open Court, April 21, A.D. 1879

Louis H. Baldy, *Clerk*

APPENDIX B:2

THE SUPPORTING AFFIDAVIT

Affidavit and Motion for Change of Venue
Cause 244-
(532. Dona Ana County)
Territory of New Mexico, County of Lincoln

Marion Turner and John Long being severally sworn depose and say severally that they have heard the foregoing affidavit read and heard the contents thereof and that the matters and things as therein stated are true.

JOHN LONG
MARION TURNER

Sworn and subscribed before me April 22, 1879

Louis H. Baldy, *Clerk*

APPENDIX B:3

CHANGE OF VENUE GRANTED

Eighth Day, Tuesday, April 22, 1879
Court met pursuant to adjournment
Present as of yesterday
243 - Murder

The Territory
VS
John Middleton
Henry Brown
William Bonny
Alias "Kid" Alias William Antrim

This Cause coming on to be heard upon the motion of the Plaintiff herein by W. L. Rynerson Esq District Attorney therefor, for a change of venue in Said Court as to said Defendant William Bonny-alias Kid, alias William Antrim, for reasons set forth in the affidavit attached to Said motion now on file herein, and the motion being submitted to the Court and the Court being fully advised in the premises, sustains Said motion Said Defendant being present with his counsel to which ruling of the Court the Defendant excepts.

It is therefore ordered by the Court that the venue in this Cause, as to the Defendant William Bonny alias "Kid" alias William Antrim herein, be and the same hereby is changed to the County of Dona Ana in the Third Judicial District, Territory of New Mexico, and it is further ordered that the Clerk of this Court make an exemplified copy of the proceedings had in this Cause in this Court and transmit the same together with the Original Papers in Said Cause to the District Court in and for the County of Dona Ana, Territory of New Mexico.

And now further comes the Said Territory by her said District Attorney and moves the Court that Isaac Ellis, B. F. Baca and Jacob B. Mathews who have been summoned to appear and testify as witnesses in Said Cause on the part of the Territory and are now present in Court be required to enter into their personal recognizance respectively to appear as such witnesses at the next Ensuing Term of the Court in and for Said County of Dona Ana, which said motion is sustained by the Court. It is therefore ordered that Said Witnesses be and they thereby are required to enter into their personal recognizance respectively in the sum of ($1,000.00) One Thousand Dollars for their appearance as aforesaid. And now comes the said Ellis, the said B. F. Baca and the said Jacob B. Mathews who in open Court each for himself does acknowledge that he is indebted to the Territory of New Mexico in the Penal Sum of One Thousand Dollars, for the payment of which well and truly to be made he binds Himself, his heirs, executors and administrators upon the condition ever that if he shall personally appear at the next ensuing Term of the District Court for the Third Judicial District of the

Territory of New Mexico to be held in and for the County of Dona Ana as a witness on the part of the Territory in Said Cause and shall remain in attendance thereat from day to day and from Term to Term until discharged by Authority of law then this obligation to be void otherwise to remain in full force and effect.

244

Now comes the Plaintiff herein by her District Attorney W. L. Rynerson Esq. and the Defendant William Bonny, alias Kid alias William Antrim, herein appearing in his own proper person accompanied by his counsel. Whereupon the said Plaintiff by her said attorney moves the court, that the Venue in this Cause be changed as to the said Defendant William Bonny alias Kid alias William Antrim for the reasons set forth in the affidavit therefor filed herein and the Court being fully advised in the premises sustains Said motion.

It is therefore ordered that the Venue in this Cause as to the said Defendant William Bonny alias Kid alias William Antrim be and the same hereby is changed to the County of Dona Ana in the Third Judicial District of the Territory of New Mexico. And it is further ordered that the Clerk of this Court make an exemplified Copy of the proceedings had in this Cause in this Court and transmit the Same together with the original Papers in Said Cause to the District Court in and for the said County of Dona Ana to which ruling and order of this Court the Defendant Excepts.

Proceedings of the Eighth Day of the District Court of the Third Judicial District held in Lincoln, New Mexico on Tuesday April 22, 1879, and found of Record in Volume B on Pages 316-317-318 of the District Court Records of Lincoln County, New Mexico.

District Court Lincoln County, State of New Mexico, Carrizozo, 13th day of October A. D. 1949

J. G. MOORE, *Clerk*
[signed]
OTELA E. VEGA, *Deputy*

Appendix C

Billy the Kid's Trial

1. The Missing Indictment
2. Request for Instructions by Defendant's Counsel
3. Judge Bristol's Instructions to the Jury
4. The Jury
5. The Verdict
6. The Sentence
7. The Death Warrant
8. The Sheriff's Return of the Death Warrant

APPENDIX C:1

THE MISSING INDICTMENT

Geraldine S. Mathisen, District Court Clerk
Third Judicial District, Phone 11, Las Cruces, New Mexico October 19, 1949
To WHOM IT MAY CONCERN:

I, Geraldine S. Mathisen, Clerk of the District Court of the Third Judicial District of New Mexico do hereby certify that I have made a due and diligent search of the records here in this office, and fail to find the indictment in Criminal Cause No. 532 entitled Territory of New Mexico versus William Bonney alias "Kid" alias William Antrim

Dated at Las Cruces, New Mexico this the 19th day of October, A.D. 1949.

[s] GERALDINE S. MATHISEN
District Court Clerk of the Third Judicial District in and for the county of Dona Ana, State of New Mexico

APPENDIX C:2

REQUEST FOR INSTRUCTIONS BY DEFENDANT'S COUNSEL

In the District Court, Dona Ana County, N. M.
March 1881 Term
Cause 532
Territory of New Mexico
vs
William Bonny, alias Kid, alias William Antrim (Murder)

Instructions asked for by Defendants Counsel. The Court is asked to instruct the Jury as follows, to wit:

1st Instruction asked.

Under the evidence the Jury must either find the Defendant guilty of murder in the 1st degree, or acquit him.

2nd Instruction asked.

The Jury will not be justified in finding the Defendant guilty of murder in the 1st degree unless they are satisfied, from the evidence, to the exclusion of all reasonable doubt, that the defendant actually fired the shot that caused the death of the deceased Brady, and that such shot was fired by the Defendant with a premeditated design to effect the death of the deceased, or that the Defendant was present and actually assisted in firing the fatal shot or shots that caused the death of deceased, and that he was present and in a position to render such assistance from a premeditated design to effect the death of the deceased.

3rd Instruction asked.

If the Jury are satisfied from the evidence to the exclusion of all reasonable doubt that the Defendant was present at the time of the firing of the shot or shots that caused the death of the deceased Brady, yet, before they will be justified in finding the Defendant guilty, they must be further satisfied from the evidence and the evidence alone, to the exclusion of all reasonable doubt, that the Defendant either fired the shots that killed the deceased, or some of them, or that he assisted in firing said shot or shots, and that he fired said shot or shots or assisted in firing the same or assisted the parties who fired the same either by his advice, encouragement, or procurement or command from a premeditated design to effect the death of Brady. If the Jury entertains any reasonable doubt upon any of these points, they must find a verdict of acquittal.

A. J. FOUNTAIN
J. D. BAIL
Attorneys for Defendant

APPENDIX C:3

JUDGE BRISTOL'S INSTRUCTIONS TO THE JURY

Territory of New Mexico District Court
3rd Judicial District
Dona Ana County
April Term A. D. 1881
Murder- 1st Degree
The Territory of New Mexico
Vs
William Bonney alias Kid alias William Antrim

Gentlemen of the Jury: The defendant in this case William Bonney alias Kid alias William Antrim is charged in and by the indictment against him which has been laid before you with having committed in connection with certain other persons this crime of murder in the County of Lincoln in the 3rd Judicial District of the Territory of New Mexico in the month of April of the year 1878 by then and there unlawfully killing one William Brady by inflicting upon his body certain fatal gunshot wounds from a premeditated design to effect his death.

The case is here for trial by a change of venue from the said county of Lincoln.

The facts alleged in the indictment if true constitute murder in the 1st and highest degree and whether these allegations are true or not are, for, you to determine from the evidence which you have heard and which is now submitted to you for your careful consideration. In the matter of determining what your verdict shall be it will be improper for you to consider anything except the evidence before you as jurors are the exclusive judges or the weight of the evidence. You are the exclusive judges of the credibility of the witnesses. It is for you to determine whether the testimony of any witness whom you have heard is to be believed or not. You are also the exclusive judges whether the evidence is sufficiently clear and strong to satisfy your minds that the defendant is guilty.

There is no evidence tending to show that the killing of Brady was either justifiable or excusable in law—as a matter of law therefore such killing was unlawful and whoever committed the deed or was present and advised aided or abetted and consented to such killing committed the crime of murder in some one of the degrees of murder.

There is no evidence before you showing that the killing of Brady is murder in any other degree than the first—

Your verdict therefore should be either that the defendant is guilty of murder in the 1st degree or that he is not guilty at all under this indictment.

Murder in the 1st degree consists in the killing of one human being by another without authority of law and from a premeditated design to effect the death of the person killed—

Every killing of one human being by another that is not justifiable or excusable would be necessarily a killing without authority of law. As I have already instructed you to constitute murder in the 1st degree it is necessary that the killing should have been perpetrated from a premeditated design to effect the death of the person killed—

As to this premeditated design I charge you that to render a design to kill premeditated it is not necessary that such design to kill should exist in the mind for any considerable length of time before the killing.

If the design to kill is completely formed in the mind but for a moment before inflicting the fatal wound it would be premeditated and in law the effect would be the same as though the design to kill had existed for a long time—

In this case in order to justify you in finding this defendant guilty of murder in the 1st degree under the peculiar circumstances as presented by the indictment and the evidence you should be satisfied and believe from the evidence to the exclusion of every reasonable doubt of the truth of several propositions.

1st- That the defendant either inflicted one or more of the fatal wounds causing Brady's death or that he was present at the time and place of the killing and encouraged—incited—aided in—abetted—advised or commanded such killing—

2nd- That such killing was without justification or excuse

3rd- That such killing of Brady was caused by inflicting upon his body a fatal gunshot wound. And

4th- that such fatal wound was either inflicted by the defendant from a premeditated design to effect Brady's death or that he was present at the time and place of the killing of Brady and from a premeditated design to effect his death he then and there encouraged —incited—aided in—abetted—advised or commanded such killing_

If he was so present—encouraging—inciting—aiding in—abetting_ advising or commanding the killing of Brady, he is as much guilty as though he fired the fatal shot—

I have charged you that to justify you in finding the defendant guilty of murder in the 1st degree you should be satisfied from the evidence to the exclusion of every reasonable doubt that the defendant is actually guilty. As to what would be or would not be a reasonable doubt of guilt I charge you that belief in the guilt of the defendant to the exclusion of every reasonable doubt does not require you to so believe absolutely and to a mathematical certainty—That is to justify a verdict of guilty it is not necessary for you to be as certain that the defendant is guilty as you are that two and two are four or that two and three are five.

Merely a vague conjecture or bare probability that the defendant may be innocent is not sufficient to raise a reasonable doubt of his guilt. If all the evidence before you which you believe to be true convinces and directs your understanding and satisfies your reason and judgment while acting upon it conscientiously under your oath as jurors and if this evidence leaves in your minds an abiding conviction to a moral certainty that the defendant is guilty of the crime charged against him: then this would be proof of guilt to the exclusion of every reasonable doubt and would justify you in finding the defendant guilty—

You will apply the evidence to this case according to the instructions I have given you and determine whether the defendant is guilty of murder in the 1st degree or not guilty—

Murder in the 1st degree is the greatest crime known to our laws. The Legislature of this Territory has enacted a law prescribing that the punishment for murder in the 1st degree shall be death—

This then is the law: no other punishment than death can be imposed for murder in the 1st degree—

If you believe and are satisfied therefore from the evidence before you to the exclusion of every reasonable doubt that the defendant is guilty of murder in the 1st degree then it will be your duty to find a verdict that the defendant is guilty of murder in that degree naming murder in the 1st degree in your verdict and also saying in your that the defendant shall suffer the punishment of death— If from the evidence you do not believe to the exclusion of every reasonable doubt that the defendant is guilty of murder in the 1st degree or if you entertain a reasonable doubt as to the guilt of the defendant- then in that case your verdict should be not guilty.

No. 532

Territory vs William Bonny alias "Kid" alias William Antrim (Murder)

Charge to trial Jury
Filed in my office this 9th day of April A. D. 1881

[S] GEORGE R. BOWMAN
Clerk

APPENDIX C:4

THE JURY

Page 390 Eleventh Day, April 8th A D 1881—Cont'd

And now there being twelve qualified Petit Jurors present and both parties declaring themselves satisfied with the Jury as it now stands the following Jury is accepted to wit:

Refugio Bernal
Jesus Telles
Crecencio Bustillos
Luis Sedillos
Felipe Lopez
Pedro Onopa
Merced Lucero
Pedro Serna
Jesus Silva
Pedro Martinez
Hilario Moreno
Benito Montoya

Twelve good and lawful men of the body of the Third Judicial District, duly drawn accepted *empanelled* and sworn to well and truly try and true deliverance make between the Territory of New Mexico and the prisoner at the bar and a true verdict give according to the evidence. And after hearing a part of the evidence the said Jury are placed in charge of two sworn officers until the opening of Court tomorrow.

Whereupon Court adjourned until tomorrow morning at 10 o'clock

[s] Warren Bristol
Judge

APPENDIX C:5

THE VERDICT

Page 391
Twelfth Day, April 9th A.D. 1881
Court met pursuant to adjournment.
Present as of yesterday
Territory of New Mexico
vs
William Bonny alias "Kid" alias William Antrim (Murder)

Now comes the Plaintiff herein by Simon B. Newcomb Esq. District Attorney therefore and the Defendant appearing in his own proper person and accompanied by John D. Bail Esq. and A.J. Fountain Esq. his attorneys and the jury empanelled yesterday in said cause being present and said Jury having heard all the evidence and the arguments of counsel and received the instructions of the Court, retire to deliberate, accompanied by two sworn officers. And after deliberation the said Jury return into Court and upon their oaths do say "We the Jury in the above entitled cause to find the Defendant guilty of murder in the first degree and do assess his punishment at death"

[s] Warren Bristol
Judge

APPENDIX C:6

THE SENTENCE

Page 406 Fifteenth Day, April 13th A D 1881—Continued
Territory of New Mexico
vs
William Bonny alias "Kid" alias William Antrim (murder)

Now comes the Plaintiff herein by Simon B., Newcomb Esq. District Attorney therefor and the Defendant appearing in his own proper person and accompanied by counsel and the Court being fully advised as to the sentence to be passed upon said Defendant in pursuance of the verdict rendered in said cause at a former day of this Term; and the Defendant being asked if he had anything to say why sentence should not be passed upon him in pursuance of said verdict says nothing.

It is therefore considered by the Court here that the said Defendant, William Bonny, alias Kid alias William Antrim be taken to the County of Lincoln in the Third Judicial District of the Territory of New Mexico by the Sheriff of said county of Lincoln and that he, the said William Bonny, alias Kid, alias William Antrim be confined in prison in said county of Lincoln, by the Sheriff of such county until on Friday the 13th day of May in the year of our Lord One Thousand Eight Hundred and eighty-one. That on the day aforesaid between the hours of nine of the clock in the forenoon and three of the clock in the afternoon he, the said William Bonny alias Kid alias William Antrim, be taken from such prison to some suitable and convenient place of execution within the said County of Lincoln, by the Sheriff of such county and that then and there, on that day and between the aforesaid hours thereof, by the Sheriff of said county of Lincoln, he, the said William Bonny, alias Kid, alias William Antrim be hanged by the neck until his body be dead.

Judgment and sentence herein was pronounced upon the said defendant at five o'clock and fifteen minutes in the afternoon of this 13th day of April A.D. 1881. Ordered by the Court that a certified record of the Judgment of the Court be transmitted to the Governor of the Territory without delay, which is accordingly done. Whereupon Court adjourned until tomorrow morning at 10 o'clock.

[s] Warren Bristol
Judge

APPENDIX C:7

THE DEATH WARRANT

Death Warrant of Billy the Kid
Ex. Rec. 506

To the Sheriff of Lincoln County, New Mexico, Greeting:

At the March term, A.D. 1881, of the District Court for the Third Judicial District of New Mexico, held at La Mesilla in the county of Dona Ana, William Bonney, alias Kid, alias William Antrim, was duly convicted of the crime of murder in the 1st Degree; and on the fifteenth day of said term, the same being the thirteenth day of April, A.D. 1881, the Judgment and Sentence of said Court were pronounced against the said William Bonney, alias Kid, alias William Antrim, upon said conviction according to law. Whereby the said William Bonney, alias Kid, alias William Antrim, was adjudged and sentenced to be hanged by the neck until dead, by the Sheriff of the said county of Lincoln, within said county.

Therefore, you, the Sheriff of the said county of Lincoln, are hereby commanded that on Friday, the Thirteenth day of May, A. D. 1881, Pursuant to the said Judgment and sentence of the said Court, you take the said William Bonney, alias Kid, alias William Antrim, from the county jail of the county of Lincoln where he is now confined, to some safe and convenient place within the said County, and there, between the hours of Ten O'clock, A. M., and three O'clock, P. M., of said day, you hang the said William Bonney, alias Kid, alias William Antrim by the neck until he is dead. And make due return of your acts hereunder.

[SEAL] Done at Santa Fe in the Territory of New Mexico, this 30th day of April, A. D. 1881.

Witness my hand and the great seal of the Territory.

[signed] LEW WALLACE
Governor New Mexico

By the governor
W. G. RITCH, Secretary, N. M.

APPENDIX C:8

THE SHERIFF'S RETURN OF THE DEATH WARRANT

Death Warrant
Territory
vs
Wm Bonney, alias Kid
Lincoln, Lincoln County, New Mexico May 24th 1881.

I hereby certify that the within Warrant was not served owing to the fact that the within named prisoner escaped before the day set for serving said Warrant.

PAT F. GARRETT, *Sheriff*
Lincoln County, New Mexico
2 Ex Rec 515

FILED. June 3, 1881
W. G. RITCH, *Sec.* N.M.

Appendix D

The Report of the Coroner's Jury

1. The Report (translation)
2. Letter from the District Attorney for the Fourth Judicial District
3. Letter from the County Clerk of De Baca County
4. Letter from the County Clerk of Guadalupe County
5. Letter from the Deputy District Clerk of the Fourth Judicial District
6. Letter from the Secretary of State of New Mexico

APPENDIX D:1

THE CORONER'S JURY (TRANSLATION)

Report of the Coroner's Jury (translation of a photostat copy of a purported original which was never filed in San Miguel County)
Territory of New Mexico Precinct No. 27
County of San Miguel

To the attorney of the First Judicial District of the Territory of New Mexico.

GREETING:

This 15th day of July, A. D. 1881, I, the undersigned, Justice of the Peace of the Precinct above named, received information that there had been a death in Fort Sumner in said Precinct and immediately on receiving the information I proceeded to the said place and named Milnor Rudolph, Jose Silva, Antonio Saavedra, Pedro Antonio Lucero, Lorenzo Jaramillo, and Sabal Gutierres a jury to investigate the matter, and, meeting in the house of Lucien B. Maxwell, the said jury proceeded to a room in said house where they found the body of William H. Bonney alias "Kid" with a bullet wound in the chest, and, having examined the body, they examined the evidence of Pedro Maxwell, which evidence is as follows: "As I was lying on my bed in my room about midnight on the 14th day of July,

Patrick F. Garrett entered my room and sat down on the edge of my bed to talk to me. Soon after Garrett had seated himself William Bonney entered and approached my bed with a pistol in his hand and asked me, 'Who is it? Who is it?' and then Patrick F. Garrett fired two shots at him, the said William Bonney, and the said Bonney fell upon one side of my fireplace, and I left the room. When I returned three or four minutes after the shots, the said Bonney was dead."

The jury has found the following verdict: "We of the jury unanimously find that William Bonney was killed by a shot in the left breast, in the region of the heart, fired from a pistol in the hand of Patrick F. Garrett, and our verdict is that the act of the said Garrett was justifiable homicide, and we are unanimous in the opinion that the gratitude of the whole community is due to the said Garrett for his act and that he deserves to be rewarded."

M. RUDULPH
President

ANTON SABEDRA
PEDRO ANTO LUCERO
JOSE X SILBA
SABAL X GUTIERREZ

LORENZO X JARAMILLO

All of which information I bring to your notice.

ALEJANDRO SEGURA
Justice of the Peace

APPENDIX D:2

LETTER FROM THE DISTRICT ATTORNEY FOR THE FOURTH JUDICIAL DISTRICT

Jose E. Armijo, District Attorney
E. R. Cooper, Assistant
Counties: San Miguel, Mora and Guadalupe
Office of the District Attorney
Fourth Judicial District
State of New Mexico
Las Vegas, New Mexico
August 14, 1951

Mr. Wm. V. Morrison 1312 Arizona
El Paso, Texas

Dear Sir:

I wish to acknowledge receipt of your letter of August 9, 1951 requesting a certified copy of the coroner's verdict on the death of Wm. H. Bonney, alias Billy the Kid.

I am sorry I cannot comply with your request because of the fact that such a record is not now, and never has been, among the records of this office. I am sorry, also that I am at a loss to direct you to the office where you could obtain a copy of such record.

Such a verdict, if it existed, should have been filed in the office of the County Clerk. However, the original San Miguel County (Which at that time comprised what is now De Baca County) has been split up so many times that it is now but a small fraction of its original size. Perhaps such a record can be found in the office of the County Clerk of Guadalupe County, (County seat being Santa Rosa, New Mexico), or in the office of the County Clerk of De Baca County (county seat being Fort Sumner, New Mexico). Both these counties were formed out of what once was San Miguel County.

I am sorry the Attorney General's office misinformed you as to such record. I have never seen such record and it is my opinion that it would be almost an impossibility to locate such a record at this late date because of the poor condition and method of keeping records at the time Billy the Kid is purported to have been killed by Pat Garrett.

Again, I am sorry I cannot be of service to you in this matter, but I do wish you success in locating such record.

Very truly yours,

[s] Jose E. Armijo
District Attorney

APPENDIX D:3

LETTER FROM THE COUNTY CLERK OF DEBACA COUNTY

County Clerk and Ex-Officio Recorder
De Baca County

Fort Sumner, New Mexico
STATE OF NEW MEXICO –ss.
County of De Baca

I, Cecil W. Williams, County Clerk within and for the County of De Baca, State of New Mexico, Do Hereby Certify that I have searched the records in my office and I fail to find anything pertaining to the Coroner's Jury Verdict in the Case of "Billy the Kid."

Witness my hand and seal of said office this 21st day of August, 1951.

[SEAL]

[S] CECIL W. WILLIAMS

County Clerk

APPENDIX D:4

LETTER FROM THE COUNTY CLERK OF GUADALUPE COUNTY

Jose M. Maestas, Jr., Clerk of Guadalupe County
Santa Rosa, New Mexico
State of New Mexico –ss.
County of Guadalupe

I, Jose M. Maestas, Jr. County Clerk within and for the County of Guadalupe, State of New Mexico, do hereby certify that I have searched the records in my office and I fail to find anything pertaining to the Coroner's Jury Verdict in the Case of "Billy the Kid."

Witness my hand and seal of said office this 21st day of August, 1951.

[SEAL]
[S] JOSE M. MAESTAS, JR. *County Clerk*

APPENDIX D:5

LETTER FROM THE DEPUTY DISTRICT CLERK OF THE FOURTH JUDICIAL DISTRICT

Office of the
Clerk of the District Court
Las Vegas, New Mexico

October 31, 1949

Mr. William V. Morrison
3120 Wheeling Street
El Paso, Texas.

Dear Mr. Morrison,

I sent your letter requesting the Coroner's Verdict of the purported death of William H. Bonney to the Clerk of the District Court of De Baca County, as there is no record in this office of any Coroner's Verdict, and we do not have the records of De Baca County in this office.

Very truly yours,

[s] CARMEN ARMIJO
Deputy District Court Clerk

APPENDIX D:6

LETTER FROM THE SECRETARY OF STATE FOR THE STATE OF NEW MEXICO

State of New Mexico
Department of State
Office of the Secretary of State
Santa Fe

November 21, 1949

Mr. William V. Morrison
3120 Wheeling Street
El Paso, Texas

Dear Mr. Morrison:

This will acknowledge receipt of your letter dated November 12th.

Our records failed to disclose the death record or Coroner's report with reference to the purported death of William H. Bonney, alias the Kid, alias William Antrim.
As requested, I am enclosing a certified copy of the Return on Death Warrant which was issued by the Sheriff of Lincoln County on May 24th, 1881.

Also enclosed is your Official Receipt in the amount of $3.00 in full payments of statements dated October 27th, and November 21st.

Yours very truly,

[s] ALICIA ROMERO
(Mrs. M. A. Romero) Secretary of State

APPENDIX E

THE REWARD

1. Governor Wallace's Official Offer
2. Governor Ritch's Refusal to Approve Garrett's Application
3. The Legislative Act

APPENDIX E:1

GOVERNOR WALLACE'S OFFICIAL OFFER

REWARD Territory of New Mexico
vs
William Bonney alias "The Kid", A Fugitive
[Indictment in Lincoln County District Court for Murder]
Executive Office
Territory of New Mexico

WHEREAS William Bonney, alias "the Kid" stands charged under indictment issued from the District Court in and for the County of Lincoln, of the crime of murder committed in said county; and

WHEREAS, the said William Bonney alias "The Kid" is a fugitive from justice

Now THEREFORE, I, Lewis Wallace, Governor of the Territory; by virtue of the power and authority vested in me by the law and believing the end of justice will best be served thereby, do hereby offer a reward of five hundred dollars ($500.00) for the apprehension and arrest of said William Bonney alias "The Kid" and for his delivery to the Sheriff of Lincoln County at the County seat of said county.

In witness whereof I have hereunto set my hand and have caused the Great Seal of the Territory to be hereto affixed this 13th day of December, 1880.

[S] LEW WALLACE
Governor
[ORIGINAL SEAL]

By the Governor
[s] W. G. Raul
Secretary of New Mexico

(Copy certified by Beatrice B. Roach, Secretary of State, August 23, 1951)

APPENDIX E:2

GOVERNOR RITCH'S REFUSAL TO APPROVE GARRETT'S APPLICATION

July 21

In the matter of the application by Patrick F. Garrett for a reward claimed to have been offered May 1881 for the capture of Wm Bonny alias the Kid

[Action on Petition Suspended]
Executive Department
Territory of New Mexico

July 21, 1881

July 20th 1881 Pat. F. Garrett, Sheriff of Lincoln County, appeared and presented a bill for $500. claiming it as a reward offered on or about the 7th of May 1881 by the late Governor, Lew Wallace, for the capture of said Bonny.

As evidence of said offer having been made the affidavit of publication thereof made by Chas. W. Green, the editor and manager of the Daily New Mexican, was presented with said bill, as also was presented a statement of the proceedings and verdict of a coroner's jury at Ft. Sumner in San Miguel County upon the body of said Bonny, captured as aforesaid, and a statement of Garrett directed to this office of his doings in the premises.

Upon examination of said papers it was deemed important that the opinion of the Attorney General be taken thereon and they were at once transmitted to that office. On the following day, the papers with the opinion of Hon. Wm. Breeden Attorney General were filed.

Said opinion is quite full. We quote the closing paragraphs as sufficient in this connection, to wit:

BILLY THE KID
$500 REWARD

"I will pay five hundred dollars reward to any person or persons, will capture William Bonny, alias the Kid, and deliver him to any Sheriff of New Mexico, satisfactory proof of identity will be required."

[S] LEW WALLACE
Governor of New Mexico"

"This certainly appears to be the personal offer of Governor Wallace, and it seems he did nothing to indicate that it was intended as an executive act, on behalf of, and to bind the Territory.

"If the reward should be paid, it is very probable, that the Legislature would approve the payment if so desired, and that no objection would be raised, or that it will provide for its payment, if it remains unpaid, at the next session thereof; but if the Governor should now direct the payment of the claim, he would doubtless expose himself to the charge of misappropriation of the Territorial funds, in case the Legislature should refuse to ratify and approve the payment." In addition, we will add as a fact that there was no record whatever, either in this office or at the Secretary's office of there having been a reward offered as set forth by Attorney General, nor was there any record on file in said offices of a corresponding reward in any form.

The opinion of the Attorney General appearing to be consistent with the law and the facts, decision is rendered accordingly and the Governor declines to allow the reward at this time. Believing how- ever, that Mr. Garrett, has an equitable claim against the Territory for said reward; further action at this office will simply be suspended until the case can be properly represented to the next Legislature Assembly.

[s] W. G. RITCH
Acting Governor New Mexico

APPENDIX E:3

THE LEGISLATIVE ACT

1882—Private Laws of New Mexico-25th Session
Relief of Pat Garrett—Chapter 101 page 191
Chapter C1
AN ACT for the Relief of Pat Garrett.

Contents

Section 1. Authorizes the payment of $500 reward for the arrest of the "Kid."

WHEREAS, The Governor of New Mexico did, on or about the 7th day of May, A. D., 1881, issue his certain proclamation in words and figures as follows, to-wit:

"I will pay five hundred dollars reward to any person or persons who will capture William Bonney, alias 'The Kid', and deliver him to any Sheriff of New Mexico. Satisfactory proof of identity will be required."

[Signed] LEW WALLACE,
Governor of New Mexico

AND WHEREAS, Pat Garrett was at that time Sheriff of Lincoln County, and did, on or about the month of August, 1881, in pursuance of the above reward and by virtue of a warrant placed in his hands for that purpose, attempted to arrest said William Bonney, and in said attempt did kill said William Bonney at Fort Sumner, in the County of San Miguel, in the Territory of New Mexico, and wherefore, said Garrett is justly entitled to the above reward, and payment thereof has been refused upon a technicality.

Be it enacted by the Legislative Assembly of the Territory of New Mexico:

Section I. The Territorial Auditor is hereby authorized to draw a warrant upon the Territorial Treasurer of the Territory of New in favor of Pat Garrett for the sum of five hundred dollars, we out of any funds in the Territorial treasury not otherwise especially appropriated, in payment of the reward of five hundred dollars heretofore offered by his Excellency, Governor Lew Wallace, for the arrest of William Bonney, alias "The Kid."

Section 2. This act shall take effect and be in force from and after its passage.

Approved February 18, 1882.

Appendix F

Affidavits

1. Severo Gallegos
2. Martile Able
3. Jose B. Montoya
4. Dewitt Travis
5. Robert E. Lee

APPENDIX F:1

AFFIDAVIT OF SEVERO GALLEGOS

STATE OF NEW MEXICO -ss.
County of Lincoln

Before me, the undersigned authority, on this day, personally appeared Mr. Severo Gallegos of Lincoln County, New Mexico, who, upon his oath, deposes and says:

That his name is Severn Gallegos, that he is past 82 years of age, that he is a son of Lucas Gallegos, deceased; that he is a half-brother of Florencio Chavez, who fought in the Lincoln County War, and rode with Wm. Bonney, known as Billy the Kid.

This affiant further states that Billy the Kid many times visited in the Gallegos Home; that he stayed there some times over night and that he ate many meals there; that the Kid and Florencio Chavez did much target practice at their home in San Patricio; that Billy was quick on the draw; that he fired a rifle left handed and six shooters with both hands; that he would shoot from the hip and that he was known to be a good shot.

This affiant further states that Billy the Kid was a small man when he was young; that he had small feet and hands with large wrists; that he had two large teeth in the front of his mouth; that he had blue-grey eyes with small brown spots in them; that his nose was straight, high cheek bones and large ears; that he had dark hair; that he stood as straight as a whip, and rode a horse straight in the saddle.

This affiant further states that he made many visits to see Billy the Kid in the Lincoln Jail; that he took berries to the jail for Billy to eat; that he saw Billy escape from the Jail in April, 1881; that he never saw Billy the Kid again until the first day of April, 1950; that after talking to Billy for several hours on April first, this affiant knows from conversation and looking him over, that Billy the Kid was the same person as O.L. Roberts who visited here in Ruidoso.

This affiant further states that he never believed that Billy the Kid was killed by Sheriff Pat Garrett; that he heard from time to time throughout the years that Billy the Kid was still living.

This affiant further states that O.L. Roberts has the same blue-grey eyes, with brown spots in them; that his nose is straight, with high cheek bones, large ears, small feet and hands with large wrists, and he stands as straight as he stood in Lincoln County days; that he is still fast on the draw; that he talks and laughs the same, and looks the same in many ways; that he has no teeth now, and his hair is nearly gray with some dark streaks in it.

This affiant further states that he is of firm belief that Billy the Kid and O.L. Roberts are one and the same person.

SEVERO GALLEGOS

X (His Mark) (L. M. W.)
Affiant

Sworn to and subscribed to before me, a notary public, this 11th day of November, A. D. 1950.

[SEAL] [s] LILLIE MAY WARD
Notary Public in and for Lincoln County, State of New Mexico.

STATE OF NEW MEXICO –ss.
County of Lincoln

Before me, the undersigned authority, a Notary Public, on this day personally appeared Mr. Severo Gallegos, known to me to be the person whose name is subscribed to the foregoing instrument and he acknowledged to me that he executed the same for the purposes and consideration therein expressed.

Given under my hand and seal of office this the 11th day of November, A. D. 1950.

[SEAL]
[s] LILLIE MAY WARD
Notary Public in and for Lincoln County, New Mexico
My commission expires, Feb. 5, 1953.

APPENDIX F:2

AFFIDAVIT OF MRS. MARTILE ABEL

STATE OF TEXAS –ss.
County of El Paso

Before me, the undersigned authority, a notary public, on this day, personally appeared Mrs. Martile Able, widow of John C. Able who died at the age of 56 years, in 1918, of the County of El Paso, and State of Texas, who upon her oath deposes and says:

That her name is Mrs. Martile Able, that she was born in Cook County, Texas, more than eighty years ago, that she was married to John C. Able, in Abilene, Texas, after which they moved to a Ranch on the Black River, south of Carlsbad, New Mexico, where they lived for about two years, Stonewall County, Texas; that years after which they moved back to Abilene, Texas; that they moved from Abilene to El Paso, Texas, about 1900, and she still resides in El Paso County, Texas.

This affiant further states that the family was well acquainted with Wm. H. Bonney, known as Billy the Kid; that Mr. John C. Able, the husband of this affiant, knew Wm. Bonney years before around Pecos, Texas, where the group of friends had a picture made in 1880, which picture is a good likeness of Wm. Bonney; that Wm. Bonney visited with the Able Family before, and after, the time it was said, Pat Garrett killed him in New Mexico; that John C. Able brought Wm. Bonney to their house on one day when he caught a, horse for Bonney to ride out; that this affiant cooked a meal that day that he ate in hiding; that Bonney rode away on the horse, that the horse came back home after Bonney made his journey; that the last time this affiant saw Wm. Bonney was about the year of 1902; that she did not see Wm. Bonney again until July 1, 1950, while he was visiting here in El Paso, at which time this affiant talked to Wm. Bonney about the old times around Pecos and other places; that he talks about the old times as we always knew them, that he laughs much the same, has the same keen blue eyes, long nose, large cars, small feet, small hands with unusually large wrists, stands and walks as straight as ever with a lively step, that he appears to be around ninety years of age, but appears much younger in general, with hair nearly gray, looks much the same only he is a little larger than when I last saw him in 1902; that he spoke about the times when John C. Able helped him and loaned money to him when he was on the dodge; that the pictures in his album from the time he was about 14, late twenties, fifties, eighties, and the present time show a marked resemblance to the old picture in our album made in 1880 at Pecos, Texas.

This affiant further states that it was generally known among friends that Billy the Kid was not killed by Garrett in New Mexico, like they said he was killed; that Billy escaped into Mexico; and that this affiant saw him after he came back to this country from Old Mexico.

This affiant further states that to the best of her knowledge, information, and belief Wm. H. Roberts, also known as Wm. H. Bonney, Billy the Kid, Texas Kid, Brushy Bill Roberts, O. L. Roberts is one and the same person as O.L. Roberts, who visited with us here during the first week of July, 1950, and further affiant says nothing.

[s] MRS. ABLE
Affiant

Sworn to and subscribed to before me, a notary public, this the 1st day of Aug., 1950 A. D.

[s] G. A. ARREDONDO
Notary Public in and for El Paso County, State of Texas.

STATE OF TEXAS -ss.
County of El Paso

Before me, the undersigned authority, a notary public, on this day personally appeared Mrs. Martile Able, known to me to be the person whose name is subscribed to the foregoing instrument and she acknowledged to me that she executed the same for the purposes and consideration therein expressed.

Given under my hand and seal of office this the 1st day of Aug. A. D. 1950.

[SEAL]
[S] G. A. ARREDONDO
Notary Public in and for El Paso County, State of Texas.
My commission expires, June 1, 1951

APPENDIX F:3

AFFIDAVIT OF JOSE B. MONTOYA

STATE OF NEW MEXICO -ss.
County of Lincoln

Before me, the undersigned authority, on this day, personally appeared Mr. Jose B. Montoya of Lincoln County, New Mexico, who, upon his oath, deposes and says:

That his name is Jose B. Montoya, that he was born on May 6, 187o, in Lincoln County, New Mexico, that his parents died when he was quite young, that he went to live with his sister, Mrs. Felicita Gabaro, and her husband, on a ranch in the Capitan Mountains, later moving to the Town of Lincoln where he went to school; that this affiant was well acquainted with Pat Garrett, John Poe, Sheriff Kimbrel, and most people in that country.

This affiant further states that he was well acquainted with Wm. Bonny, known later as the Kid, and Billy the Kid, that Bonny stayed, from time to time, at the home of this affiant in Capitan Mountains, and Lincoln Town, that he watched Billy the Kid target practice often, that he would throw quarters into the air while Billy the Kid would shoot them with his pistols; that Billy was a good shot, and fired pistols with either hand; that Billy the Kid was a small man with large ears, a long straight nose, big teeth, small feet, small hands with large wrists off of which he could slip handcuffs; that he stood as straight as an arrow, was a good dancer and singer; that the negro, George Washington played the guitar, and negro Bates played the fiddle; that Juan Patron was guard over Billy after Sheriff Kimbrel arrested him; that Sheriff Kimbrel was a friend of Billy; that Pat Garrett beat Sheriff Kimbrel in the election for Sheriff; that people said Sheriff Kimbrel was too friendly with Billy the Kid; that the Kid broke jail at Lincoln by killing the two guards, Olinger and Bell, escaping to Fort Sumner, N. M., where some people said Pat Garrett killed Billy the Kid, but many people did not believe that Garrett killed him; that the Kid escaped from Fort Sumner into Old Mexico.

This affiant further states that he did not believe the story of Garrett killing the Kid; that he and another man by the name of Green saw Billy the Kid at a bull fight in Juarez, Mexico, in 1902, and both of them knew the Kid; that the Kid was well dressed, wearing a large hat and buckskin jacket, and was talking to two Mexican officers; that a man in El Paso told them later that the Kid had been in El Paso three times before; that this affiant did not see Billy the Kid again until talking with him today while he was visiting with Wm. V. Morrison and the Kid in Carrizozo, N. M.

This affiant further states that to the best of his knowledge, information and belief Pat Garrett did not kill Billy the Kid, because Billy the Kid had too many friends in that country, and for other reasons including the fact that this affiant saw Billy the Kid in 1902 at Juarez, and talked with him personally today; that Wm. Bonney, alias Billy the Kid, alias O.L. Roberts, is one and the same person as 0. L. Roberts; that he talks and laughs, looks much the same, only older than he did before.

[SEAL]
[s] Jose B. Montoya
Affiant

Sworn to and subscribed to before me, a Notary Public, this 3rd day of July, A. D. 1950.

[s] Otto E. Prehm
Notary Public in and for Lincoln County, State of New Mexico.

STATE OF NEW MEXICO –ss.
County of Lincoln

Before me, the undersigned authority, a Notary Public, on this day, personally appeared Mr. Jose B. Montoya, known to me to be the person whose name is subscribed to the foregoing instrument and he acknowledged to me that he executed the same for the purposes and consideration therein expressed.

Given under my hand and seal of office this the 3rd day of July, A. D. 1950.

[SEAL]
[s] Otro E. Prehm

Notary Public in and for Lincoln County, State of New Mexico.

My commission expires, February 13, 1951

APPENDIX F:4

AFFIDAVIT OF DEWITT TRAVIS

STATE OF TEXAS
County of Gregg

Before me, the undersigned authority, on this day, personally appeared Mr. Dewitt Travis, Longview, Texas, who, upon his oath deposes and says:

That his name is Dewitt Travis, that he is 63 years of age, that he was personally acquainted with Wm H. Roberts, also known as Wm. H. Bonney, "Kid," "Billy the Kid," Texas Kid, Hugo Kid, Brushy Bill Roberts, and O.L. Roberts, who died on December 27, 1950, at Hico, Hamilton County, Texas.

This affiant further states the following facts with reference to the above-mentioned Wm. H. Roberts:

I have known him all of my life, having been raised with him and being around him, more or less, since my early childhood. I knew him to be honest, upright, truthful, polite and mannerly. He did not use tobacco or alcoholics. He was not a large man. He stood about five feet and eight inches, weighing about one hundred and sixty-five in late years, standing as straight as an arrow, and walking with a brisk step all of his life without the use of a cane. He was fair complected with high cheek bones, long straight nose, large ears with the left ear protruding farther away from the head than the right ear, blue grey eyes keen and shifty, dark hair graying in late years, peculiarly shaped teeth with two large teeth protruding outward from under the upper lip and a large tusk on each side of his upper jaw, the teeth having been extracted in 1931 by Dr. Cruz, Gladewater, Texas. He had small feet and wore a size seven boot, small hands with unusually large wrists, well-shaped fingers and hands. He was a very muscular and well-built man, quick as lightning, calm and collected, ambidextrous but preferably left handed, quick on the draw, shooting a pistol with either or both hands, a good shot with a rifle, which he fired left handed. I have seen him shoot and I will say he was a very good shot. I have seen him in skirmishes in which he was level headed, calm and collected, never appearing nervous. He was a likeable fellow, always smiling and in good humor, looking much younger than he actually was in years.

He taught me to swim. It was during swimming in cold water that I noticed many scars on his body. He pointed out some of the scars, telling me how they were received. I remember a bullet scar about two inches in length across the top of his head a couple of inches from the forehead which he said was received in the gun battle with Garrett's posse in Fort Sumner, N. M., on the night of July 14, 1881, when Garrett made the claim of killing him. During this gun battle he also received a bullet in the left shoulder, which scar remained prominent. He had a scar about an inch long across the back of the right hand near the knuckle joints; a scar across the first knuckle on the forefinger (trigger finger) of the right hand; one scar inside on the kneecap of the left leg; two scars inside the shin near the lower part of the left leg and a bullet lodged in the muscle; one scar high up on the right hip received during the battle when Sheriff Brady was killed in Lincoln; and several other scars on his body.

His name was not O.L. Roberts, and he was not the son of the family in East Texas. They died thinking Bill was their son, but he was not. This happened in my lifetime, so I am sure of what I am saying. My father, Elbert Travis, and Brushy Bill's father, "Two-Gun Roberts" fought together in the Civil War. I have known him intimately all my life. He used different names at various times.

I do not recall the name he was using when he ranched in Old Mexico. He came back to Texas about 1884 and took the name the Hugo Kid while on the Anti-Horse Thief trail at Hugo, Oklahoma. He rode in the Wild West shows of Buffalo Bill and Pawnee Bill, later starting a Wild West show of his own. He ranched in Arkansas and Oklahoma in later years, moving to Gladewater, Texas, where he was well liked by everyone. Later on, he moved back to Hico, Hamilton County, in the community where he spent his childhood days. He would not admit that he was "Billy the Kid," New Mexican outlaw, until shortly before his death. But his intimate friends knew all the time that he actually was the New Mexican outlaw. I have seen him shoot and remove the hand cuffs from his hands like he did in the days of old.

The affiant further states that to the best of his knowledge, information, and belief the said Wm H. Roberts, alias Wm. H. Bonney, alias "Kid," alias "Billy the Kid," alias Brushy Bill Roberts, alias O.L. Roberts are one and the same person. And that he was not killed by Sheriff Pat Garrett in Fort Sumner like they said he was killed in 1881, and further this affiant says nothing.

[S] DEWITT TRAVIS
Affiant
Sworn to and subscribed to before me, a notary public, this 12th day of December A. D. 1951.
[SEAL]
{s] MRS. ETHEL MARTIN
Notary Public in and for the County of Gregg, State of Texas

STATE OF TEXAS -ss.
County of Gregg

Before me, the undersigned authority, a Notary Public, on this day personally appeared Mr. Dewitt Travis, known to me to be the person whose name is subscribed to the foregoing instrument and acknowledged to me that he executed the same for the purposes and consideration therein expressed.

Given under my hand and seal of Office this the 12 day of Dec., A.D. 1951

[SEAL]

[s] MRS. ETHEL MARTIN
Notary Public in and for the County of Gregg, State of Texas
My commission expires, June 1, 1953

APPENDIX F:5

AFFIDAVIT OF ROBERT E. LEE

STATE OF LOUISIANA –ss.
Parish of E. Baton Rouge

Before me, the undersigned authority, a notary public, on this clay, personally appeared Mr. Robert E. Lee, of Baton Rouge, Parish of East Baton Rouge, State of Louisiana, who upon his oath deposes and says:

That his name is Robert E. Lee, that he is 76 years of age, that he was born near Corsicana, Texas, the son of James Lee of Virginia, that he was kidnapped by a band of horse thieves, and traders, at the age of 15 years, that, after being liberated from the band in the summer of 1889, he stayed at the ranch in New Mexico for a few months later drifting to "Scout's Rest Ranch," North Platte, Nebraska, which was owned by Colonel Wm F. Cody, known as Buffalo Bill; that Buffalo Bill hired this affiant at the ranch; that this affiant worked in Buffalo Bill's Wild West Show as body guard for Col. Cody; that Buffalo Bill's show was also known as "Congress of the Rough Riders of the World," with about six hundred people under his tent City outside the World's Fair Grounds at Chicago, Illinois, during the Exposition there in May, 1893.

This affiant further states that the first time he saw Wm. Bonney, alias the Kid, alias Billy the Kid, alias Texas Kid, was in the summer of 1889, at a ranch across the road from Fort Selden, New Mexico, when the Kid and his ranch pals rescued this affiant from the hand of thieves as they were camping at the ranch, doctoring their stallion; that the Kid was staying over at the ranch house; that William Bonney and his pals liberated this affiant at the ranch, and also disarmed the kidnappers then and there.

This affiant further states that it was generally known to him, and among friends of the Kid—some of whom were Buffalo Bill Cody, who hired the Kid in 1885, and subsequently; Pawnee Bill, or Major Gordon W. Lilly; T. B. Omohundro (Texas Jack) and Mexican Joe, both of whom worked with the Kid at Buffalo Bill's Place; Belle Starr; Indian Jim; Cherokee Bill; Ozark Jack; Miss Lou Mulhall; the James Brothers; John Trammel, who cooked for the Kid's father and his friends during the Civil War; Tex Moore; and many other old timers—that Wm. Bonney was not killed by Pat Garrett and his deputies in 1881, as stated by hearsay for many years; that the Kid escaped from Ft. Sumner into Old Mexico where he lived with the Yaqui Indians in Sonora; that Billy the Kid assumed the name of the Texas Kid when he returned to this country from Old Mexico; that the Texas Kid worked in Texas, the Indian Territory, the Black Hills of Dakota, Idaho, and divers other places with intermittent trips back to Mexico, where he had ranches at different times, all of which facts were generally known to the Kid's friends.

This affiant further states that the Kid, New Mexican outlaw, was riding in Buffalo Bill's Wild West Show in Chicago, Illinois, in 1893; that the Kid was one of the best riders in the show; that the Kid obtained the name of Brushy Bill, the Scout, for his good work in the Anti-Horse Thief Association, sometime before the performance in Chicago in 1893; that Buffalo Bill fought Indians with the Kid's father; that Buffalo Bill was well acquainted with the mother of the Kid; that he hired the Kid because he was well acquainted with the pioneer Roberts family in Texas and wanted to help the Kid go straight.

This affiant further states that William H. Roberts, alias William H. Bonney, alias Kid, alias the Texas Kid, alias Brushy Bill Roberts, is a man who stands about five feet and eight inches, weighs about one hundred and sixty pounds, has dark hair, almost white at present, blue eyes with hazel spots in them, large ears, prominent straight nose, and high cheek bones; that the large crooked teeth are no longer in his mouth; that he has small feet, small shapely hands with large wrists; that he is a well-built man, standing and riding straight as an arrow, and walking with a lively step; that he is about ninety years of age but looks much younger; that he always appears in good humor, laughing quite a bit and smiling when he talks; that he has a soft and sort of high-pitched voice; that he was a good singer and dancer in his younger days; that lie is always friendly and has a lot of friends; that he is a man of good habits, refraining from the use of alcohol and tobacco, is well mannered and a nice man in general; that lie has a cool temperament, is steady nerved; that he is a good shot with a pistol with either hand, but preferably left handed; that he has a good record; that he has not been known to be in trouble since killing his two guards in his escape from the Lincoln County, New Mexico, jail in 1881.

This affiant further states that the last time he saw Wm. H. Roberts, alias Wm. H. Antrim, alias Wm. H. Bonney, alias Kid, alias Brushy Bill Roberts, alias O.L. Roberts, was at New York City in January, 1950. We both were there at the Jesse James Press Conference at that time.

This affiant further states that William Bonney was never shot and killed by Pat Garrett, or any other Garrett. No Sir, for I worked with him in the Colonel Cody Show, and I took orders to him from Colonel Cody. Don't you think Colonel Cody and I knew just who he was? Folks, I say take it or leave it, Billy the Kid is still riding, or the Kid will ride again. I know him just awful well. Many of the old timers said it was only hearsay that Pat Garrett killed Billy the Kid; that Wm. H. Roberts, alias Wm. H. Antrim, alias Wm. H. Bonney, alias Kid, alias Billy the Kid, alias Texas Kid, alias Brushy Bill Roberts, alias O.L. Roberts, the son of "Wild Henry" Roberts, is one and the same person as O.L. Roberts with whom I visited in New York City in January of 1950.

This affiant further states that to the best of his knowledge, information and belief the above-mentioned Billy the Kid was not killed by Pat Garrett at Maxwell's Home in Fort Sumner, New Mexico on July 14, 1881.

[s] ROBERT E. LEE
Affiant
Sworn to and subscribed to before me, a notary public, this the 5th day of July, A. D. 1950.

[SEAL]
[s] FLETCHER T. HINTON
Notary Public in and for Parish of East Baton Rouge, State of Louisiana.

STATE OF LOUISIANA
Parish of East Baton Rouge

Before me, the undersigned authority, a notary public, on this day, personally appeared Mr. Robert E. Lee, known to me to be the person whose name is subscribed to the foregoing instrument and he acknowledged to me that he executed the same for the purposes and consideration therein expressed.

Given under my hand and seal of office this the 5th day of July, A. D. 1950.

[s] FLETCHER T. HINTON
Notary Public in and for Parish of East Baton Rouge, State of Louisiana
My commission expires at death

ABOUT THE AUTHOR

Daniel A. Edwards grew up in a suburb of Tampa, FL before moving to the deep south and then finally to the Philadelphia, PA suburbs. Since childhood he has been fascinated with the outdoors and the early American frontier lifestyle. He has a beautiful wife and two amazing children.

THANK YOU FOR READING!

If you enjoyed this book, we would appreciate your customer review on your book seller's website or on Goodreads.

Also, we would like for you to know that you can find more great books like this one at www.CreativeTexts.com

Printed by Amazon Italia Logistica S.r.l.
Torrazza Piemonte (TO), Italy